THE FISHERMEN'S CHAPEL

Frontispiece   View across Saint Brelade's Bay, showing the church from the north-east and the restored Fishermen's Chapel to its immediate left. In the foreground the base of the original circular churchyard is visible, disappearing under the nineteenth-century sea wall.

Photo: Warwick Rodwell

THE FISHERMEN'S CHAPEL
SAINT BRELADE
JERSEY

ITS ARCHAEOLOGY, ARCHITECTURE, WALL PAINTINGS AND CONSERVATION

by

Warwick Rodwell

with sections by

Ursula Fuhrer, Gottfried Hauff
and Sven Mieth

and contributions by

Margaret Finlaison
and Juliet Rogers

Société Jersiaise
and
The Rector and Churchwardens of Saint Brelade
1990

Published by Société Jersiaise 1990
© Warwick Rodwell 1990

ISBN 0 901897 19 1

For

Doctor E. Clive Rouse
M.B.E., F.S.A.

who initiated the study
of the wallpaintings in
The Fishermen's Chapel

Front cover: Fifteenth-century painting depicting King Herod, on the vaulted ceiling of the Fishermen's Chapel.
Photo: Robin Briault

Produced by Alan Sutton Publishing Ltd., Stroud, Glos.
Printed in Great Britain.

CONTENTS

LIST OF TEXT-FIGURES

All line-drawings and monochrome photographs in the text are referred to as figures.

LIST OF COLOUR PLATES

Front cover:
Fifteenth-century painting depicting King Herod

Frontispiece:
View across Saint Brelade's Bay, showing the church and chapel from the north-east

PREFACE

The Fishermen's Chapel – *La Chapelle ès Pêcheurs* – is one of the best known buildings in the Channel Islands, and every year it is visited by thousands of pilgrims and tourists. It is not a grand or imposing structure, but a small granite chapel, perched on the cliff edge above Saint Brelade's Bay. Alongside and overshadowing the chapel is the much larger parish church. These two ancient ecclesiastical buildings, lying in the same churchyard and no more than a few feet apart, present a curious spectacle, one which is repeated nowhere else in the Channel Islands.

Externally, the Fishermen's Chapel is a plain, rectangular structure with no sign of ornamentation or suggestion of the glory that it holds within. But once inside, the visitor is confronted with an experience of unparalleled delight: the walls and the stone-vaulted ceiling are covered with Old and New Testament scenes, executed in bright colours. For more than six hundred years these paintings have survived the ravages of time and man, and although they are now far from complete, their impact is nevertheless stunning: the message they conveyed to medieval worshippers is still there to be read today.

Medieval churches were frequently adorned with paintings based on the scriptures, but in most parts of Europe religious art was savagely depleted by sixteenth-century reformers. Nowhere were the adverse effects of the Calvinist Reformation more acutely felt than in the Channel Islands, with the consequence that 'popish' church furnishings and decoration were more thoroughly and systematically destroyed than in England. There are only scraps of medieval wall painting surviving in five of the islands' churches and chapels which, altogether, cover no more than a small fraction of the area represented by the murals in the Fishermen's Chapel. These are indeed a remarkable survival.

No less remarkable is the fact that the chapel exists at all today. Again, the post-Reformation destruction of chapels in the Channel Islands was a thorough process: dozens were razed or ruined. However, by an accident of history the Fishermen's Chapel was converted into a sixteenth-century armoury, and later into a workshop. The paintings gradually fragmented and disappeared behind a film of dirt and salt incrustation, and the entire history of the chapel faded from both memory and record. At the end of the nineteenth century the building was rescued and converted into a meeting room, but it was not until 1915 that the paintings were rediscovered, when plaster was being hacked off the walls, during the process of 'restoration'. By another accident of history the paintings were again saved from the brink of destruction, this time by a German artist who was a refugee in Jersey during the First World War.

Following earthquake damage in 1926, a further restoration programme was carried out by the Reverend J.A. Balleine, and the chapel was finally reinstated as a place of worship in 1935. Gradually, as the decades passed, the medieval paintings began to deteriorate once again, and by 1972 it was clear that a crisis of conservation existed. A report on the paintings and their condition was prepared by Doctor E. Clive Rouse, the leading English wall paintings conservator of the time. Emergency treatment of the most endangered areas was carried out by Ann Ballantyne. But further work was pointless unless the root of the problem was tackled. This was a structural matter: the roof leaked.

Moreover, the whole building was in dire need of internal refurbishment. It would have been all too easy to carry out a few running repairs and make some token changes in the hope that the dull and uninspiring atmosphere within the chapel might somehow be improved. Much more was needed: wall and floor finishes, lighting and furnishings were all haphazard and fundamentally unsympathetic to the building. But to carry out far-reaching changes required not only vision and scholarship, but also the assembly of a skilled team and the raising of a prodigious sum of money to fund the project. The Rector of Saint Brelade, the Reverend Michael Halliwell, took the lead and, with the active support of his Churchwardens, determined to embark upon a thorough programme of repair and conservation.

At the same time the opportunity was seized to carry out a detailed archaeological study of both the building and its site, in an attempt to recover something of its lost history and associations. Over the course of the past century, much legend had accrued about the chapel, its origins, and Saint Brelade as a person, but virtually all was without substantive evidence; fact, fiction and hypothesis had become inextricably intertwined. A completely fresh appraisal was needed.

Consequently, between 1982 and 1987, an integrated programme of research and investigation, conservation and repair, refurbishment and revitalization, took place with an interdisciplinary and internationally recruited team. The results of their findings have now been distilled and are presented in this volume. The church of Saint Brelade generously funded the entire investigation, while the cost of producing this report has been shared between the church and the Société Jersiaise.

Warwick Rodwell   Saint Brelade
                                                                                      May, 1989

ACKNOWLEDGEMENTS

This book is the result of a collaborative venture, which would have been impossible without the goodwill and co-operation of many people. The project was initiated by the Rector, the Reverend Michael Halliwell, whose profound and active interest in the Fishermen's Chapel, and determination to achieve an imaginative and scholarly restoration, was the driving force throughout. We also enjoyed the continuous support of the Churchwardens, Major B. St C. Russell-Jones and Mr David Ling, and of the Ecclesiastical Assembly and the Parochial Church Council of Saint Brelade.

Throughout the project the Church's Architect, Mr David Barlow, gave constant support and skilfully co-ordinated all the diverse requirements and interests of a complex interdisciplinary study. Likewise, the builder, Mr Harry Tumblety, unfailingly responded to requests to provide an unusual variety of equipment and skills, and to work with teams of archaeologists and conservators. Mr John Cronin, the Verger, also provided much timely assistance.

The preliminary conservation and study of the paintings was undertaken by Doctor Clive Rouse, and his continued interest and kindly assistance, during retirement, were much appreciated. Collaboration with the teams of conservators has been an instructive pleasure, and my particular thanks go to Gottfried Hauff, Ursula Fuhrer, Madeleine Katkov and Christoph Oldenbourg. Assembling the successive teams was no easy task, but was deftly accomplished from London first by Canon David Bishop and then by Peter Burman, formerly Secretary of the Council for the Care of Churches. My personal thanks are also due to the latter for introducing me to the project.

The members of the conservation team, and co-authors of this report, wish to express their thanks to all those who made the conservation project and publication possible, and additionally wish to thank Jonathan Berwick for assistance with translation.

The archaeological team which carried out the excavations was almost entirely drawn from the membership of the Société Jersiaise, to whom thanks are due for much hard work and the loan of equipment. I am particularly grateful to the successive chairmen of the Archaeology Section of the Société, Mrs Deirdre Shute and Mrs Janine Tanguy, for co-ordinating this work. Mrs Shute has also carried out detailed and painstaking searches of the ecclesiastical records of the parish. For the benefit of extended discussions of the archaeology of Jersey churches I am indebted to the late Mrs Joan Stevens, Miss Jean Arthur, Mrs Kirsty Rodwell, Peter Bisson and Christopher Aubin.

In preparing this report I have received specialist assistance from Mrs Margaret Finlaison with the pottery finds, Doctor Juliet Rogers with the human skeletal remains, Doctor John Renouf with geological matters, Mr D. Corbel on numismatics, and Mr Robin Briault with the photography of the wall paintings. Important photographic evidence has also been kindly provided by Mr Geoffrey Parker, Mr L. Le Moignan and Mrs E.M. Bois, from the collections of the late Mr F. de L. Bois. Finally, I must thank my wife, Christine, for her assistance both on the excavation and with subsequent work on the finds; and the many friends in Jersey who have generously offered us their hospitality over the course of several years.

1. HISTORICAL INTRODUCTION

Medieval Jersey was endowed with a generous provision of ecclesiastical buildings, comprising twelve parish churches, the Abbey of Saint Helier, seven small priories, and a multiplicity of chapels. In this last class there is firm evidence for around fifty, but only a handful of these sites now exhibits any architectural remains (Stevens, 1977). Pre-eminent amongst the survivors is the Fishermen's Chapel in Saint Brelade parish, a small, plain rectangular structure (Fig. 1). Although well visited, widely appreciated and the subject of frequent mention in antiquarian literature, surprisingly little is certainly known about the history of the building or its site. No medieval or

Fig. 1.   The Fishermen's Chapel from the south-west, after restoration. The south transept and chancel of Saint Brelade's Church are seen on the left.

Photo: Warwick Rodwell

1

Fig. 2.   General view of Saint Brelade's Church and the Fishermen's Chapel from the south-west, in 1982. The temporary roof which then protected the chapel can be seen here.

Photo: Warwick Rodwell

early modern historical references are unequivocally associated with the chapel, and even its dedication has been lost from record. Widely differing estimates have been made of the chapel's age – ranging from the mid-sixth to the thirteenth century – and there has been rampant speculation regarding its origin and associations. Its topographical situation, on the cliff edge and within Saint Brelade's churchyard, has long evoked interest: at the closest point church and chapel are separated by only two metres (frontispiece; Figs. 2–4).

Antiquarian Descriptions of the Fishermen's Chapel

It comes as no small surprise to discover that the earliest mention of the chapel by name is no older than 1817, or two hundred and seventy years after its desecration. While no specific record of that desecration survives in relation to the chapel, there can hardly be any serious doubt that the building ceased to have a religious function soon after 1547, the year of Edward VI's abolition of all Chantries and Parish Fraternities. The fact that the chapel's dedication slipped from local recall in the interval is not wholly remarkable.

Jean Poindestre, in his *Discourse on the Island of Jersey* (1682), relates that 'there were heretofore about 25 Chappells', mentioning five by name, but he did not refer to the Fishermen's Chapel amongst these. Poindestre concluded 'I do not remember of any other undefaced, there remaining at this day nothing but ye very foundations to be seene of above Twenty more dedicated to divers Saints, whome it would be easy but needless to rehearse' (Poindestre, ed. Nicolle, 1889, 31).

Likewise, in Philippe Falle's *Account of the Isle of Jersey*, first published in 1694, we learn that there were then 'above twenty chapels, of which the greater part are now in rubbish. Of those that are left standing there are two of special note'. He then described the chapels at La Hougue Bie and Notre Dame des Pas (Falle, 1694, 119). There is no mention of the Fishermen's Chapel, either here or in Philip Morant's substantially revised edition of Falle's work, published in 1734, and reissued in 1797. Morant was an antiquary and local historian of immense capability (better known in England for his monumental *History of Essex*, 1768). It is therefore difficult to view the repeated omission of any reference to the Fishermen's Chapel as purely coincidental. The implication must surely be that the history, the dedication and even the religious nature of the building in Saint Brelade's churchyard had been wholly forgotten: in the seventeenth and eighteenth centuries the erstwhile chapel was nothing more than a gun shed associated with a battery on the sea wall.

The earliest allusion to the Fishermen's Chapel – then named La Chapelle ès Pêcheurs – is contained in William Plees's description of 1817, *An Account of the Island of Jersey*. He wrote in some detail about the paintings on the vaulted ceiling, which were obviously then exposed to view, concluding, 'the chapel is now employed as an armory for the parochial artillery, so that the whole of these antique designs cannot be seen unless when the guns, &c. are drawn out; and even then, the greater part of the figures being nearly effaced, it is difficult to identify the occurrences to which the paintings refer.' (Plees, 1817, 342–5).

What Plees has to say about the origin of the chapel's name and it assignation to fishermen is interesting: 'This chapel is supposed to have taken its name from the number of fishermen residing in the neighbourhood . . . Another account of the chapel is, that it was frequently the resort of Norman fishermen, who had a priest residing near it to perform the ministerial offices . . . The former of these traditions seems the more probable account'. The writer was clearly reporting local folklore which, as often in cases of this nature, was internally inconsistent. These 'traditions' bear the hallmarks of *post hoc* inventions, promulgated to fulfil the need to explain the origins of a building whose history had passed wholly from memory.

J.N.R. de la Croix, in his history of Jersey (1859), gave a substantial description of the chapel, enthusiastically referring to it as 'antique et isolée sur le bord de la mer, et incontestablement un des premiers édifices consacrés au culte du vrai Dieu', and again as 'la plus ancienne, du moins la plus remarquable de ces chapelles', but he was unable to supplement his observations with any firmly recorded evidence (de la Croix, 1859, I, 153 and 164–5). Down to the middle of the nineteenth century, and beyond, the building was most commonly referred to merely as 'an old chapel' or 'The Ancient Chapel' (Fig. 5). The antiquarian interest and vagueness attending the chapel's origin and circumstances were summed up by a visiting member of the Ecclesiological Society in 1849:

'The greatest ecclesiological treat [in Jersey] is the old chapel of St. Brelade's in the same churchyard: it is of immense antiquity. Indeed, it might be of any age, so entirely is it devoid of distinctive date-marks, except that

Fig. 3.   A mid-nineteenth-century watercolour showing Saint Brelade's Church and the Fishermen's Chapel from the south-west, before the restoration of either building was begun.

From a copy in Saint Brelade's Church

vague pointed vaulting. These chapels, of which there are several in the Channel Islands, are of course all desecrated. St. Brelade's is a carpenter's shop, the carpenter being the parish clerk. It has a rude chancel arch; but is most remarkable for the fragments of fresco remaining upon the plaster ceiling. These frescoes appear to be of the fourteenth century. . . . I understand that a few years ago this interesting decoration was nearly perfect: very little indeed now remains, and that little in a state of very rapid decay.' (Anon., 1850, 181–2).

The Oxford architectural historian, E.A. Freeman, writing in 1845, was brief in his description of the chapel, but a little more precise in his view as to its date: 'In the churchyard stands a small Romanesque chapel, now desecrated; the roof is of the common pointed barrel vault, but adorned with some paintings of later date.' (Freeman, 1845, 64). John Hayward, the Exeter architect, who was responsible for restoration work in several Jersey churches, published his observations of the early 1860s. He unfortunately had little to say about Saint Brelade's: 'it has been surmised that the present churches replaced earlier chapels, and the curious Fisher's Chapel as it is called, at St. Brelade's, affords some support for this. This chapel is certainly a very early structure, and although close to, it is quite detached from, the church, and it was internally decorated with wall painting, which is now almost entirely defaced by time and damp' (Hayward, 1867, 201). In 1884 P.B. Hayward was appointed architect for the restoration of the chapel.

These last three references make no allusion to the use of the chapel as an armoury, since the guns would have departed in *c.* 1844, when the military arsenals were opened; hence the availability of the building for use as a carpenter's shop before 1849. This activity was, however,

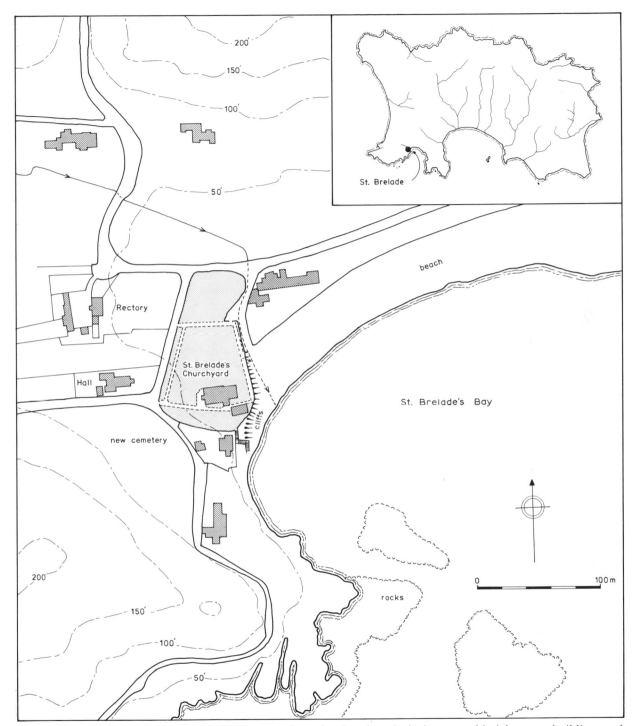

Fig. 4.   Plan of the western part of Saint Brelade's Bay, showing the principal topographical features, buildings and present extent of the churchyard (stippled). The Fishermen's Chapel is the detached building in the south-east corner of the churchyard.

Fig. 5.   View of Saint Brelade's Church and 'The Ancient Chapel' from the west, *c.* 1850, showing the secularised
appearance of both buildings.

From the collection of the late F. de L. Bois.

over by 1861, and in that year the *Jersey Independent* reported: 'This chapel deserves better treatment from the old harridan who exhorts a fee for its exhibition. This interesting relic of the past has been suffered to be encumbered with old ladders, faggots and beanstalks, a crab-pot and a three-legged stool . . . some lively bantams and a motherly cat in the straw'. These miscellaneous secular uses continued until 1883–84.

Meanwhile, scholars continued to take an interest in the chapel. William Burges, architect and artist, visited and made drawings of the paintings, which he exhibited in London in 1848, when he lectured to the Royal Archaeological Institute on the subject of wall paintings.[1] A few years later, in 1864, the paintings were described in the magazine *The Builder* (Anon. 1864), and the principal scenes were noted in C.E. Keyser's handbook of medieval wall paintings (Keyser, 1883, 145). The earliest published illustrations of the paintings are, however, a pair of very crude sketches accompanying de la Croix's account (de la Croix, 1859, I, 339 and 362) (Fig. 16).

Early Topographical Illustrations

Various engravings and photographs exist of Saint Brelade's Church prior to its restoration of 1895–1900, many of which show also tantalising glimpses of the Fishermen's Chapel. While a few distant views include the east end of the chapel, there are better and closer depictions of the west end, seen not as it is today with a small window, but with a pair of solid wooden doors, under a broad segmental arch (Figs. 3, 5 and 6): this was the entrance created in the sixteenth century for the passage of cannon. Unfortunately, no detailed early views of the chapel are known, and there are no measured drawings apart from a plan of *c.* 1880 in the library of the Société Jersiaise. This plan shows the building in its unrestored form (Fig. 7); the opening at west end was seven feet wide, and the original north door was infilled, as were two of the four windows. Other illustrations appear to indicate that all the original windows were blocked while the chapel was in use as an armoury. The oldest view of the chapel, seen from the north-east in 1798, shows no openings in the two visible sides (Fig. 8).

Fig. 6.   The earliest known photographic view of the chapel, taken from the west, and dating from the 1860s or '70s. Note the iron-studded doors in the west wall.

From the collection of the Société Jersiaise.

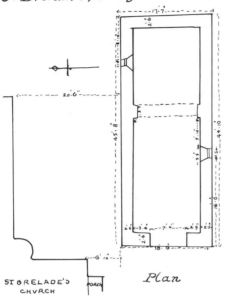

La Chapelle des Pêcheurs,
St Brelade's, Jersey.

Plan

ST BRELADE'S
CHVRCH

Fig. 7. The earliest known plan of the chapel, prior to its restoration in 1884. Note the wide entrance for cannon at the west end; also the north doorway and two of the chancel windows (east and south) remain infilled, while the other two have been reopened.

From the collection of the Société Jersiaise.

Stead del.

Fig. 8. View of Saint Brelade's Churchyard from the north-east, in 1798. The Fishermen's Chapel (arrowed) is the low, windowless building between a house (Le Coleron) in the centre of the picture and the church on the right. In front of all these the military wall can be seen cutting off the eastern end of the circular churchyard, with a flight of steps descending to the sea. Compare with *frontispiece* and Fig. 109.

After Stead, 1798

Fig. 9. The interior of the chapel, looking east, *c.* 1895–1900. The chapel was then used as a meeting room and temporarily housed the wall-tablets which had been removed from Saint Brelade's Church. From a demi-postcard view.

From the collection of L. Le Moignan

The earliest internal view of the chapel, a photograph dating from the period 1895–1900, shows the east end in its fully plastered state, with only faint traces of the paintings visible. The blocked windows had been reopened, a new concrete floor laid, and the sanctuary marked by a step; there were no liturgical furnishings, but stacked against the east end were several marble memorial plaques that had recently been taken down from the walls of the parish church (Fig. 9; and McLoughlin, 1982, 118).

The Restorations of 1877 to 1918

The extensive works undertaken during this period are poorly documented but knowledge of them is essential to an understanding of the archaeology of the chapel, and the conservation record of the medieval wall paintings. The earliest reference to repairs to the chapel is contained in the minute book of the Ecclesiastical Assembly for 1877, when the churchwardens were instructed to put in hand and necessary repairs to the roof 'and other parts' of the old chapel in the cemetery (*l'ancienne Chapelle dans le Cimetière*).[2] Nothing more is known of this work.

Then, in 1883, a fresh initiative was taken: a special committee of distinguished people (including the Bailiff of Jersey) was set up to organise and oversee the rehabilitation of the Fishermen's Chapel (*ladite Chapelle des Pêcheurs*). The committee was expressly charged with the tasks of preserving the existing fabric and carrying out a simple restoration. No funds were to be sought from the parish rates, but had to be raised by subscription.[3] Who instigated this restoration is not recorded: it may have been the recently appointed rector, Josué Le Sueur (1882–92). Progress was evidently not rapid, and six months later the restoration committee instructed the rector to make contact with P.B. Hayward, the Exeter-based ecclesiastical architect, who was then in the island.[4] Shortly afterwards, Hayward was commissioned to prepare a report on the condition of the chapel, specify the works to be carried out, and supply an estimate of the cost.[5]

Unfortunately, Hayward's report has not survived, but it was duly received and debated by the restoration committee in July 1884; the proposed work was authorised and a sub-committee appointed to put it in hand.[6] It is curious that there are no further references to the project in the minutes of the Ecclesiastical Assembly, but it is presumed that the work was carried out forthwith. Even so the chapel was not restored for worship, but for use as a meeting room by both the Ecclesiastical Assembly and the Parochial Assembly (Balleine, 1946, 115). The minutes of the former body record that on 30th August 1887 the Assembly held its first meeting in the chapel, from which it may be deduced that work had been completed. Thereafter, until 1944, the Ecclesiastical Assembly held, on average, no more than one meeting in the chapel each year, other venues being the parish church or, sometimes, a hotel.[7]

Restoration had clearly not begun when La Société Française D'Archéologie visited in July 1883, and a contemporary architectural description of the chapel was published in the account of its proceedings (Anon., 1884), along with a separate paper on Jersey churches. The latter refers to the chapel as having been rendered and limewashed externally 'within the last twenty years' (possibly in 1877?), noting also that the original north doorway was still walled up with stone, and the murals were in poor condition (de Gruchy, 1884, 341).

Having completed a thorough-going restoration of Saint Brelade's Church in 1900, the indefatigable Rector, John A. Balleine, turned his attentions in the opening decade of the present century to further improvements in the Fishermen's Chapel. In 1905 the London architect Adolph Curry was commissioned to report on the condition of the building: his primary concern was the leaking roof, which was covered with slates, set directly onto the outer surface of the stone vault (Fig. 76).[8] Curry recommended repairing the roof *in situ*, rather than relaying it, because:

'To take the slates off would also necessitate the removal of the mortar bedding underneath, which is . . . next to impossible without damaging the existent inside plaster. I doubt whether we have a workman who would refix these stone slates as well as they are now – they varying so much in size – some being double the width of others, having been cut in situ. (This is an art which, in the present day, is quite unknown to our local craft).'

Curry recommended that the joints between the slates be raked out and repointed, estimating the cost to be about £50. The Civil Assembly of the parish budgeted £40 towards this work in the year 1905–6.[9] However, the repairs were not effected until 1908, when secondhand slates matching the existing ones were purchased from Cherbourg.[10]

Over the course of a generation, local knowledge of the mural paintings seems to have lapsed, and they had evidently become almost totally obscured by grime and accretions of salts, followed perhaps by limewashing of the lower parts of the side walls and the east end in the early 1900s (although no traces of limewash were observed to overlie the final polychrome layer during the 1980s conservation work). At any rate, it is certain that by 1915 there was little if anything readily visible on the walls (as opposed to the ceiling vault). According to Balleine, there was said to have been a severe thunderstorm in 1918, following which traces of polychrome were seen in the saturated plaster on the east wall (Balleine, 1932, 33).[11]

By extraordinary good fortune, a German art historian and artist, who was living at 'Bay View' in the parish at the time, heard of the discovery. Alfred N. Oppenheim from Frankfurt am Main was on holiday at Saint Brelade in July 1914, and found himself obliged to remain there for the next

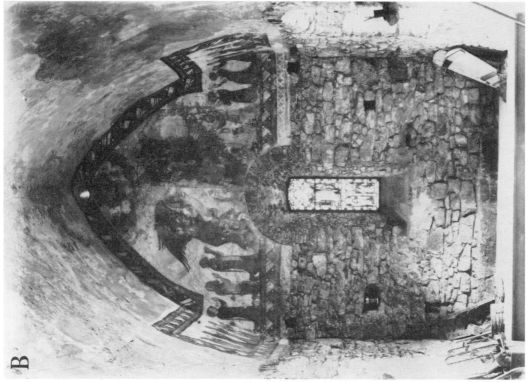

Fig. 10. Two early views of the interior of the chapel, looking east. The chancel walls and arch had recently been stripped of plaster, and the painting of the Annunciation exposed and retouched.

A. A retouched postcard of c. 1920, showing the chapel furnished as a meeting room.
From the collection of Saint Brelade Parish

B. A closer view of the east wall, taken in 1928 when the chapel was being restored following earthquake damage. Five of the original putlog holes are visible here.
Photo: E. Guiton: from the collection of the Société Jersiaise

four years as a First World War refugee. He examined the exposed traces of polychrome and was able to persuade Balleine to allow him to carry out further tests, and subsequently to expose considerable areas of painting. Oppenheim records:

> 'I began (in July 1915) to examine the remains of mural decoration, traces of which were visible on the whole vault and walls. Under the conviction that the main subject would have adorned the wall behind the altar, I started with this eastern part, where only a chaos of dirt and dust covered colour-remains was to be seen. By carefully washing away old dirt I discovered two superimposed coats and characters of paint' (Oppenheim, 1916, 4).

By March 1916 Oppenheim had completed the task of exposing the surviving paintings, and wrote a detailed account of their subject matter. Although he developed a close acquaintance with Balleine, he received no remuneration for many months of work, was given no credit for his labours in Balleine's published account of the restoration of the chapel, and was sadly the object of nationalist hostilities in the local press.[12]

It was decided to remove the very fragmentary remains of the upper paint layer on the east wall (which belonged to the mural of the later period), in order to uncover the earlier painting below, which was then subjected to substantial retouching. Postcards printed around 1920 record the interior of the chapel as Oppenheim left it (Fig. 10). At this date the chapel was still only furnished as a meeting room, with wooden benches around the walls. The postcards also reveal a tragedy: Balleine had started the process of hacking off the ancient plaster from the chapel walls, with a view to exposing and pointing the masonry, as he had done throughout the parish church. At the east end of the chapel the readily accessible plaster, to a height of 2.7 m, was entirely removed, without noticing the paintings on it; these had included life-size figures of saints flanking the east window. Only the tips of their haloes remain today. After Balleine's death in 1941, Oppenheim was able to reveal the sad truth. He wrote, 'In 1915 [Balleine] told me during a visit to the chapel that he had decided to order the decayed plaster of the building to be entirely knocked down in order to renovate the interior of the chapel . . . I asked the rector's consent to let me investigate the east wall, the lower part of which had already fallen victim to the mason's tools.'[13]

The Earthquake and its Aftermath, 1926 to 1935

On 30th July 1926 an earthquake shook the Fishermen's Chapel and the sea wall (which is also the churchyard wall). It was observed that fissures had appeared in the chapel's masonry, including a crack from the ground to the apex of the vault, through the south-west window.[14] A local architect, P. Bown, was commissioned to report upon the damage to the chapel and nearby sea wall. Bown concluded that the damage to the chapel was due to:

> 'the giving way of part of the retaining wall holding up the ground in the vicinity of the chapel. This wall has been built at different times . . . the older portion which is unfortunately the section upon which the stability of the Fishermen's Chapel depends is now in a very bad state. It has cracked and bulged in several places . . . the mortar having perished and large tree roots . . . have further added to its weakness by thrusting out certain portions of the same.'

Bown recommended that the sea wall be rebuilt, section by section, at a cost of approximately

£400.[15] A six-foot length of wall was reconstructed as a trial run,[16] following which the architect reported that this was insufficient and more needed to be done.[17] There is no further mention of the work in the minute book of the Ecclesiastical Assembly, although the remainder of the wall was certainly repaired (Fig. 111). While this work was in hand, Balleine was responsible for the fabrication of another piece of pseudo-history: he claimed that the flight of stone steps leading down to Saint Brelade's Bay from the house which adjoins the churchyard on the south ('Le Coleron') was an ancient sanctuary path, or so-called *perquage*, from the church to the sea. As part of the 1927 repair work, Balleine duly built a gateway in the churchyard wall – where there was none previously – and commandeered the steps (Figs. 4 and 98).

The minute book of the Ecclesiastical Assembly contains no further account of work that was done to the chapel itself. But a massive campaign of repairs was carried out, the cracks in the walls having prompted Balleine to embark on a scheme totally to underpin the foundations. He had already carried out similar operations on parts of the parish church in the 1890s. His published accounts of works on both buildings, and of the archaeological observations made at the time, are valuable for the light they shed on evidence discovered in the most recent excavations; these findings are discussed in chapter 4. Balleine's description implies that the whole interior of the chapel was dug out, with the bed-rock being laid bare at an average depth of six feet below floor level: 'the concrete floor lately laid down is very thick and rests on some three feet of macadam, the human remains having been carefully removed and reverently re-buried in the churchyard' (Balleine, 1932, 37). It would thus appear that the archaeological deposits beneath the chapel had been largely, if not entirely, destroyed.

Upon completion of the underpinning and reflooring, the chapel was fitted out for worship: the sanctuary step, a massive piece of Mont Mado granite 4.35 m in length, which had been introduced in the 1880s and was said to have come from Saint Helier's Church, Jersey, was left in position, and altar rails of polished granite erected upon it in 1930. An altar of rough stone was built against the east wall (Pls. 1 and 2). Its top was one of several medieval stone altar-slabs recovered from Mont Orgueil Castle; at least seven of these slabs had been taken from various Jersey churches in about 1550 and dumped at the castle, since they no had place in the new Calvinist liturgy. The altar-slab in the chapel, which possibly dates from the fifteenth century, was transported there in 1929, having previously served as the cover for a well at the castle (Fig. 95).

A full complement of stained glass windows, by the local artist H.T. Bosdet, was installed around the same time. Three of them are dated by inscriptions to 1930, although the designs were prepared as early as 1914–15.[18] The north window depicts 'Saint Brendan's' boat amongst icebergs and is entitled 'St. Brelade en Voyage', the south chancel window is untitled but shows Saint Brelade holding a thanksgiving service on the Isle of Birds, and the south nave window represents the saint as a student, 'La Jeunesse de St. Brelade'. Until 1987 there was a depiction in the west window of 'Saint Brendan' landing on Jersey and being welcomed by a local 'chieftain'. There was a firm equation between Saint Brendan, the legendary voyager, and Saint Brelade in the iconography of all these windows (Balleine, 1932, 30). The east window (also removed in 1987) contained a representation of Christ calling his disciples, Saint Peter and Saint Andrew, and was installed *c.* 1915.

Balleine's restoration of the chapel proceeded slowly, as funds permitted. The work was once again paid for privately, and not through the parish rate; hence the absence of records in the minute book of the Ecclesiastical Assembly. The task was finally completed in 1935, when the rededication of the chapel was carried out on 22nd September by the Bishop of Winchester (in whose diocese the Channel Islands have lain since 1499).[19] Thus 388 years of desecration and secular use came to an end (Pls. 1–2).

John Balleine was Rector of Saint Brelade for half a century (1892–1941), and it was during this period that a great volume of legendary material relating to the origins and construction of the parish church and the Fishermen's Chapel was promulgated. Two of the leading architectural historians of the mid and later nineteenth century had pronounced the chapel to be Romanesque: first, E.A. Freeman in 1845 (see p. 4), and then J.T. Micklethwaite, on the occasion of the Royal Archaeological Institute's visit to Jersey in 1897,[20] proposed a date in the late eleventh or twelfth century. A.N. Oppenheim (1916, 1) also drew attention to the chapel's Romanesque style, suggesting that it was built between the eighth and the tenth centuries. Notwithstanding, Balleine continually referred to the chapel as sixth century through the nine editions of his guide book (Balleine, 1932, *et seq.*), and postcards bore captions dating it variously to about A.D. 550 and A.D. 600 (Fig. 10A).

The basis of this dating was simple: 'Saint Brelade', he surmised, was a rendering of 'Saint Brendan', the renowned Irish missionary-saint who settled in Brittany. Balleine then made a direct association between Saint Brendan and the foundation of the Fishermen's Chapel, citing as his evidence a verbal opinion given by two visiting French antiquaries that the structure dated from the mid-sixth century (Balleine, 1932, 30). Moreover, the subconscious association between Saint Brendan and the Fishermen's Chapel was visibly reinforced by the stained glass windows of 1930. The west window even represented 'St. Brendan landing perhaps on the very spot, and a Jersey Chieftain embracing Christianity through his ministry'. Sadly, notwithstanding all these displays of patriotic antiquarianism, and published assertions, there is still no scholarly basis for much of the chapel's legendary history that has been so extensively promulgated since about 1900.

Shortly after Balleine's death, Major N.V.L. Rybot – Jersey's doyen archaeologist of the first half of the twentieth century – drafted a new guide to Saint Brelade's Church and the Fishermen's Chapel. He tackled the problem of myth-making head-on:

'The fact that nothing precise is known of the origin and purpose of this obviously ancient building has permitted, and still permits, anyone who lists to advance a theory of his own. Those who claimed that it dated from the sixth century and connected its site with an unrecorded visit by the much-travelled Saint Brendan, were so satisfied with their claim that they welcomed the installation, early in the present century, of a series of admirable stained glass windows representing scenes from the Saint's life.

When the chapel's foundations were underpinned in 1927, many human remains were disturbed, among them being thigh bones which had "belonged to people about seven feet high". Two of the skulls, it was noted, had "cracks in the forehead – the result of having been hit with some heavy stone or implement by the defending natives who killed their owners and buried them where they fell".

Let us hope that this spirited action took place before, and not during or after good Saint Brendan's visit.

But that is not all. Some of the human bones were mixed with the teeth of horses and the tusks of pigs. "It thus appears that the custom then prevalent was that if a man died owning a horse, the animal was killed and buried with its master, and if he only possessed pig, it was likewise put to death and buried with its former owner".

We include all this information because we think that fiction is stranger than truth, and usually much more entertaining. Other and less spectacular theories suggest that the chapel was either an oratory or a private chantry erected in the XIIth or XIIIth century.' (Rybot, 1948, 22–3).

Unfortunately, Rybot died before this guide-book went to press, and it has languished ever since.

His citations of archaeological impossibilities and implausible speculations were but examples: there are many more relating to both church and chapel. It has long been clear that an entirely fresh appraisal of the material, without preconception, is overdue.[21] The evidence – old and new – is re-examined and discussed in chapter 8.

Deterioration and Rejuvenation, 1972 to 1988

The visible deterioration of the wall paintings in the 1950s and '60s gave rise to mounting concern, and by 1971 the old roof was leaking again.[22] In the following year the Rector and Churchwardens commissioned Doctor Clive Rouse to make a detailed report on the paintings.[23] Further investigations and reports followed in 1973 and 1975,[24] and in the latter year the first stage of remedial treatment was begun, with the securing of areas of paint and plaster that were in imminent danger of falling. It was quickly diagnosed that the principal cause of deterioration was the penetration of salt-laden rainwater through the porous roof slates. The moisture, once trapped under the slates, could only soak through the stone vault and into the facing plaster upon which the paintings were executed. The constant transpiration of water through the painted surface not only weakened its key, but also led to the deposition of a crust of salts and residues. Progressively this obscured the colourful pigments, which appeared gradually to be fading. If fact the colours were not fading, but merely disappearing behind an opalescent screen.

Two courses of action were necessary. First, to prevent any further ingress of water through the stone vault and, secondly, to allow the vault to dry out slowly and establish a chemical equilibrium over the course of several years. Both objectives were achieved by erecting a temporary roof of corrugated asbestos sheeting over the entire chapel (Fig. 2). While the drying out process took place plans were laid not only for the full-scale conservation of the paintings, but also for the complete refurbishment of the chapel.

It was recognized that a unique opportunity now presented itself for carrying out a thorough archaeological investigation of the upstanding fabric of the chapel, and to re-examine such buried evidence as might have survived the drastic underpinning operation of the 1920s. In 1982 a preliminary assessment of the archaeological potential of the whole church and chapel complex was made, and followed by trial excavations.[25] Full-scale excavation of the interior of the chapel took place in 1984, and an area of the graveyard between the church and the chapel was opened up in 1985.[26] The results of these investigations are given in chapters 4 and 5.

Meanwhile, conservation of the mural decoration and medieval plaster was carried out over four summer seasons, between 1982 and 1985,[27] and is described in detail in chapter 7. Upon completion of this work the chapel was reroofed, a new granite floor was laid down, a specially designed lighting scheme was introduced, and an entire new suite of furnishings was commissioned. The whole project was finally completed by Easter 1988, and once again achieved by subscription without the need to call upon the parish rates.

2. A BRIEF DESCRIPTION OF THE CHAPEL

The Exterior (Fig. 1)

The chapel is a simple rectangular structure, 14.0 m by 5.6 m (46 by 18½ feet) externally, composed very largely of pink granite boulders which were quarried in the immediate locality. Some have roughly dressed faces. The construction is basically random rubble with little hint of coursing, although some of the 'lifts' in which the walls were raised can be detected with difficulty. There is no use of ashlar or other prepared dressings for the quoins (Fig. 11). The chapel is unbuttressed, and displays no decorative features with the exception of the two gable-crosses.

The one to the west is octagonal shafted (Figs. 12 and 77B) and, although it is absent from illustrations ante-dating c. 1884, there is nevertheless reason to doubt whether it is so recent in origin: the stone, which is Chausey granite, is decidedly more weathered than the late nineteenth-century gable crosses on the parish church.[1] The east gable-cross is badly weathered and is clearly ancient (Figs. 13 and 77A); it has arms of squarish section, and rises from the apex of

Fig. 11. The south-east quoin of the chapel, showing its rough rubble construction. The very small stones were inserted as gap-fillers when the rendering was stripped and the masonry pointed in 1884. See also drawing, Fig. 65.

Photo: Warwick Rodwell

Fig. 12. The late medieval cross of Chausey granite on the western gable of the chapel. Probably removed from the church and placed here *c.* 1884. See also drawing, Fig. 77B.
Photo: Warwick Rodwell

Fig. 13. The early medieval Jersey granite cross on the eastern gable of the chapel; the groove around the upper arm is a fault-line in the rock. The cross probably dates from about the twelfth century. See also drawing, Fig. 77A.
Photo: Warwick Rodwell

a large triangular block of local granite. There is nothing to support the contention that the form of the cross represents a fully robed monk (Balleine, 1932, 23). Its form and splayed base may indicate a twelfth-century date.

The gabled roof has a pitch of forty-five degrees and is now finished with grey Burlington slates from Cumbria. Until 1985, it was covered with slates of dark blue-grey colour, probably of Norman origin. These were bedded in mortar directly on the extrados (outer curve) of the ceiling vault. Below the eaves of the roof on the north and south sides is a plain, horizontal band of masonry (eaves-course) which projects *c.* 5 cm beyond the line of the wall face and is supported by a course composed of thin pieces of granite (Fig. 65).

The chapel is provided with a north doorway (Fig. 14), set hard against the north-west corner, and the interior is lit by five small windows. One is set centrally in each gable wall, there are two in the south wall, and one in the north, towards the north-east corner. The doorway and windows all have low, segmental heads and simple jambs, formed entirely out of small pieces of cut granite. In

Fig. 14.   The north doorway with its late medieval segmentally-arched head; heavily restored in 1884, when the present door was made. See also drawing, Fig. 69.

Photo: Warwick Rodwell

Fig. 15.   The north chancel window in its late medieval form, but retaining the early medieval sill-stone. The rebuilding of the outer arch with small, brick-shaped stones probably dates from 1884. See also drawing, Fig. 66E.

Photo: Warwick Rodwell

size and regularity, the dressings of these arches superficially resemble brickwork, rather than masoncraft. None of this work is original, being neither coursed with the adjacent walling nor in character with it. The large sill stones of the north, east and south-east windows are the only original features associated with these openings (Fig. 15). The slight bulge visible in the masonry around and over the north doorway provides further evidence that its arch and jambs are not contemporary with the wall, but are later introductions.

While the doorway and windows all certainly perpetuate ancient features, it is difficult to estimate the age of the visible masonry owing to the thoroughness of the 1884 restoration. There must be a strong presumption that the very regular, brick-like masonry, particularly of the window jambs, belongs entirely to the late Victorian restoration, not long prior to which the chapel had been plastered on the exterior (p. 10). This is attested by early illustrations. It is most probable that the chapel was originally fully plastered on the exterior, and that this covering had fallen away during centuries of neglect.

The loss of the rendering will have exposed the generally irregular nature of the masonry, and the wide, mortar-filled joints between the granite boulders doubtless appeared unsightly. To counter this, the grosser joints were packed during the restoration with small pieces of stone as part of the task of pointing the masonry. Thus the external texture of the wall surfaces must have been considerably altered through restoration (this process is equally apparent on the parish church), at the same time largely obscuring the evidence for the constructional lifts in the masonry. Doubtless many putlog holes associated with the scaffolding erected by the original builders of the chapel were also plainly revealed when the rendering was removed in 1884; they too have now been obscured.

At the base of the south wall a horizontal band of comprehensive refacing can be seen; this was undertaken in the late 1920s, when the ground here was lowered and a 'dry area' created for better drainage. The most substantial alteration to the chapel effected in 1884 is, however, the most difficult to discern: it is at the west end. The former opening here for the entry of cannon was *c.* 2.2 m (7 ft) wide, and had a low segmental arch (Figs. 3, 5, 6 and 7). This doorway was infilled with masonry and was so skilfully integrated with the general restoration of the exterior that no trace of its arched head or jambs can now be made out, with the possible exception of one projecting stone at the base of the southern jamb.

Some old illustrations depict a small opening in the centre of the west wall, immediately above the door arch. The aperture is usually shown as squarish in shape, although in one drawing it is exaggerated to form a tall, round-headed window. There is little doubt that what was actually visible was a 'ghosted' outline of the surviving uppermost portion of the former west window, antedating the insertion of the large doorway. This window was fully reinstated in 1884, using the east window of the chapel as a model, even to the extent of employing a large, deceptively original-looking granite boulder for the sill (Fig. 66B). The jambs of the reconstituted west window are so similar in stone and in constructional technique to those now at the east end that the contemporaneity of the two features seems assured. In other words, this is another pointer to the likelihood that the neat jambs of all except the south-west window are nineteenth-century renewals.

The Interior (Pls. 1 and 3)

Upon entering the building, two important constructional features are immediately apparent, neither of which is evidenced on the outside. First, the chapel is structurally divided into two cells by a transverse arch carried on a pair of pilasters and, secondly, the building is not truly rectangular in plan, but has aberrant angles and a markedly skewed east wall. The transverse (or pilaster) arch separates the interior into a rectangular nave and a square chancel. The form of the interior therefore resembles that of a small two-celled parish church, with a slender chancel arch. The chancel is lit by the north, east and south-east windows, and the nave by the west and south-west windows, and the door when open.

The walls of the nave are now entirely covered with lime plaster, much of which was applied in 1984–85 as a replacement for a hotchpotch of mortars and cements, dating from 1884 and later works. These patchings largely obscured the constructional features of the walls, and no more than a hint of the outline of the former west doorway could be discerned. Substantial areas of medieval plaster and painting still survive on the upper halves of the nave walls. The formerly bare rubble walls of the chancel and the pilaster-arch have also been replastered, with the result that a unified texture and finish have once again been imparted to the interior of the chapel. Previously, the rough masonry exposed in 1915 had been limewashed.

The nave and chancel are ceiled by a continuous barrel-vault of pointed form; this is of the same height and profile both east and west of the pilaster-arch. The vault rises directly from the tops of the north and south walls, with no offset or other form of demarcation. The vault is cracked in places, and there were formerly many modern cement repairs, all now removed and made good with lime mortar (Figs. 80–82). The vault retains much of its medieval plaster, although large areas of original surface have been lost. Medieval plaster is also well preserved on both gable walls, above window level.

Apart from the painted decoration, the interior of the chapel, like the exterior, is devoid of architectural embellishment. The windows are all widely splayed and have plain, round-headed rear-arches, contrasting with the segmental-headed arches that are now visible externally. The window openings are all ancient except, of course, at the west end where the jambs, splays and sill were reconstituted in 1884, but the round head itself is original. The north doorway has a segmental rear-arch (matching its external arch), which is plastered and carries traces of painted decoration. The heavy oak door and its frame date from 1884.

The chancel arch, which bears no mouldings or ornament, follows the profile of the vault. The pilasters and the arch itself are of simple rectangular cross-section; there is no elaboration at the base of the pilasters, while their tops are crowned by thin slabs of stone which project only very slightly. These slabs are hardly significant enough to be termed 'imposts'. Examination of the exposed masonry clearly demonstrated that the walls, pilaster-arch and ceiling vault were all of contemporary construction. Moreover, the complement of five windows and a north doorway is original, although the external apertures of the windows and the head of the doorway have all been modified in the late Middle Ages. The large west doorway, probably inserted soon after *c.* 1550 and dismantled in 1884, was the only major structural modification carried out in the entire history of the chapel. The evidence is discussed in detail in chapter 5.

3. THE WALL PAINTINGS

'The curious in antiquities may find wherewithal to speculate upon, in the vestiges of some rude paintings that are still to be discovered on the walls of the chapel, and which, in their day, were no doubt thought to embellish them'.(Inglis, 1834, 76)

Loss and Rediscovery

While there can be no doubt that the paintings in the Fishermen's Chapel should have been obliterated from view with a coat of limewash in *c.* 1550, there is no direct evidence that this ever happened. Even though the chapel had fallen out of liturgical use, the murals, if left uncovered, would have constituted an unacceptable display of 'popery' within the precinct of the parish church. Once converted into an armoury, it is most unlikely that the interior of the former chapel was ever again redecorated. Nineteenth-century descriptions and accounts of Alfred Oppenheim's work in 1915 seem to indicate that there was virtually no painted decoration visible on the east wall or on the side walls, and that these areas had possibly been limewashed over. The vaulted ceiling, on the other hand, was probably not masked with limewash.[1] The likely reason for this difference is readily appreciable: it would have been very easy to limewash the walls and east gable from a ladder, but access to the vaulted ceiling would have required scaffolding.

Gradually, as dampness penetrated through the failing roof structure into the vault and walls below, the limewash will have flaked away, and further portions of the decoration must have re-emerged into view, not that they would have been easy to see with all the windows blocked up. An oblique reference to this situation was made in 1844: the paintings 'are now so much defaced that very little can be traced out, except when the strong light of the sun shines into the building' (Baker, 1844, 171).

The rafters and battens supporting the late medieval slated roof decayed until a point was reached, sometime in the eighteenth or the early nineteenth century, when it was determined to relay the slates on a bed of mortar, directly on the vault (p. 91). For a time, this doubtless improved conditions inside the chapel, and if the vault dried out substantially, a good deal of loose paint and limewash would have flaked away of its own accord. This is likely to account for the inferences that the paintings were in tolerably good condition in the earlier nineteenth century (p. 4; Anon., 1850, 182).

The earliest attempt to describe and interpret the subject matter of the paintings appears to have been by William Plees in 1817:

'The interiour of the chapel has been ornamented with a variety of figures, displaying different scenes from the New

21

Testament. These figures are about four feet in height, and painted in colours on the plastered walls; but time, accident, and perhaps wantonness, have nearly effaced them. On the right [nave, south] is still distinguishable an angel, having in one hand a scroll, on which is an inscription in Gothic characters. He holds this towards a female, whose hands are uplifted in the attitude of praying: behind her, on a curvated pole, is a reading desk, with a book open, in which are some nearly illegible letters. We may venture to suppose this to represent the annunciation.

'On the left-hand wall [nave, north] is a man, crowned, with an antique sword in his right hand: from his mouth issues a scroll, on which is inscribed *herod le roy*. His garments are of an olive colour, and over them is a scarlet robe flowing to the ground. On the lower part of the same wall is Jesus Christ, bearing his cross, depicted with yellowish hair, and his head surrounded with a glory.

'Over the entrance which is opposite to the west, is the figure of a man robed with a number of naked persons round him; some at full length, others just emerging from the ground. This is doubtless a representation of the general resurrection. The figures of this composition are smaller than those on the side walls. All are tolerably well proportioned; but, like many other ancient religious portraits, there is little expression in the features of those personages. The figures are mere sketches; but the colours appear to be well preserved.' (Plees, 1817, 343–4).

The next substantial description of the chapel's decoration was published by de la Croix in 1859, in which he first states that there were four paintings, and later refers to a dozen. He describes the Resurrection above the west doorway, the Annunciation on the south wall, Herod and the Massacre of the Innocents, and Christ carrying the Cross, on the north wall. The descriptions and interpretations given by de la Croix are fuller than those of Plees, and are accompanied by a pair of crudely executed line drawings of the scenes on the north wall of the nave (Fig. 16; de la Croix, 1859, I, 164–7, 338–9 and 361–2).

Fig. 16.   The earliest known illustration of paintings in the Fishermen's Chapel, 1859, showing part of the north side of the nave vault (Slaughter of the Innocents, and the Flagellation). These are very schematic and inaccurate in many details, but the areas of damage and paint loss outlined correspond closely with the surviving evidence. The two drawings were originally printed separately, but are reproduced here in register. In the lower tier the line which appears to cut off the figures at the knees probably represents an intruded fixture, since the paintings continue further down the wall. The label 'Flagellation, Crucifixion' is the artist's addition (the last scene is not the Crucifixion, but the Carrying of the Cross). Compare with Pls. 16 and 23.

After de la Croix, 1859.

Fig. 17. Nave vault, north side: the Slaughter of the Innocents. Detail of Herod, before conservation (1977); compare with Fig. 16 and Pl. 16.

Photo: Geoffrey Parker

Another first-hand description was published in *The Builder* in 1864, where it was stated that,

'The paintings were apparently confined to the vault.[2] Along the apex is a line of scroll foliage. Each side of the vault is divided into three long horizontal lines of painting, executed in red outlines with considerable artistic skill, on the ground of pale buff-tinted plaster, the subjects running continuously without separation. . . . On the north side, so far as they remain, seem to relate to the Passion of Our Lord. Beginning at the west end, we have first the 'Trial before Herod'. . . . The next subject is the 'Binding of Our Lord'. The second row begins with the 'Scourging', next the 'Bearing the Cross'. The lower line of the painting is obliterated. On the south side of the vault, the subjects . . . relate to the Nativity. Beginning at the west end, in the first subject is seen a portion of a royal figure, but the subject is so far obliterated as to be undecipherable. The next as an 'Annunciation'. At the west end of the chapel is 'St. Michael weighing the Souls'. The vacant spaces in the background between the figures are powdered with a very simple pattern consisting of five small circles.' (Anon., 1864, 733).

Further details, not previously noted, appear in later accounts: thus in the 1883 description of the Nativity (Adoration) scene on the south side of the nave, Mary, Joseph and the infant Jesus are all mentioned (there is now nothing remaining of Jesus), and reference is made to the presence of Joseph's name in Gothic script. Likewise, the names of the Magi in the Adoration scene are said to be recorded (Caspar alone remains today) (Anon., 1884, 444). The same account supplies the explanation for the complete lack of any reference to paintings in the chancel: the east end of the chapel was in darkness, and the visiting party complained of its inability to procure a torch, but concluded that there were the severely effaced remains of a painting on the east wall. This account provides further evidence that the chapel windows were still blocked at this date.

But the opening-up was soon to come, and when Keyser listed the paintings, he was the first to note what he believed to be the Assumption of the Virgin, on the east wall (Keyser, 1883, 143).[3] None of the published nineteenth-century accounts refers to the Old Testament cycles on the south side of the chancel, or the Entry into Jerusalem, on the north side. These, and other less well preserved scenes, must have been substantially hidden from view.

Subject Matter and Iconography
by Gottfried Hauff

In the course of studying the wall paintings of England, the painted decoration of the Fishermen's Chapel was soon considered by antiquaries to be of great art-historical importance. Except for two much more fragmentary decorations – one at Saint Clement's Church, and the other at the chapel at La Hougue Bie – these are the only surviving wall paintings in Jersey, and they are certainly the most outstanding. They are mentioned, for example, in the *List of Churches having Mural Decorations* (Keyser, 1883), and a photograph of the east wall painting was published in *Englische Malerei des Mittelalters* (Borenius and Tristram, 1927, 40–1; pl. 76).

It has long been recognized that there were paintings of two different periods in the chapel. Previous accounts of the iconographical aspect of the paintings have, however, been very sketchy. There have been only two serious attempts to explain the iconographical programme of the paintings of the Fishermen's Chapel: the first was by Alfred Oppenheim in 1916[4], and the second by Doctor Clive Rouse in 1975.[5] On both occasions the paintings were in a rather poor state of preservation, large parts being obscured by incrustations, or disfigured by cement patchings.

Today, after their conservation and restoration, it has become necessary to make a third attempt, which will be more detailed and specific and will differ in some points of interpretation from the earlier ones.

THE PAINTINGS OF THE EARLIER PERIOD

I.1 THE ANNUNCIATION (Pls. 4–7)

East wall.

The painting of the east wall, and its two continuations which extend onto the north and south walls of the chancel as far as the windows, show a representation of the Annunciation, together with the family of the donors of the decoration. The Virgin Mary, clothed in a red robe, is holding her hands in a gesture which can be seen to be one of greeting, and is turning her head towards the archangel Gabriel. She bears two symbols, a lily and a vase, representing, respectively, the rod of Jesse and (for Mary) the vessel of incarnation. A lectern, in front of which the Virgin is standing, supports an open book with an inscription.

The complete text of this quotation from Psalms 51:15 reads: *Domine labia mea aperies. Et os meum annunciabit laudem tuam*, 'O Lord, open my lips. And my mouth shall shew forth thy praise'.

The painted architecture in the background may be interpreted as symbolizing either a sacred or a secular building, representing either the home of the Virgin, or the Church (Pl. 6). On the left, the archangel, who is holding a scroll in one hand, is depicted in a pose which may be interpreted as kneeling or approaching in a devout attitude (Pl. 5). The inscription on the scroll, now blank except for the first initial, *A*, must originally have been a quotation from Luke 1:28, *Ave Maria gratia plena*[6], ['And the angel came unto her and said'] "Hail, Mary, thou that art highly favoured, the Lord is with thee; blessed art thou among women". The angel's other hand is raised in a declamatory gesture.

Above these two figures, God the Father is seen, clothed in red, and surrounded by a nimbus of clouds, his right hand raised in benediction, his left carrying an orb (Pl. 7). Rays of light extend from him towards the Virgin. The dove, symbol of the Holy Spirit, commonly appears with the rays, or directly above the Virgin's head, in paintings of the Annunciation from the thirteenth century onward; it does not, however, appear here.[7]

On a smaller scale than the Virgin and the archangel, are depicted fourteen figures of the donor's family, kneeling, and with their hands raised in prayer (Pls. 5–6 and 8–9). It has been proposed by Oppenheim that the donors are members of the de Carteret family, the seigneurs of Saint Ouen's Manor. There is no evidence to support this conjecture, and the hypothesis is improbable (Oppenheim, 1916, 24; for further discussion see p. 142).

1.2 UNIDENTIFIED FIGURES

East wall.

The scene of the Annunciation is framed with an elaborate bent-riband, with an additional frieze of black quatrefoils on the lower border (Pl. 4). Below, on the north side of the window, is a fragment of a red halo, which suggests that the figure of a saint – or more than one – was depicted on the lower part of the east wall.

1.3 UNIDENTIFIED

South wall.

The only other piece of decoration from the earlier period is to be found on the lower tier of the south wall of the nave (not illustrated). Some fragments of saints are preserved there, with red haloes on a white background. The latter is decorated with red trefoils, very similar to the quatrefoils of the border described above. The red and yellow frame is again analogous to the outer part of the frame on the east wall.

There is no clue to the meaning of the scene, but its size suggests that it may have been part of a sequence running along the wall of the nave. Judging by the colours, the tiny fragmentary traces of painting surviving in the area below these figures probably belong to the same scheme of decoration. This would indicate that even larger parts of the chapel may possibly have been covered with decorations of the earlier period.

THE PAINTINGS OF THE LATER PERIOD

There is much more evidence remaining of the paintings of the later period than of the earlier one, enough to understand the overall iconographical concept. The east wall, above the altar, formerly carried a representation of the Virgin Mary. The side walls and vault of the chapel were covered – and these paintings are still partially preserved – with two cycles from the Old and New Testaments, respectively: the Fall of Man and the Life of Christ. The west wall carries a painting of the Last Judgement.

The two cycles on the vault and flanking walls are presented in two tiers on either side of the apex, and are horizontally separated from one another by ornamental friezes. Those of the chancel are decorated with a continuous, red, scallop-shaped (or pelta) pattern (Pl. 10 and Fig. 19), and those of the nave with a black ivy-scroll pattern (Pl. 11 and Fig. 20). The chancel arch, which forms a vertical subdivision, is covered with a colourful plant-scroll, possibly representing a fig tree bearing fruit (Pl. 31 and Fig. 21).[8] The white background to the tiers carries various decorative combinations of black and red florets, and crescents, similar to those in medieval tapestries.

The cycles are, in our opinion, to be read starting in the chancel with the upper tier at the east end of the south wall, and moving westwards, after which they continue along the opposite (north) wall, from west to east. The cycles then jump down to the lower tier – which has mostly perished – and start again in the south-east corner (Fig. 18).

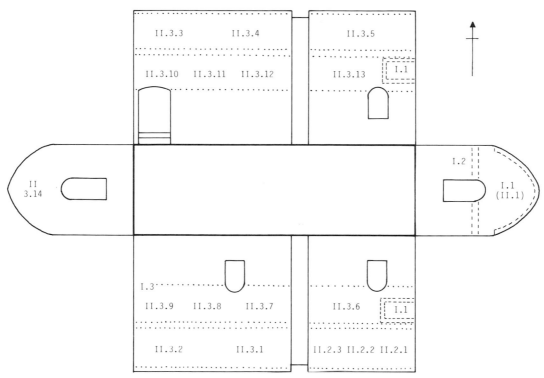

Fig. 18. Key diagram to the iconographic programme of wall painting in the chapel.

Fig. 19. The scallop-shaped pattern used to define the decorative tiers on the chancel vault. See also Pls. 10 and 22.

Fig. 20. The ivy-scroll pattern and *S* motifs decorating the crown of the nave vault. See also Pls. 11–13.

Fig. 21. The plant-scroll pattern decorating the soffit of the chancel arch. See also Pl. 31.

II.1 VIRGIN AND CHILD

East wall.

As mentioned above, the east wall today displays only a painting of the earlier period. The subject matter of the later painting, which was removed in 1915, can no longer be established with any certainty. Oppenheim asserts that 'only parts of the surroundings were visible', mainly pieces of 'a *fond à fleurons* mingled with red crescents', 'parts of a throne', 'flanked . . . on either side . . . by a white-winged angel', clad in a 'long red garment and playing on a long trumpet, and in the upper part by two smaller flying angels, clothed in yellow, their censers swinging and crossing the frame lines'. Nothing else was left of the main subject, except a few lines 'defining the two haloes'. Oppenheim concluded, 'there appears . . . no doubt that here an enthroned Virgin and Child had been represented' (Oppenheim, 1916, 8–9).

In later descriptions of the chapel,[9] this lost painting is mentioned as having portrayed the Assumption of the Virgin Mary, but no reason or evidence is put forward for this different interpretation; and it must be said in support of Oppenheim that an isolated representation of the Assumption would be rather exceptional.[10] It is therefore probable that Oppenheim was correct in identifying the painting on the east wall as depicting the Virgin and Child.

II.2 OLD TESTAMENT CYCLE

Chancel vault, south side, upper tier.

Only fragments of the Old Testament cycle, originally consisting of three scenes, are preserved. Nevertheless the subjects of two of these scenes can be discerned, and one deduced. The background shows a red floral brocade pattern.

II.2.1 Adam and Eve (Pl. 10)

In the first scene, reading from east to west (i.e. from left to right), two nude figures are portrayed, simply standing one beside the other. They are Adam and Eve. Long blonde hair and bare breasts, one of which she is covering with her left hand, show the figure on the left to be Eve. The other figure (Adam) is also covering his breast with his arm and hand. Moreover, a fig leaf with which he covers his nakedness has also been preserved. It may be assumed that the figure of Eve originally held a similar leaf (Fig. 22). Unfortunately, only a single letter, *A*, remains of the inscription which originally ran above Adam's head, and probably above Eve's too. The scene must be interpreted as a representation of Adam and Eve, the First Parents. It is a relatively uncommon scene. From a comparison with many similar medieval cycles, we should expect the Creation of Adam, possibly combined with the Creation of Eve (Kirschmann, 1970, 42).

II.2.2 The Fall Of Man (Pl. 10 and Fig. 24)

The second (middle) scene of the cycle from the Old Testament shows the Fall of Man. It must have been painted in the stereotyped, symmetrical version of the time, with the two figures shown on either side of the Tree of Knowledge[11] (Fig. 23). In our example, Adam is standing on the left, covering his breast with one hand; his name is still partially legible above his head.

Eve, with long blonde hair, is standing on the right, again covering her nakedness with a fig leaf. With the other hand (now lost), she was most probably holding the apple. The Tree

Fig. 22.   Adam and Eve. Reconstruction of scene II.2.1.

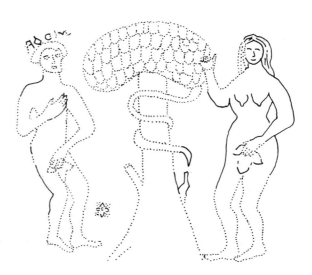

Fig. 23.   The Fall of Man. Reconstruction of scene II.2.2.

of Knowledge, together with the serpent of temptation, originally between the two figures, have both perished. Only the tip of the snake, which must have been depicted coiling around the tree, can still be seen.

II.2.3 Identification Uncertain

The last scene of the cycle (on the extreme right) can no longer be determined. However, following the traditional sequence, it would have depicted the Expulsion from Paradise. In the medieval tradition this episode portrays Adam and Eve expelled by a cherub brandishing a flaming sword (Kirschmann, 1968, 67). A piece of architecture, such as a door or a wall, symbolizes the division between paradise and the profane world.

Fig. 24.   Detail of Eve from the Fall of Man (II.2.2).

Photo: Robin Briault

II.3 THE LIFE OF CHRIST

The first and smaller section of this cycle, depicting the infancy of Jesus, survives in
fragments large enough to identify the three scenes with certainty. They all have a
background *à fleurons* with simple red and black florets. In addition, the first two scenes
have a row of stencilled upper-case letters *S* running along the top edge. The letter has
been interpreted by Oppenheim (1916, 16) as an abbreviation of *Sanctus* (Fig. 20 and Pl. 11).

II.3.1 The Annunciation (Pls. 11–12)

Nave vault, south side, upper tier, left panel.

Compared to the painting on the east wall, this later depiction of the same event, following a slightly different concept, has a more dramatic effect. The Virgin is standing on the right in front of her lectern, both hands raised, turning her head in an attitude of surprise towards the archangel (Fig. 25). She is wearing a red robe and a coat with a fur lining, a symbol of her royalty. Rays of light beam down towards her, and the fragment of a bird's wing indicates that a dove, representing the Holy Spirit, was originally visible directly above her head. The lectern bears an open book. The first word of the inscription is still decipherable as *Domine*, from which it may be assumed that it originally quoted Psalm 51.

There is no architectural detail to define the setting of this scene. On the left of the Virgin there is still a fragment of the lily. However, because of the large lacunae, we cannot know whether there were originally more attributes represented. The depiction of the archangel, who has his name *Gabriel* written above his head, follows a specific late Gothic type (Kirschmann, 1968, 639).

Not only does he have wings with long feathers, like his counterpart in the fourteenth-century painting, but his whole body, including arms and legs, is covered with grey feathers (Pl. 12). His face is that of a youthful man, and he wears a red head-dress with a small cross. A scroll, probably originally bearing an inscription of the angel's greeting, has all but perished, and the words are no longer legible.

Fig. 25.   The Annunciation. Reconstruction of scene II.3.1.

II.3.2 The Adoration Of The Magi (Pls. 13–14)

Nave vault, south side, upper tier, right panel.

Although most of the painting is lost, the original composition of the scene depicting the Adoration of the Magi can be reconstructed to a large extent (Fig. 26). Reading the painting from the left, the first figure is Joseph. He is wearing a red hat, above which his name appears (Pl. 14).

The female figure with the red halo who is next to him must therefore be Mary. There follows a large lacuna, and then fragments of two male figures, two of the Magi. They are clad in colourful, contemporary medieval clothes:

Fig. 26.   The Adoration of the Magi. Reconstruction of scene II.3.2.

tight-fitting hose and short jackets with huge, sagging sleeves (so-called bombarde sleeves). The name of one of the kings still appears above his crown: *Caspar*.

There are fragments of a chalice which he is holding in his right hand. Of the first extant king, Oppenheim reported that above his head was 'written in Gothic letters the name . . . Melchior' (Oppenheim, 1916, 12). The inscription has since perished. The first of the Magi, who must therefore have been Balthasar, has totally disappeared. The same is true of the main figure of the scene – the infant Jesus – and there is no way of telling how and where he was originally situated. The child was probably seated on Mary's lap, following a certain medieval tradition of representation influenced by the French mystery plays. In this tradition, the first of the Magi kneels in front of Mary and the child; the second turns back and points out the star to the third, who stands upright, looking towards the child (Kirschmann, 1968, 542).

II.3.3 The Slaughter Of The Innocents (Pl. 15)
Nave vault, north side, upper tier, left panel.

The cycle now continues on the opposite wall with the scene of the Slaughter of the Innocents. King Herod is seated on a throne and is further identified by a scroll bearing the inscription, *Herodes Roy*.

He is wearing a crown and the very fashionable, two-coloured robe. In his right hand he holds a bare sword, symbolizing his ordering the slaughter (Pls. 16–17).

Further on are fragments of two men in armour and a female figure. No definite trace of the slaughtered innocents themselves is visible today, but the painting suggests that the soldiers were originally depicted each holding a child; or holding a single child between them, with one hand each, and a weapon with the other hand (Fig. 27). The female figure on the right, dressed in a long robe and wearing a bonnet, is holding a *battoir à ligne* raised above her head. She is to be interpreted as the child's mother, trying to defend it against the soldiers. The inclusion of a *battoir à ligne* in this scene is assumed to indicate a link with the districts of Cotentin and Avranches.[12]

Fig. 27. The Slaughter of the Innocents. Reconstruction of scene II.3.3.

II.3.4 Unidentifiable Scene (Pl. 18)
Nave vault, north side, upper tier, right panel.

Very little of the following scene is discernible. There are a few fragments of the background and of what appears to have been a figure. Somewhat to the right of this figure are the remains of another, rather shorter than the first, with long blonde hair and a halo, dressed in a long red garment and a long grey coat. Both halo and garments indicate that the figure could represent either Jesus or the Virgin Mary (Pl. 19). As the scene is placed between the Slaughter of the Innocents and Christ's Entry into Jerusalem, there is quite a choice of possible subjects, of which the most common were the Flight into Egypt, the Presentation of the infant Jesus, the Boy Jesus in the Temple, and the Baptism of Jesus. Each of these scenes was used to represent either the conclusion of Jesus's infancy or the commencement of his public ministry.

The section recalling the Passion of Christ makes up the larger part of the life cycle, and originally consisted of about nine scenes. Today only five of these can be identified with any certainty from the remaining fragments.

II.3.5 The Entry Into Jerusalem (Pl. 20 and Fig. 28)
Chancel vault, north side, upper tier.

The painting of the Entry into Jerusalem covers the whole upper tier of the chancel vault; the background is a decoration of red crescents. The scene shows Christ in the middle, astride a small donkey, with his right hand raised in a gesture of blessing, and his left hand holding the reins of the animal (Pl. 21). As in the other scenes of the Passion, Christ is portrayed with long, wavy blonde hair, a short blonde goatee, and a halo with a cross inset. Of his retinue, fragments of only one figure remain, a male figure with a red head-dress walking behind Christ.

To the east, the picture is filled with painted architecture representing the city of Jerusalem (Pl. 22). It is composed of towers decorated with flags, roofs with red and white tiles, a high city wall, battlements, etc. There is a kneeling figure in the gateway, his arms raised to welcome Christ, and another figure on one of the towers, throwing down flowers in greeting.

Following our proposed order in reading the cycles painted on the north and south sides of the chapel, we conclude that the Passion of Christ now continues in the lower tier on the south side. Unfortunately, there is not a single scene preserved on this side which can be identified with

Fig. 28.   The Entry into Jerusalem. Reconstruction of scene II.3.5.

certainty. However, all the fragments remaining show the simple background *à fleurons*, which seems to be characteristic of the Life of Christ cycle. Furthermore, the fact that the end of the cycle, from the Flagellation to the Crucifixion, is depicted to a quite detailed extent on the north side suggests that the earlier Stations of the Cross were almost certainly also depicted in the cycle.

II.3.6 Identification Uncertain
Chancel vault, south side, lower tier.

There are only three small isolated fragments of the scene, or scenes, that once covered the southern lower tier of the chancel vault. The eastern fragment, adjoining the earlier painting on the east wall, shows an area of background *à fleurons*, part of an arm and the hand of a figure holding a round object, only partially preserved. The second fragment is situated at the upper border of the tier. It shows the lines of two haloes and parts of the inscriptions above them, which originally bore the names of the figures depicted. The second of these could possibly be the name *Petrus*.

The third fragment, which is at the lower border, consists of different colours and lines which must have been part of the long robes of figures. The second and third fragments together indicate that in the middle of the panel there were originally several figures standing upright, at least two of them saints.

Oppenheim recorded the existence of another fragment, 'a round beardless head, wearing a black cap, and parts of an inscription'. He interpreted this figure as David. He also mentioned a 'big hand, holding a stick or shaft of a lance; probably the fragment of a representation of Goliath' (Oppenheim, 1916, 15). Unfortunately, the 'David' fragment was removed by Oppenheim, which precludes any further investigation of his hypothesis. However, it must be said that a representation of David and Goliath in this place seems highly improbable. It would stand totally isolated, without any iconographical connection with either the Old Testament cycle or the Passion of Christ cycle. Moreover, how are we to explain the presence of two or more saints in the scene?

Finally, the simple black and red floral pattern of the background is found, elsewhere in the chapel, only in scenes from the New Testament. In a cycle such as we have here, one would expect the Entry into Jerusalem to be followed by the Last Supper or Judas's Betrayal of Christ. Judging by the extant fragments, the latter is more likely. The figures seem to have been depicted standing, not sitting at a table. Furthermore, for reasons of aesthetic balance, a table would very probably have extended for the whole width of the panel; and if that were so, the area around the hand that is carrying an object – an area which clearly bears the general pattern of the background – would have been part of the table's surface.

II.3.7, 3.8 and 3.9 Identifications Uncertain
Nave vault, south side, lower tier.

The only surviving fragment in the west corner of the lower tier on the south side of the nave displays a section of background *à fleurons* and the depiction of some object, the meaning of which cannot be deciphered.

We assume that for reasons of symmetry this lower tier on the south side originally carried the same number of scenes as that on the north side, as is true for the upper tier. Hence, we deduce that there were once three scenes here, and would expect these panels to depict events from the Passion of Christ that occurred before the Flagellation. Possible themes would be the Mocking of Christ, Christ before Caiphas, Christ before Pilate, or the Crowning with Thorns (Kirschmann, 1977, 40).

The Passion cycle leads on to four scenes on the lower tier of the north side of the chapel which are preserved well enough to be identified. They all have the simple background *à fleurons*.

II.3.10 The Flagellation (Pls. 15 and 23 and Fig. 29)
Nave, north side, lower tier.

The Flagellation is the first of three surviving scenes. Here, Christ is depicted standing naked in front of the column of flagellation, which forms the central axis of the painting. His body is covered with weals as a result of the lashing, each weal showing three red droplets of blood. These marks, together with the halo with the cross inset, and the blonde hair and beard previously mentioned, are characteristics of Christ throughout the rest of the Passion cycle (Pl. 24). Two rogues, dressed in fashionable medieval clothes, are standing on either side, holding the whips in their hands. The one on the left is depicted actually striking Christ on the shoulder with his whip, which has knots or nails in its thongs.

Fig. 29.   The Flagellation. Reconstruction of scene II.3.10.

II.3.11 The Carrying Of The Cross (Pl. 25 and Fig. 30)
Nave, north side, lower tier.

The next scene, a painting of the Carrying of the Cross, seems similarly to have been composed of three figures. Christ is pictured in the middle, and again seems to be naked, carrying the cross on his left shoulder. The surviving fragments of paint around the cross-beam must belong to a human figure. In many medieval renditions of this scene, Simon of Cyrene is shown helping to carry the cross (Kirschmann, 1970, 650), but whether we have a representation of Simon here, or of a soldier, or some other figure altogether, cannot be determined any more.

Fig. 30.   The Carrying of the Cross. Reconstruction of scene II.3.11.

II.3.12 The Nailing Of Christ To The Cross (Pl. 26 and Fig. 31)
Nave, north side, lower tier.

The few remaining fragments of the scene show several features that are common characteristics of a representation of the Nailing of Christ to the Cross (Kirschmann, 1970, 600). He is depicted with outstretched arms, lying on the cross. Surviving fragments of the painting suggest legs and feet and the soldiers' swords, similar to one in the previous scene. It can be deduced that there were four or five kneeling figures arranged around the figure of Christ, and one standing to the right-hand side. These kneeling figures must have been soldiers, depicted nailing or binding Christ's arms and legs to the cross.

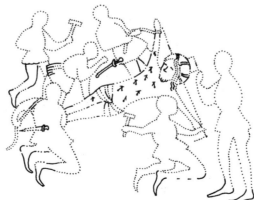

Fig. 31.   The Nailing of Christ to the Cross. Reconstruction of scene II.3.12.

II.3.13 The Crucifixion (Pl. 27)
Chancel, north side, lower tier.

In the chancel, where we find the first station of Christ's Passion depicted (viz. his entry into Jerusalem), we also find the final scene of this cycle, the Crucifixion, in the lower tier. The few remaining fragments in the middle of the panel show Christ on his Cross, wearing a green loincloth. There is an inscription below his right arm, and this probably reads, *Hodie eris m(ecum) i(n) p(aradiso)*, 'Today you shall be with me in paradise', the words of Christ to one of the thieves (Luke 23:43).

Some traces of brown colour further to the right seem to have belonged to the crossbeam of one of the two crucified thieves. Medieval representations of the Crucifixion often included the thieves, one on either side of Christ, and this was probably the case here (Fig. 32).

Fig. 32.   The Crucifixion. Reconstruction of scene II.3.13.

II.3.14 The Last Judgement (Pl. 28 and Fig. 33)
West wall.

As in so many places of worship with mural paintings, the west wall of the chapel displays a large painting of the Last Judgement, which confronts us on leaving the building (Kirschmann, 1972, 520). Christ, the judge of the world, is shown seated on a throne with his torso and his feet exposed to reveal the wounds of his crucifixion (Pl. 29). Much of the upper part of the figure is lost, but according to the traditional type his head must have been surrounded by a halo with a cross inset, as in the Passion cycle, and his forearms raised to show the marks of the nails in his hands. Some of the *arma Christi* are displayed on either side: the three nails and the lance on one side, and the lower part of what could have been the cross, or the stick with the sponge, or the ladder of the deposition, on the other.

The area below the majestic representation of Christ the Judge contains a considerable number of figures painted on a smaller scale, of which twenty-seven are at least partially intact. The two largest represent archangels. They are placed on either side of the window and are clothed in strange garments; each has a head-dress decorated with a small cross. They are proclaiming the Day of Judgement with their long trumpets (Pl. 30). All the remaining figures are depicted naked

Fig. 33.   The Last Judgement. Reconstruction of scene II.3.14.

and turning towards Christ, their arms raised in prayer as they emerge each from a small black coffin. There are women with long blonde hair, men with short hair, two figures who appear to have tonsures and may represent monks, two with plain round caps, two mitred bishops, two figures wearing large hats who must be noblemen, and two with long tipped hats who are probably ladies. Finally, there is even a king with his crown.

Altogether, this depiction constitutes a fair cross-section of medieval society. None of the figures shows any sign of despair so that, presumably, they represent the Blessed, who have been resurrected from the dead, adoring Christ. This very restricted version of the Last Judgement, which excludes violence, presupposes the omitted scenes of Christ's own resurrection and the apocalyptic separation of the Blessed from the Damned.[13] According to Fournée (1964, 130), it is characteristic of painting in northern France at this time.

Dating and Stylistic Observations
by Sven Mieth

No satisfactory attempt to date the paintings of the Fishermen's Chapel by examining the costumes and the stylistic features has yet been made. Previously suggested datings vary considerably. The Annunciation on the east wall, exposed by Oppenheim, has been variously dated between *c.* 1315 and 1425. For the later paintings in the chancel and the nave, dates between *c.* 1400 and 1450 have been suggested.[14] Unfortunately, we too are far from able to offer exact dates. However, we tend to the view that the older painting was executed during the third quarter of the fourteenth century, while the later painting can be dated to around 1425.

THE FOURTEENTH-CENTURY PAINTING

While the clothing depicted in the fifteenth-century painting must remain problematic, since the artist could have based his work on patterns and design books that were already antiquated, the clothing depicted in the Annunciation on the east wall may well reflect the contemporary fashion. It is extremely unlikely that the donors would have allowed themselves to be depicted in anything but their best and newest clothing, in what might be termed a 'representational' picture. Unfortunately, fashions in the Middle Ages did not change as frequently as they do today.

The knight (the second kneeling figure behind Gabriel, Pl. 5) wears a bright, tight-sleeved and tight-waisted *pourpoint* (doublet), an example of which is still extant today, made for the Blessed Charles de Blois (Enlart, 1916, 56; pl. 76) De Blois's *pourpoint* dates from *c.* 1360. However, the donor figure of the priory church of Friardel, Calvados, who is very similar to our knight, wears a comparable jacket, and this ex-votive picture from the same region is dated to *c.* 1385 (Thibout and Deschamps, 1963, 193; illus. CCXII-1). Similarly, the clothing of the figure in front of the knight permits us to draw no firm conclusions. There are numerous examples in France dated between 1350 and 1375 of this *houppelande* (a formal outer garment) with a hood *à cornette* thrown back. Similar also in their posture, are the kneeling figures of the de la Grange memorial in Avignon, *c.* 1370 (Enlart, 1916, 77; pl. 56). In any event, the Annunciation on the east wall could not have been executed much later than 1375.

The depiction of a wedding celebration in the *Très Belles Heures de Notre Dame* (*c.* 1380) represents a point at which Ladies' fashions changed (Scott, 1980, 84; pl. 56). It is useful to compare this scene with the Annunciation in the Fishermen's Chapel. The sleeves of the ladies' clothing are still tight-fitting and bite into the tops of the arms. The neck-lines, too, are decidedly plunging. Yet the female donor figures in the Annunciation picture (Pl. 6), as distinct from the ladies in the *Très Belles Heures*, do not show the swollen bellies that became fashionable around 1380 (Scott, 1980, 84f).

Another useful clue is provided by the hair-styles. Since ladies first began to comb their hair forwards, covering the ears with plaits and leaving the neck free, around 1345 – whereas the hair had previously been knotted at the neck – the coquettish style of the ladies' hair in the Annunciation is, apart from the evidence of their clothing, probably the surest confirmation of the dating that we have suggested: between *c.* 1350 and 1375.[15]

A further clue to an approximate dating is supplied by the architecture in front of which the Annunciation takes place. A brief sketch of the development of the iconography of the Annunciation in the fourteenth century may be useful here.

While artists of the High Middle Ages liked to depict this event in the open air, or in front of a neutral building, we observe a tendency to interiors in fourteenth-century northern France and in the territory of present-day Holland. Towards the end of the century, these settings became church interiors.[16] E. Male suggests that this tendency can be explained in terms of the propagation of new literary sources (Male, 1908, ch. 1, p. 3f). However, the formal initiating factor for the way in which this theme was developed in the north appears to have been an *Announcement of the Virgin's Death* by Duccio. In the *Book of Hours of Jeanne d'Évreux* (1325/28), Jean Pucelle took over

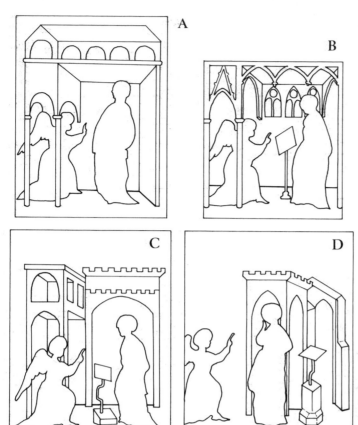

Fig. 34. The architectural setting of the Annunciation. A. Jean Pucelle, *Book of Hours of Jeanne d'Évreux*; B. Jacquemart de Hesdin, *Très Belles Heures*; C. Disciple of Jean Pucelle(?), *Bréviaire de Belleville*; D. Detail of the Annunciation on the east wall of the Fishermen's Chapel.

Duccio's L-shaped architectural setting for his portrayal of the Annunciation (Robb, 1936, pl. 15). Pucelle's portrayal gives the impression that the angel has entered the Virgin's room from the left; the Virgin is shown standing, in a posture similar to that of the Virgin in the Annunciation on the east wall of the chapel. Pucelle's kneeling angel is placed under a portico, behind which a wall runs to the right, serving as a background to the Virgin. The whole edifice is crowned with a roof (Fig. 34A). If we eliminate the roof and pierce the wall with traceried windows, we have an interior immediately recognizable as that of a church (Fig. 34B). That is exactly what was executed *c.* 1390 by Jacquemart de Hesdin in the *Très Belles Heures* of the Duc de Berry (Robb, 1936, pl. 21). Between Pucelle and Hesdin, however, lie years of fumbling attempts and experiments, some of which seem even to have been retrogressive.

The artist of the *Bréviaire de Belleville* (1343) may actually have trained in Pucelle's workshop (Robb, 1936). Again in his Annunciation, the angel kneels. This time, however, he is placed in front of the portico. To his right stands the lectern which separates the Virgin from the angel. The wall behind the Virgin is battlemented and the roof has disappeared, so that it is difficult to identify the architecture still as an interior (Fig. 34C). In our opinion, a solution like that found by the Pucelle disciple could have been known to the artist of the Annunciation in the chapel. Apart from the finer points of the elaborate architecture depicted in the *Bréviaire*, the scheme used by the artist in Jersey is exactly the same. To fit his composition to the east wall he had to do no more than shift the architecture of the Pucelle disciple one 'step' to the right, so that now the Virgin – instead of Gabriel – appears in front of the portico. The battlements that define Mary in the *Bréviaire* would in this case remain in place, whereas the lectern would have to be moved along, i.e. to its position to the right of the Virgin (Fig. 34D). This close resemblance to the composition in the *Bréviaire* which we have described would permit the supposition that the Annunciation in the chapel is to be dated to *c.* 1340, if the artist had not made a conscious effort to give the background wall a new appearance.

By means of the buttress shown behind the first kneeling figure, the gable and the pointed archway in the wall, it seems that the artist intended to give the viewer the impression that the portico adjoined an ecclesiastical building. However, this is the resolution of the L-shaped ground plan that we should expect, as the Hesdin example shows, sometime after 1350.

THE FIFTEENTH-CENTURY PAINTING

The clothing style of the Virgin and of Christ hardly changed between the eleventh and the fifteenth centuries. However, the remaining figures provide clues for the dating of the later painting; in particular, Herod, the servants in the Passion scene, and the Three Wise Men (Magi).

Herod's extremely long Bombard sleeves are characteristic of the male fashion of the Burgundy court between *c.* 1390 and 1430. At that time, however, the belt was mostly worn more loosely and below the waist and, as compensation for the over-long sleeves, the skirt reached down to cover the legs. Hence, the very obvious contrast between the quantity of material in Herod's sleeves and his skin-tight breeches makes him appear rather strange and top-heavy (Pl. 16). It may be supposed that the artist wished to allude to the perverse, vain character of this figure; and indeed in his treatment of the Magi the disproportion between the fashionable sleeves and the skirt is not so extreme. Although poorer in detail, their clothing is nevertheless just the same as that of the Three Wise Men of Saint Bonnet-le-Château, Loire, and that painting was executed *c.* 1425.[17] Since there is a noticeable tendency in these figures of the later painting in the chapel to articulate the folds of the jackets and skirts, and since the waist is cut tight, and the material at the shoulders is beginning to puff out a little, it may be argued that the later paintings in the Fishermen's Chapel, too, were executed towards the end of the period mentioned, that is when men's clothing fashions began to change.

The sixty to seventy years that separate the two occasions on which the chapel was decorated are coincident with a deterioration in the quality of painting. The Annunciation in the chancel is without doubt the finer painting; while the decoration of the fifteenth century may exercise a certain charm on the viewer, it is nonetheless very rustic and appears to have been hastily executed. Furthermore, within the decoration of the fifteenth century, a deterioration in quality is discernible. In the eschatological scene (Last Judgement), for example, the Redeemer and the figures closest to him have been relatively skilfully painted (Pl. 29). Further down, however, the painting becomes uncertain, and the two trumpeting angels that form the lower border are indeed crudely executed (Pl. 30). It is quite possible that a master reserved for himself the most important parts on the west wall, below the apex, and that he allowed an apprentice to work further down.

A purely aesthetic judgement of the fifteenth-century painting would, however, be unfair, for it is not without importance as a historical document. Apart from the fact that this decoration appears to be the earliest example of the century in the field of wall painting of a complete Passion cycle in the artistic sphere of Normandy,[18] it reflects the new, contemporary relationship to reality which equally influenced such widely diverse aspects as the artist's treatment of space, and the piety of the work.

Since a fragment of fourteenth-century decoration is still to be seen on the south wall of the nave (p. 26), whereas no traces of earlier painting have been discovered on the vault, it is unlikely that there ever were fourteenth-century paintings on the vaulted ceiling. The earlier decoration would have been confined to the lower regions of the chapel: possibly a single tier beneath the Annunciation in the chancel ran along the four walls, above a fairly low skirting or dado. The only painting that can claim to have reached up from the lower tier into the white-washed vault is the Annunciation on the east wall.

The general impression the earlier painting strives to give is tectonic. It subjugates itself to the actual architecture and 'fits in' with it. A small example of this is described above, the case of the Annunciation, where the placing of the figures and the architectural settings are determined by the space (p. 39). The strong ornamental, geometric bands that traced the main lines of the architecture and isolated the figures, as in the Annunciation, would have contributed significantly to the strong tectonic effect.

In contrast to this, the later painting appears to have been inspired by a completely different style. Presumably the whole chapel, with the exception of the skirting area, was covered with painting in the fifteenth century. The ornamental division into tiers (or levels), with overflowing, nervous foliage or with restless, meandering lines, seems to detract from the architectural effect rather than enhance it. This is most apparent in the chancel arch. Here, the vine of fig leaves and fruit is furthest removed from the abstract, geometric designs of the fourteenth century. This decoration detracts from the effect of the arch by creating an illusion of rampant, luxuriant Nature, albeit crudely observed (Pl. 31).

Like the ornamentation, the figures too, tend to detract from the architecture. Whereas in the earlier Annunciation both the architectural setting and the figures have been adapted by balanced distribution to the available space prescribed by the architecture, this is not so in the later painting. The Gabriel figure, that so dramatically bursts into the later Annunciation scene on the south wall, for example, explodes the fixed order by overlapping the ornamental band with its left foot, placing its weight there (Pl. 12). In this way an illusion is created that the angel is stepping into the picture, and we can see that the artist was trying to draw the viewer into the event that is being depicted. The same intention appears again in the scene portraying Christ's entry into Jerusalem. Instead of being presented in profile, looking towards Jerusalem, the donkey on which Christ rides appears to be glancing directly at the viewer (Pl. 21). This attempt to remove the distance between subject and viewer by creating an illusion (which, in the case of wall painting, means freeing itself from the architecture) is not seen anywhere on the east wall.

The features described above are an expression of the new intentions in painting which, in the light of works produced in the great centres – Flanders and Italy – can be understood as a turning to Nature and to the study of Nature. We cannot speak of a serious study of Nature in the case of the chapel painting, although the artist has indeed used his modest skill to draw the believer into the reality of salvation history by giving this as contemporary and vital a form as possible.

All the essential stages of salvation history have been used by the artist for this purpose: the Fall of Man, the Incarnation (or Infancy) of Christ, his Passion and Death on the Cross and, finally, Christ in Glory (implying his resurrection). Only the miracles and preaching of Christ seem to have been omitted. However, the artist's chief interest is in the Passion; that is evident from the numerical proportion of the Passion scenes.

The Fall	Incarnation	Infancy	Passion	The Last Judgement
–Adam and Eve	–Annunciation	–Slaughter of the Innocents	?	–Christ in Glory and the Resurrection of the souls
–Temptation	–Adoration		–Entry into Jerusalem	
–Expulsion		?	?	
			?	
			?	
			?	
			–Flagellation	
			–Carrying of the Cross	
			–Crucifixion	
Total 3	2	1–2	8–9	1

Even in his choice of scene with regard to the Infancy of Christ, the artist shows his predilection for the Passion: he selects neither the Presentation in the Temple nor the Boy Jesus teaching the Elders (i.e. the scenes that, at most, focus on Mary's suffering), but an event that clearly foreshadows the Passion: the Slaughter of the Innocents. The blood sacrifice seems to form the core of the artist's Infancy narrative: he affirms the ancient tradition that the Innocents were the first Christian martyrs, baptized in their own blood instead of water. The scene on the west wall, depicting Christ in Glory, also makes reference to the sacrifice of Christ's blood that flows so profusely from his wounds in all the extant Passion scenes: the Redeemer, surrounded by the instruments of his Passion, displays his stigmata. Although the Passion has always been an important thematic cycle within Christian art, the intensity and breadth with which it appears in the chapel is really quite remarkable. It can be viewed as an expression of the new piety that evolved in France and elsewhere at the beginning of the fifteenth century.[19]

This increasing preoccupation with the sufferings of Christ at the beginning of the fifteenth century is to be seen in the growing popularity of the mystery plays, which primarily took the Passion as their subject to edify the spectator. The desire of the faithful to draw closer to Christ through vivid contemplation of his sufferings is not least an achievement of the Franciscan Order and its efforts to reach the hearts of simple people, through the senses, especially the visual. Indeed, it was to the *Meditationes Vitae Christi*, a book by an unknown Franciscan at the beginning of the fourteenth century, that the Passion plays of the following century owed the great number of new visual images that they presented.[20]

The Rouen Passion Play of Arnoul Greban, for example, is based on the *Meditationes Vitae Christi* which, incidentally, in most editions omits the miracles and preaching of Christ, as our artist seems also to have done. The Nailing of Christ to the Cross, one of the most moving of the new scenes which Greban took from the *Meditationes*, appears to have inspired the artist in the Fishermen's Chapel. 'Prenez moi', says the captain to the four,

'. . . ces deux gros cordons,
Que j'ay à son poignet serrés,
Et tirez tant que vous pourrez,
Vous quatre – jusqu'aux nerfs des joindres
Tant que vous faciez la main joindre
Au pertuis qui est fait pour elle.' (Male, 1908, 19)

To judge from the fragments that remain, Arnoul's passage on the Nailing to the Cross reads like a close description of what is portrayed in the chapel. On the captain's orders, Christ's supine body is stretched with ropes in a gruesome way so as to fit the cross (note the remaining fragment of the rope, *c.* 30 cm above the place where the feet of Christ must have been; the apparent four, or perhaps five, kneeling soldiers; and the figure standing on the right-hand side, not kneeling: Fig. 31).

A further scene that enjoyed great popularity with Arnoul and others is a long, sentimental parting of Christ from his mother when he went up to Jerusalem from Bethany (Ragusa, 1961, 305). Since there is unquestionably a narrative-thematic connection between the Expulsion of Adam and Eve by the angel, depicted in the chancel, and the subsequent Annunciation by Gabriel, on the south wall of the nave, it would not be surprising to discover that the artist had thematically connected the other scenes that face one another. The remaining figure of the scene that followed the Slaughter of the Innocents appears, indeed, to be shifted extremely far to the right and focuses its attention in this direction. One could read this as a gazing after Christ, who is entering Jerusalem in the distance. In other words, the Annunciation, as the moment in which Mary receives the son, would be linked to the moment of her separation from him, depicted opposite.

This supposition, by which Mary establishes herself, as it were, as a link in the chain of salvation history, is also supported by the fact that other scenes which face one another in the chapel apparently also correspond thematically. This can be maintained in the case of the Adoration of Magi: opposite them, their antitype, Herod, is situated at the same height in the chapel. Just as the Three Kings render worship to the new-born child, so Herod strikes the new-born children of Bethlehem with his hatred. The entry of Christ into the earthly Jerusalem on a modest donkey – according to the *Meditationes*, an animal reserved to the poorest (Ragusa, 1961, 306), and therefore a paradigm of divine humility – is placed directly opposite and at the same height as the Fall and the ignominious Expulsion from the earthly paradise, which was the consequence of human pride. Moreover, to the extent that one may assume that the scene depicting Judas's kiss of betrayal was situated beneath the story of Adam and Eve, a connection with the Crucifixion scene opposite is not hard to draw. Whereas, on the one side, the most heinous treachery is shown, on the other in the Crucifixion scene, the loyalty of the believer is rewarded with the promise, *Hodie eris m(ecum) i(n) p(aradiso)*, 'Today you shall be with me in Paradise' (Luke 23:43).

With the exception of the Annunciation and the supposed Parting scene, all these depictions which face each other follow the archetype-antitype scheme. On account of the Virgin Mary's integrity and closeness to Christ, the scheme certainly cannot be extended to include the Annunciation, Parting and Eschatological scenes. By departing from the overall scheme in these scenes, however, the artist has emphasised the unique place of Christ and of his mother in salvation history. Thus, too, the uniqueness and prime importance of Christ's Passion is asserted, the main section of which is developed in the lower tier in the nave. Pairing – or even the construction of an archetype-antitype scheme – could hardly have been employed here. Here, to the west of the chancel arch, the faithful were supposed to be able to witness and lament, at close proximity, the sequence of Christ's physical sufferings; whereas the more remote upper tier exacted a reflective mode of viewing, involving making distinctions between right and wrong.

In this regard it may be useful to recall the basic optimistic tone of the eschatological scene on the west wall. It seems never to have been the artist's intention to depict a division of the resurrected into the Blessed and the Damned. Considerations of the fate of the unjust are omitted.

With its portrayal of Christ, surrounded by the adoring and displaying his stigmata, the west wall does not lead one so much to the contemplation of the final triumph of justice – which is usual in a Last Judgement scene – as to the contemplation of Christ's triumph over suffering and death: his own and that of all Mankind.

Materials, Painting Technique and the Sequence of Decoration
by Gottfried Hauff

Apart from their religious and art-historical significance, the technical aspects of mural painting have received increasing attention during recent decades. Of special interest are questions concerning the methods and techniques employed for the execution of the paintings, for instance: what were the materials used? Did the painters apply their colours on a damp rendering (*a fresco* technique), or on a dry ground (*a secco* technique), using a binding medium for the pigments, or did they paint in lime? Another issue, more specific to the Fishermen's Chapel, is how we should imagine the respective appearances of the successive systems of painted decoration throughout the history of the building.

In order to shed some light on these questions, a technological study was carried out during the course of the conservation project, consisting basically of three types of examination:

1. The stratigraphic examination of the different layers of rendering and painting. This was carried out at many points on the vault and on the walls, in places which yielded good evidence; for example, at the margins of losses of rendering, where a cross-section of all the different strata was visible.

2. The analysis of the composition of the renderings. This was carried out both *in situ* and in the Jersey States Analyst Laboratory.

3. The close examination of the surface of the paintings. This was done with the naked eye and a magnifying glass, with the help of reflected light at various angles of incidence to the surface.

As a result of these examinations, the stratigraphy and the composition of the materials of the various decorations of the Fishermen's Chapel can be systematized as follows.

The support for the paintings – i.e. the walls and vault of the chapel, together with the chancel arch – is made of granite rocks set in a coarse, dense and hard mortar. This matrix consists of one part lime and four parts filler, namely sand with additions of stones, gravel, and whole and crushed shells (Fig. 36). In the case of the vaulted and arched parts of the building, which were constructed on formwork, the coarse mortar formed a continuous undercoat, an *arriccio*. Where the *arriccio* was exposed it still clearly showed the imprints of timber shuttering on the surface, and even some chips of wood remained (Figs. 35 and 73; see further pp. 87–9). In places, the same coarse plaster mix was used to level up sizeable depressions in the *arriccio*, which were caused by the overlapping planks of the shuttering.

The next stratum is formed by a similarly dense and hard, but distinctly finer, finishing plaster, the *intonaco* (Fig. 36). This consists of one part lime and one part filler, namely sand with additions of fine gravel and crushed sea-shells, and was applied over the whole shutter-marked surface of the *arriccio* and the rough surface of the walls. On top of the *intonaco* lies the first

Fig. 35.   Chancel arch. Imprints of wooden shuttering in the *arriccio*.
Photo: Warwick Rodwell

Fig. 36.   Nave vault. Detail of south side, showing the two basic layers of rendering. The loss of
the *intonaco* has revealed the underlying *arriccio*;
in the middle is a chip of wood from a shuttering
board.
Photo: Gottfried Hauff

limewash. Both the limewash and the surface of the *intonaco* show corresponding marks of brush-strokes, thus indicating that the limewash was applied when the *intonaco* was still damp. In places where the limewash had become visible again – and this was the case especially on the vault of the nave – a dark, and apparently sooty patina could be observed on the surface.

The limewash must have been exposed for quite some time. The signs therefore point to the first interior decoration, applied soon after the erection of the chapel, being merely limewash on a lively, uneven ground of *intonaco*. There were no traces of polychromy observed on this layer, but it must of course be remembered that most of the original surface is now covered by succeeding layers of decoration: the existence of figural or ornamental wall paintings cannot be ruled out with certainty at that stage.

Next comes the second layer of limewash, which also shows the marks of brush-strokes. This layer served simultaneously as the painting-ground, as a white background for the earlier wall

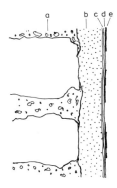

Fig. 37. Cross-section through wallplaster with paintings of the earlier period uncovered. Key: a. wall; b. first *intonaco*; c. first limewash; d. second limewash; e. paint layers of the earlier decoration.

Fig. 38. Nave vault. Detail from the Adoration of the Magi. On top of the worn first *intonaco* are fragments of the second *intonaco*, carrying the third limewash layer and traces of the later poly-chromy.
Photo: Gottfried Hauff

paintings and, in the areas without polychromy, simply as white colouring. The polychrome paintings themselves were built up in one or more layers of paint (Fig. 37). So, according to our observations, the chapel was redecorated in a second phase with a coat of whitewash and polychrome paintings on the east wall and on at least part of the south wall of the nave.

On top of all these layers a second stratum of *intonaco* could be observed on the vaulting of the chapel, *c.* 1 cm thick at the apex, and gradually thinning down towards the springing-line (Fig. 38). This layer consists of one part lime and about four parts filler, in this instance just sand and gravel. As a final general layer, extending over the whole surface of the walls and vaults, there is a third limewash, which again serves as a painting-ground and general background for the later polychrome wall paintings (Fig. 39). Thus, in the third and final phase of decoration an additional coat of intonaco was applied to the vaulting, and the whole interior of the chapel was whitewashed and adorned with a fresh set of wall paintings (Fig. 40).

The painting method employed to execute the final decorative scheme was, according to our observations, basically the same as in the earlier period. As the stratigraphy shows, in each case a coat of limewash was applied to the surface which was to be painted. Then a preparatory drawing of the figures, objects and ornament was executed in black colour. The existence of a preparatory drawing is especially evident where the outline was changed during the subsequent painting process. In such cases the preparatory drawing was covered up with an additional application of limewash, and a corrected version was drawn.

Fig. 39.   Nave vault. Detail from the Adoration of the Magi, showing marks of brush-strokes of the third limewash, the painting-ground and general background of the later polychromy.

Photo: Gottfried Hauff

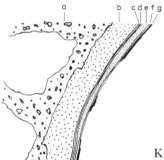

Fig. 40.   Cross-section through the earlier and later paintings on the vault.
Key: a. vault; b. first *intonaco*; c. first limewash; d. second limewash; e. second *intonaco*; f. third limewash; g. paint layers of the later decoration.

These *pentimenti* can be observed in the paintings of both periods where, in the course of time, the covering limewash has worn off again (Figs. 41 and 42). Generally, the preparatory drawing seems to have been rather sketchy, just defining outlines, and not including details, incarnates, or the like. The forms circumscribed were then either left white or infilled with flat colours which were modelled afterwards, mainly by adding white highlights and black lines for shadows. The outlines were finally corrected and, where necessary, reinforced. For this work, and for drawing facial features and the hair of the figures, a dark red colour was used in the earlier paintings, while the artists of the later period just carried on using black colour. The ornamental friezes separating and framing the paintings of both periods were, judging by their marked irregularities, executed freely without the use of stencils. The repetitive letter *S* was, however, stencilled, as were some of the floral motifs.

Fig. 41. East wall. Detail of the Annunciation, showing preparatory drawing of the earlier period. An example of a *pentimentum* is seen here as the two feint lines extending below the hand of the archangel.

Photo: Gottfried Hauff

Fig. 42. Chancel vault. Detail of the Fall of Man, showing preparatory drawing of the later period, defining the outline of the figure of Eve. Another example of a *pentimentum* is seen in the two thin, curving lines below the right breast of the figure of Eve.

Photo: Gottfried Hauff

The painters' palette was evidently almost the same in both periods. The colours red, yellow, brown, black and white were used in all the paintings. Only a green colour appears exclusively in the later decoration. Considering that no precious pigments such as azurite or lapis lazuli could be observed, the colours must have been prepared from conventional and comparatively cheap mineral pigments of types popularly used in medieval wall painting; i.e. the different earths, such as red ochre, yellow ochre and terre-verte, as well as lime white and one of the several kinds of carbon black.

Comparing the paintings of the two periods generally, the earlier ones were executed in a more delicate manner, using differentiated colour tones; while bright, flat colours, combined with a strongly calligraphic momentum, are the characteristics of the later paintings.

There are few pieces of evidence from which the actual painting technique can be judged. In the case of the earlier period, the grounds of rendering and of the first limewash had been in place long enough to acquire a substantial patina. Consequently, they must have been basically dry, or just dampened, before the surface was again whitewashed. Only the limewash onto which the pigments were applied was probably still quite fresh, judging from the generally good adhesion of the polychromy.

The layers of actual polychrome are quite thick, opaque at the surface, and in some places they came away in little flakes. Together, these observations indicate that the paintings must have been executed using the technique of 'lime-painting'. In this technique the pigments are mixed with water and lime-water or milk-of-lime (sometimes also with the addition of an organic medium, such as casein or oil), and applied to the fresh limewash.[21] By comparison with the true *fresco* technique of the time, this was a rapid and relatively inexpensive method of decorating large areas.

In the case of the later paintings, stratigraphical examination has shown that a new layer of *intonaco* was applied, which could be taken as a sign that the painters' intention was to work *a fresco*. However, the fact that this *intonaco* is found only on the vaulting, and not on the walls, suggests that its purpose was merely to cover up some areas of damage. This new layer might still have been damp when the interior of the chapel was whitewashed, thus causing a certain fresco-effect in the relevant areas. Still, the fact remains that the paintings as a whole were executed on a limewash.

In a number of scenes – for instance those of Adam and Eve – the preparatory drawing is, unfortunately, almost all that is still preserved of the original painting. From this recurrent phenomenon we can, however, deduce that at least the preparatory drawing was carried out while the limewash was still damp. Again, the opaqueness of the surface and the thickness of the layers of paint speak for the assumption that the pigments were mixed with lime-milk. So, in spite of the new *intonaco*, the basic technique is, again, that of lime-painting.

To sum up: the conclusions drawn from technological examination, and from the dating through archaeological and stylistic observations, indicate that the Fishermen's Chapel had, throughout its history, three successive forms of interior decoration. Three times the walls and vaults, covered by a lively, uneven rendering, were painted with white limewash: i.e. probably in the twelfth, fourteenth and fifteenth centuries. At least twice – in the two later periods – the chapel was adorned with polychromatic wall paintings. These were executed using the lime-painting technique, the most common method for relatively simple, popular wall paintings of the Gothic period in northern Europe.[22]

4. ARCHAEOLOGICAL INVESTIGATIONS

Prior to the beginning of this project, there had never been a major archaeological investigation carried out on a church or chapel in the Channel Islands, with the consequence that almost nothing was known about the nature and quality of the evidence that might be expected. There had, however, been a tantalising series of observations and interpretations made by Rector Balleine during his restoration projects both at Saint Brelade's Church and at the Fishermen's Chapel. Insofar as we know, there was no archaeologist involved in these works, no proper records were made, no contemporary photographs have been traced, and the artefacts recovered at the time have been lost.

Balleine's guide-books to the church (1907 and 1932) and chapel (1932) contain the only record of the evidence discovered – and, for the most part, also destroyed – during the restorations. Moreover, it is clear that Balleine had access to various records which appear to have been lost since his death in 1941. Although the minute books of the Ecclesiastical Assembly are extant from 1828 onward, they contain very few references to the Fishermen's Chapel.[1] This is largely on account of the fact that both rectors Le Sueur and Balleine personally organised their restorations, collecting the funds from private sources, rather than from the parish rates. Hence, there was no obligation to keep records.

Previous Discoveries and Hypotheses

Balleine's notes concerning the chapel, although brief, contain many puzzling statements, all of which were studied carefully at the beginning of the project: some of his observations about the building seemed to be structurally impossible, while many of his historical deductions were archaeologically implausible (see also pp. 14–15). His account of the chapel's foundations belongs to the first category:

'The foundation-walls of the chapel had an average depth of three feet below the floor-level but, unlike the walls above the floor, which were quite solid, the lower walls consisted of large stones placed over each other, without compacting mortar of any kind. This discovery was first made along the south wall and was a matter of surprise, but when a similar state of things was found to exist under the north wall a very primitive system of drainage was brought to light. There being no gutters, the rain had for centuries dripped down the outer walls on to the soil, drained itself through the open wall-work below ground, then through the soil below the chapel floor, to find its outlet through the foundations of the wall on the opposite side' (Balleine, 1932, 35).

Had this really been the case, the interior of the chapel would have been a permanent quagmire; in any case, the natural drainage pattern here is from west to east, not from north to south.

51

Not surprisingly, the excavations yielded numerous bones: 'Not only was the whole space below the floor filled with human remains, but it was found that the walls themselves rested upon human skulls, thigh-bones and dust. Mixed with these remains were the teeth of horses and the bony snouts of pigs'. Balleine then advanced his contention that animals were killed and buried with their former owners (p. 14). He placed great emphasis on bones which were found close to the bedrock, assuming that they were of immense but unspecified antiquity; large thigh-bones he attributed to seven-foot giants, and the skulls he claimed 'were of an uncommon type'.

Under the south wall of the chapel, near to its centre, Balleine reported finding 'three rough stones, the longer one four feet, the others two feet in length, laid in the form of a cross, at right-angles to the wall'. He declared these stones to be 'the emblem of Christianity', placed there by the builders of the chapel. It is more likely that they were the displaced remains of a cist-grave, possibly prehistoric. 'Various fragments of ancient pottery urns and some Stone Age implements' were reported, without further description; they have since been lost. The so-called 'urns' are likely to have been sherds of domestic pottery, rather than sepulchral vessels. The find, however, that attracted most speculation was a 'semi-circular erection' under the chapel floor at the east end, on the site where the stone altar was subsequently placed. The structure was of stone 'held together by a clammy kind of yellow clay, and the soil, loose stones and bones at the base showed signs of burning'. Balleine's imagination rioted: 'Could this have been a heathen altar of sacrifice?' He regarded the discovery as one of signal importance and caused a square enclosure of concrete to be constructed around the feature, 'as a protective measure against interference by inquisitive visitors to the chapel'.

Clearly, the workmen had found a hearth or furnace of some kind, and the rector's enthusiasm was quickly tempered when a second, exactly similar structure turned up below the floor midway along the north wall: 'One of the workmen, in carefully pursuing the excavation at that spot, suddenly felt the thrust of his pick-axe arrested by some impediment, and then, with difficulty, unearthed the base of a large rusty iron cauldron'. Balleine concluded soberly: 'these two erections had been built as cooking-sites by the garrison at the time of the military occupation of the chapel. The iron cauldron had been one of their cooking utensils, and thus departed the theory of a prehistoric "altar of sacrifice"!' Although the second hearth was evidently removed, the first was said to have been preserved and protected by a concrete enclosure, which Balleine 'mentioned for the information of any who may hereafter have occasion to displace the flooring – a work which would entail great energy'. That occasion came in 1984, when great energy was duly applied to breaking up the red-painted concrete floor, as part of the refurbishment works.

Excavations inside the Chapel, 1982 to 1984 (Figs. 43–46)

Balleine's account of his discoveries in the late 1920s was more intriguing than instructive. While on the one hand there seemed to be an overwhelming case for carrying out fresh excavations under modern scientific conditions, there was, on the other hand, great apprehension concerning the academic viability of such a project. In view of the recorded extent and depth of trenching that had been carried out around the walls, both inside and outside the chapel, it was felt unlikely that any stratified deposits could be encountered in a meaningful relationship to the foundations. Six *sondages* were cut through the concrete floor at various points around the walls of the chapel, and

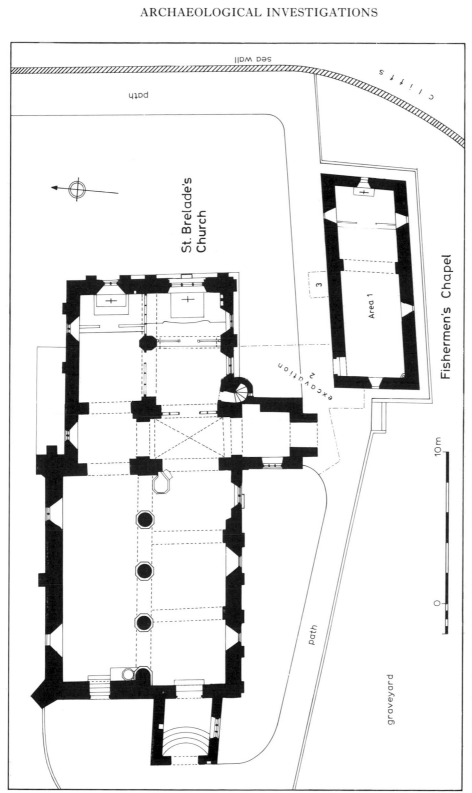

Fig. 43. Plan showing the relationship between Saint Brelade's Church and the Fishermen's Chapel, and the locations of the three areas of excavation, 1982–85.

Fig. 44.   General view of the interior of the chapel, looking west, during excavation in 1983. The foundation offsets can be seen around the bases of the walls, and beneath them the rugged concrete underpinning of the 1920s. The trenches for the underpinning have been excavated, leaving a central baulk which mostly comprised the backfilling of an earlier, unreported excavation trench.

Photo: Warwick Rodwell

Fig. 45.   General view of the interior of the chapel, looking east, during the excavation
of the surviving archaeological deposits in front of and under the sanctuary step.

Photo: Warwick Rodwell

one was cut through the asphalt path outside, to the north. As anticipated, nothing but backfilled soil and rubble, against the concrete-encased foundations, was encountered.

By November 1983 the concrete floor had been wholly removed, and it was decided to conduct small-scale excavations in the chancel, to relocate Balleine's hearth. Somewhat surprisingly, stratified deposits were revealed, albeit in a fragmentary state. The results were considered to be sufficiently encouraging to authorize full-scale excavation of the chapel's interior, which took place in March and April, 1984 (Rodwell, 1987). In the following account of the excavation all archaeological features of significance are described, and are locatable on the accompanying plans and section drawings (Figs. 46–47). All features and layers are identified by a consecutive series of *feature numbers*, prefixed 'F' (full descriptions of these are contained in the excavation archive.

The method of excavation employed was to remove Balleine's concrete floor (F3) and the macadam upon which it rested (F4, compacted layers of broken stone), leaving only the granite sanctuary step and its massive concrete foundation (F1, F2. Fig. 48). It was impracticable to attempt the removal of these without considerable disturbance to the adjacent stratification. Beneath the macadam was a deposit of loose, gravelly soil containing human bones, bricks and other recent debris (F5). Along the central axis of the chapel this layer was very thin, but towards the walls it merged with the filling of the wide and deep trenches dug in 1927–34 for underpinning the walls.

These trenches (F8, F9) were emptied, leaving a long tongue of seemingly undisturbed archaeological deposits running west from the sanctuary step (plan, Fig. 46A). In the base of each trench a massive concrete and rubble apron was revealed, built against the chapel's foundations (F22, F23). East of the sanctuary step a different situation obtained. Here, a three-sided enclosure of shuttered concrete (F7) was found, defining an area of *c.* 1.8 m by 1.3 m adjacent to the east wall (Fig. 46B). Within and all around this enclosure was loose gravelly soil (F6), containing pieces of burnt brick and stone, and lumps of clay: some had been fire-reddened but were still plastic, while others were burnt hard. None of this material was *in situ* but it, and similar debris found elsewhere in the chancel and the nave, was evidently derived from one or more post-medieval hearth structures. The bricks suggest a date no earlier than the eighteenth century.

Continued excavation failed to reveal Balleine's semi-circular hearth but, instead, a vertical-sided pit (F10) was found to have been cut within the concrete enclosure, and taken down to the bedrock. This pit had been sunk in order to underpin the central part of the east wall (F11), and in so doing Balleine's hearth had been totally destroyed (Fig. 46B). Upon removal of the concrete enclosure, a pair of trenches (F12, F14) was found (roughly beneath its north and south walls); these were associated with two small areas of underpinning of the east wall (F13, F15). Underpinning trenches for the north and south walls of the sanctuary were also found (F19, F16). On the north side an important discovery was made. Here, the workmen had not troubled to tunnel under the massive granite sanctuary step, as they had done on the south, with the result that a short length of the chapel's northern foundation had escaped underpinning. Thus, fortuitously, a small area of stratified deposits remained intact against the north wall. Elsewhere, not only had trenching destroyed all stratigraphic relationship between the chapel's foundations and other archaeological features, but the foundations themselves had been heavily daubed with cement and partially concealed by the concrete apron (Figs. 44–45).

Having removed all twentieth-century disturbances around the walls of the chapel – and they extended to nearly three-quarters of the gross floor area – it was hoped that the remaining central baulk would be largely composed of medieval deposits. However, it was quickly discovered that there had been an unrecorded trench dug along the central axis of the chapel, from its west wall to the sanctuary step. This trench, which had been taken down to bedrock, was begun at the west end, where it was 60 cm (2 ft) wide, and progressed eastwards, increasing in width to 95 cm (3 ft) at the sanctuary step. The trench had been dug in six approximately equal lengths (Fig. 46A, F21a-f). As each section was excavated, so the previous one was backfilled and a crude revetment of rocks built across the trench, to prevent the loose spoil from tumbling back into the area currently being worked.

It was clear from the debris found in the backfilling that the trench had been dug in modern times, certainly after the introduction of the granite step in *c.* 1884. There can be no doubt that it was an early antiquarian excavation. It could hardly have been undertaken in the 1880s by Rector Le Sueur, since fragments of his concrete floor were discovered in the backfilling. The alternative, that it was a wholly unrecorded activity of Balleine's in *c.* 1927–30, seems inescapable (Fig. 48). Between the disturbances caused by this excavation and the underpinning trenches, only narrow slithers of stratified archaeological deposits remained intact, standing to an average height of 90 cm

Fig. 48. View east towards the sanctuary step, during excavation, showing the two surviving east-west ridges of medieval and later deposits between the modern underpinning trenches and the unreported excavation trench in the centre of the chapel.

Photo: Warwick Rodwell

above bedrock. Under the sanctuary step and to the east of it was a larger block of undisturbed material. The full extent of the surviving deposits is shown on plan (Fig. 46A). Additionally, the badly damaged remains of several graves were located in the bottoms of some of Balleine's trenches.

STRATIGRAPHIC SEQUENCE BENEATH THE CHAPEL FLOOR

Despite the fact that less than four square metres of archaeological deposits survived inside the chapel (9 percent of the floor area), by good fortune sufficient remained for an outline history of the building to be established, although accurate dating remains problematic.

PRE-CHAPEL FEATURES

The exposure of the bedrock in the bottoms of Balleine's trenches enabled the pre-chapel topography of the site to be reconstructed. The rock here is bright pink granite, the surface of which is broken and gravelled. The gentle ground slope from west to east across Saint Brelade's churchyard reflects the underlying geology, and beneath the chapel the rock tilts towards the cliff, with a fall of 50 cm along the length of the building (reconstructed in profile in Fig. 49A). Overlying the rock are deposits of coarse and fine sand (F100) which were laid down in early prehistoric times. Most of this sand had been dug away within the chapel, but several pinnacles of it survived, to varying heights, between the trenches and graves, and below the north wall of the chancel where underpinning had not taken place.

The maximum thickness of the sand deposit was 65 cm, on top of which would originally have been a turf layer, but this did not survive within the chapel. Both the sand and the prehistoric turf line were, however, discovered in excavations outside the building, displaying a classic podsol profile (p. 69). Below the turf, the sand was banded and stained as a result of leaching from the surface. At the top was a thin, hard layer of dark brown panning, below which lay firm brown sand, merging into loose sand of pale yellow colour; and at the base was gravelly sand (Fig. 49, layers F100a, b and c, respectively). These deposits have been studied and reported upon by Doctor John Renouf.[2]

The prehistoric lithic implements which Balleine recorded (p. 52), but now lost, were presumably found in this sand, or in later deposits derived from it. No stone artefacts were recovered from the sand layers in 1984, but tiny chips of flint – a geologically alien material to the site – were observed in the backfilled trenches.

Some of the surviving pinnacles and ridges of sand were found to be supporting thin layers of black soil and crumbly, yellow clay-like material (loess). These compact layers with smooth surfaces were clearly floor levels, varying in thickness from a few millimetres to four or five centimetres (F31-F35; Pl. 34). There were four locations where such layers were preserved beneath later deposits: near the centre of the west end; just west of the pilaster-arch; in the chancel, against the foundation of the north wall; and in a strip across the centre of the sanctuary (plan, Fig. 46D; sections, Figs. 47B, 47D and 49). The most significant of these survivals was the area under the sanctuary step, where the stratigraphic relationship between the early floors and the chapel's foundations could be determined. Here, the lowest two floors were seen to pass under the foundation, and were clearly older than the existing building. Moreover, there were other deposits

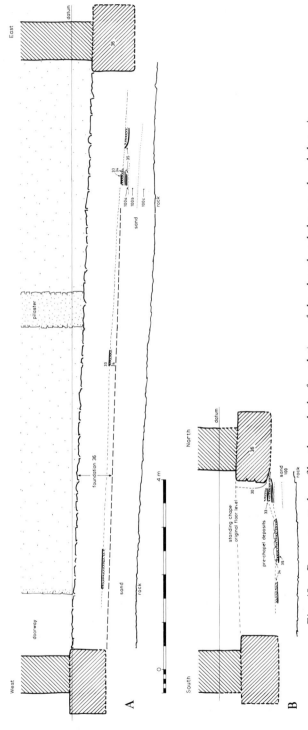

Fig. 49. Reconstructed profiles through the foundations of the chapel and the pre-chapel deposits.

A. East-west profile against the north wall, with outlying features projected, showing the eastward slope of the bedrock, the overlying sand (F100), the pre-chapel floors (F30–35), and the foundations (F36).

B. North-south section, taken on the line of the sanctuary step, showing the southward slope of the foundations and the level of the pre-chapel deposits.

on top of these floors, which were not found elsewhere in the chapel. These included, first, several interleaved layers of clay and soil (F32); secondly, a mixed layer of sand, clay and dark soil (F31); and, thirdly, cut into all these was a narrow construction trench (F30) for the footings of the chapel's north wall (section, Fig. 47D).

The floors and other layers just described all demonstrably belonged to a building antedating the present chapel. Apart from limpet shells there were no finds to provide any indication of the age of these deposits. The surviving island of deposits in the sanctuary was of further interest on account of the fact that several pieces of stone were embedded into the clay floor here (F34), and there were negative impressions where others had been removed (Figs. 46D and 49B). These stones presumably belonged to a construction that had been placed on top of the clay floor, and had sunk into it. It may be no coincidence that this was directly beneath the position where the medieval altar would have stood. Since the clay floor (F34) was present in each of the surviving islands of early deposits, and since it was overlain by the foundation of the north wall, it is reasonable to suggest that we are here glimpsing the remains of a previous building on the site, which was apparently no smaller than the present chapel. The potential significance of this discovery is discussed on pp. 131–2.

THE FOUNDATIONS OF THE CHAPEL

Of the construction trenches dug to receive the stone foundations of the present chapel only a slither remains (F30). It is, however, reasonable to assume that the contemporary ground surface from which the building was erected equated more or less with the top of the existing foundations.

The foundations (F36), which vary from 1.2 to 1.4 m in width, are considerably broader than the walls they support, the difference being shown by ground-level offsets both internally and externally. The builders made no attempt to construct the foundations to a true level, and merely followed the lie of the land. Not only do the foundations slope down to the east, but also to the south. As would be expected, the highest point of the foundation is at the north-west corner of the chapel, from which it slopes 43 cm to the north-east corner and 11 cm to the south-west. The south-east corner is the lowest of all, being 52 cm below its diagonal counterpart (for profiles see Figs. 49, 60 and 61). The depth of the foundations was difficult to ascertain, owing to Balleine's concrete encasement, but where visible the north foundation was 75 cm deep, the south at least 80 cm, and the east 90 cm.

Nowhere did the foundations reach bedrock, and the builders' intention was evidently to rest the chapel on the firm surface of the sand (but on the east there was only sandy clay, hence the deeper foundation). The composition of the foundations could be glimpsed in places. Granite boulders had been tightly packed into the construction trench, without employing mortar of other binding material in the lower courses. The uppermost course, however, was bedded in a stiff, yellow sandy clay (without added lime), and the top of the foundation levelled off with the same material. It was this dry-stone construction with voids – not uncommon in early buildings – that Balleine misinterpreted as a form of primitive drainage (p. 51).

Balleine also recorded that, as part of the underpinning work, he caused the foundations to be widened by building offsets at the base of the walls (p. 150). This was shown to be untrue, the offsets being part of the original broad foundation. Nowhere have they been increased in width, although the open joints were filled with a liberal application of thin cement, and in places the uppermost course of stone was reset (additionally, along the south wall of the chancel the offset was raised by adding a single course of stone, F37, Fig. 47C). Externally, the offsets have also been raised by casting concrete gutters directly onto them (Figs. 49, 60 and 61). While the north and south walls exhibit foundation offsets of equal width, both internally and externally, the offsets at the east and west ends are very irregular in plan (Fig. 46D). This is a result of the foundations having been laid out as a true rectangle, while the chapel itself is of trapezoidal plan. The significance of this is discussed on p. 94.

When the chapel was underpinned, Balleine sought to anchor the structure to the bedrock, and is said to have tunnelled under the foundations by about two feet (60 cm) from each side, but this could not be verified, and it is clear that on the north side of the sanctuary the reinforcement was of more modest character. Here, the concrete apron (F20) overlies an undisturbed child burial (F71). Doubtless further traces of archaeological deposits, including some ante-dating the chapel, are inaccessibly sealed below the foundations and the concrete.

MEDIEVAL AND LATER FLOORS

When the chapel was completed its floor level would have been at, or fractionally above, the top of the foundation offset, with a marked slope down to the east, and a lesser inclination towards the south. It was therefore initially puzzling to discover that all surviving floors – and not just those antedating the present chapel – lay well below the expected level. Also, upon excavation, it was found that the sequence of floors within the building belonged only to the later medieval and post-medieval periods (as evidenced by the artefacts recovered from them), and that these directly overlay the pre-chapel floors. Taken at face-value, the evidence would appear to indicate that the present chapel and its succession of earth floors could not originate earlier than the fifteenth century. On several counts, such a suggestion would be nonsensical. Without pre-empting a full discussion of the chapel's dating, it can safely be asserted that the building is no later than the twelfth century. There is thus a gap of three or more centuries in the internal stratigraphy of the chapel.

There can be little doubt as to the sequence of events leading to this anomaly. During the later medieval refurbishment of the chapel a drastic reduction of the internal floor level took place. This involved not only the removal of an accumulated series of earlier medieval floors, but also the destruction of most of the pre-chapel deposits (F30–32). Exactly how great a depth of material was removed cannot now be ascertained, but it must have been upwards of 70 cm.

The reduction of the floor level will have necessitated entry via steps, as is still the case, and the previously-unseen foundation offsets will have protruded as bench-like features alongside the walls. Indeed, this may well have been a deliberate intention: the offsets, topped with planks, would have served admirably as late medieval wall-benches. This facility has now been recreated in the latest restoration (Pl. 3).

Subsequent to the internal reduction, fresh deposits accumulated: clay floors, trampled earth layers, builders' debris, and the upcast material from grave digging (Pl. 34). The nature and depth of these deposits naturally varied from place to place and, owing to their fragmentary condition, archaeological correlation cannot now be achieved. This is a common phenomenon in church excavations, even when better preservation obtains (Rodwell, 1989, ch. 7).

In outline, the sequence of events seems to have been thus: after the floor was lowered building works took place, depositing a layer of debris which contained fragments of mortar and wallplaster (F39, Fig. 47B). This deposit was sealed by a floor of yellow clay (F40), followed by further earth floors. Many graves were then dug inside the chapel and the punctured floors successively repaired. At a later stage a complete resurfacing of the floor in clay was undertaken (F60, Fig. 47A). After the cessation of interments the chapel was evidently neglected and a layer of vegetable mould accumulated (F64), and on top of this at the east end was a deposit of gravel and fallen plaster, containing pieces of roofing slate, clay pipe stems and ivy roots (F63). Finally, the uppermost layer was a deposit of brown mould, composed of decayed wood (F65). Clearly, this was the floor surface of the nineteenth-century carpenter's workshop (p. 4).

BURIALS IN THE CHAPEL

According to Balleine, burials were found everywhere under the chapel floor (p. 52), an observation borne out by the 1984 excavation. The fragmentary remains of twelve articulated skeletons were recorded, all lying on or close to the bedrock. Additionally, more than five hundred disarticulated bones were recovered from backfilled modern trenches; these represented not less than eighteen individuals, and probably many more. Since Balleine stated that the human remains encountered in the works of 1927–35 were collected and reinterred in the churchyard, it is uncertain what proportion of the total skeletal assemblage from the chapel has been recovered. From the intercutting pattern of graves in the western part of the chancel, it is evident that burial took place over several generations at least, and a reasoned guess might suggest that a minimum of fifty – and perhaps a hundred or more – medieval interments had been made inside the chapel. A report on the skeletal remains is given in Appendix 1.

The burials comprised men, women, children and babies and, in so far as the meagre evidence goes, they were all interred within the present chapel, in the later medieval period. Every grave yielded fragments of wallplaster or structural mortar, demonstrating that the interments took place after building works had caused this material to be released from the fabric. Several graves yielded fragments of Normandy stoneware dating from the fifteenth or sixteenth century. None of the graves would, when intact, have projected under the foundations, although Balleine claimed that human bones were recovered from beneath the walls.

While mindful of the severe limitations of the evidence, the disposition of excavated graves accords well with what we know of later medieval burial practice inside churches. The greatest concentration of burials was in the chancel, west of the altar; there was none under it. A continuous line of graves probably ran westwards down the axis of the nave, and traces of some on this line were recorded near the west end. At the centre of the chancel, just east of the pilaster-arch, and where the 1920s(?) excavation trench widened out, there had apparently been some larger feature of interest. Here, two superimposed graves were found (F66, F67) and, unlike the remainder of the graves in the chapel, they did not follow the building's axis, but were markedly skewed towards the north-east (Figs. 46C, D). The misalignment of these interments suggests that when they were made there were obstacles – probably flat stone grave-covers – already existing in the floor to either side. In such circumstances, when space was constricted, the simplest solution was often to dig the new grave on a squinted alignment, in order to avoid the obstacles.

These graves, however, cut into a yet earlier feature which had been constructed of granite boulders (F70, Figs. 46D and 47A). Several pieces of stone lay flat on the sand and one large, squarish block stood upright on its edge and was aligned on the chapel's axis. These stones may be interpreted as the remains of a stone-lined cist built in the centre of the chancel, the most prestigious position in any chapel. No trace of the associated skeleton remained. It is likely that this was one of the primary graves, if not the first, in the sequence of burials in the building. When the upright stone was removed, fragments of mortar derived from the fabric of the chapel were found embedded in the sand below it. This presumed cist-grave is not, therefore, likely to be substantially older than the other interments. Several other large pieces of granite were found loose in the backfilling of the old excavation trench in this area. They too may have been derived from the cist.

Ten out of the twelve recorded skeletons were contained in wooden coffins, including the two babies buried closest to the altar (F71, F72, figs. 46 and 50). Insufficient remained of grave F81 to determine whether a coffin had formerly existed, and the only instance were the body was certainly uncoffined was grave F73, on the north side of the altar. Here, a child's legs remained in a very narrow grave, without sufficient space for a coffin (Fig. 50). Traces of the bottoms of at least three additional coffins were noted in the sections, but without surviving skeletal remains.

Evidence for coffins was provided in two forms: lines of brown crumbly humic material resulting

Fig. 50. The fragmentary archaeological deposits surviving beneath the sanctuary floor, after the removal of modern fills. Beneath the concrete foundation for the sanctuary step (top of picture) can be seen the bell mould and the lower legs of the burial in grave F74. In the centre, the scale (75 cm) rests on the possible altar foundation (F34) of an earlier chapel; to the right are the remains of grave F73, and to the left grave F72. West is at the top.

Photo: Warwick Rodwell

from decayed wood, and iron nails. Unfortunately, little could be learned of coffin construction. The incompletely excavated baby's coffin (F71) yielded one lid nail and one side-to-end nail at the south-east and south-west corners. The more complete adult graves (F66, F67, F69, F74 and F77) all yielded large iron nails. In the adult group one grave (F76) failed to produce nails, and only the slightest traces of the coffin bottom survived.

Some evidence of a burial sequence was obtained from the cluster of graves on the south side of the chancel (Fig. 46D). Grave F74 was later than both the baby F72 and an adult F75. The latter, however, was cut through by another adult, F77, and that in turn was severed by F78. The intermediate grave in this chain (F77) contained a large sherd of a jug of Normandy stoneware, placed centrally over the lower legs (Fig. 51). Whether this was a deliberate, symbolic inclusion is uncertain;[3] the vessel dates from the later fifteenth or early sixteenth century (Appendix 3).

Fig. 51. The fragmentary remains of skeleton 11 in grave F77, with a large sherd of a pottery jug placed across the lower legs. The foot-end of the coffin is seen here, represented by a thin line of soil-staining resulting from the decay of the timber.

Photo: Warwick Rodwell

THE BELL FOUNDRY (Pl. 35)

Beneath the sanctuary step, and wholly untouched by nineteenth- and twentieth-century disturbances, was found a rectangular pit 1.4 m by 1.1 m (F26, Figs. 46C, 47A and 47C). It had been cut through graves and adjacent floors. The uppermost interleaved fills of sandy soil (F28) contained many small fragments of burnt clay and bell-mould, and beneath these the rim of the fired-clay mould was found to be *in situ* (F29, Figs. 50, 52 and 53). Curiously, the mould had not been constructed on the flat base of the rectangular pit, but rested on 15 cm of sandy soil. Similar material filled the pit (F26), but was separated from the clay mould by a vertical-sided timber lining, octagonal in plan and 85 cm across (F27). The constructional sequence was thus: the rectangular pit was excavated to a depth of 1.2 m below floor level, but was presumably found to be marginally too deep, and 15 cm of loose filling was put back. Then an octagonal timber lining was placed in the centre of the pit and secured by backfilling soil around it. Finally, the bell mould was

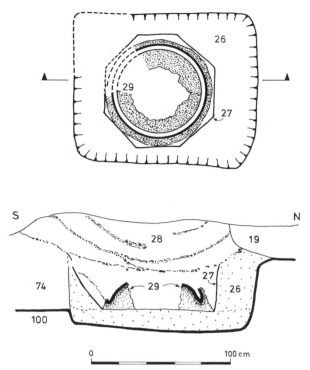

Fig. 52. Plan and section (looking west) through the bell casting pit of 1754.

constructed of raw clay, reinforced with pieces of tile, inside the timber lining. The tiles and other debris – notably clay-pipe stems – found in the filling suggest an eighteenth-century date.

The mould was made in the usual way, and the bell cast by the *cire perdue* or 'lost wax' process. First, the inner core of clay and brick was formed, and the profile of the bell was modelled upon it in wax, complete with decoration and inscription. The thickness of the wax layer reflected the intended thickness of the wall of the bell. An outer envelope (cope) of wet clay was applied and left to harden; then the mould was opened and the wax layer removed. The mould was reassembled, ready to receive the molten metal; a fuller description of the founding equipment is given in Appendix 2 (cf. Diderot, 1753 and Blagg, 1974).

In due course, the bell was cast and the mould smashed to extract it. Many of the semi-baked clay fragments were thrown back into the ground, while the lowest part of the mould remained *in situ* in the base of the pit, exactly preserving the form of the bell-mouth. This structure was not removed or damaged during excavation, and has been reburied. The mouth diameter of the bell was 70 cm ($27\frac{1}{2}$ ins), and an approximate reconstruction of the profile has been attempted from the fragments of mould recovered (Fig. 54). The historical identity of the bell is discussed on p. 147.

Immediately adjacent to the bell-casting pit would have been the furnaces in which crucibles of molten bell-metal were prepared, ready for pouring. Such was almost certainly the identity of the semi-circular hearth structure found by Balleine against the east wall of the chapel, his 'heathen altar of sacrifice', around which a protective concrete enclosure was built, albeit to no avail (p. 52). It can be deduced from debris recovered from the backfilled trenches in the chancel that the

Fig. 53.   The bell casting pit excavated to show the eastern half of the octagonal inner lining and the base of the bell-mould.

Photo: Warwick Rodwell

furnace was built of stone and brick fragments, bonded in clay. Blobs and splashes of bell-metal were also recovered from disturbed levels at the east end of the chapel.

The other hearth, containing the remains of an iron cauldron, reported by Balleine against the north wall of the nave is less likely to have been connected with bell founding and is, as he observed, more probably a legacy of the military occupation of the chapel. Small blobs of lead and pockets of grey ash found in the disturbed upper levels indicate that lead melting also took place in the chapel at some relatively late date. Whether the melting was in conjunction with roof plumbing for Saint Brelade's Church, or for the manufacture of musket-shot, cannot be determined.

Excavations Outside the Chapel, 1985

As the final stage in the restoration of the Fishermen's Chapel approached, it was decided that improvements to the surface-water drainage system were desirable, which would involve taking up the tarmac paths adjoining the chapel on the north and west. The existing paths and drains were laid by Balleine in *c.* 1935, and on various occasions further trenches had been cut in the area in

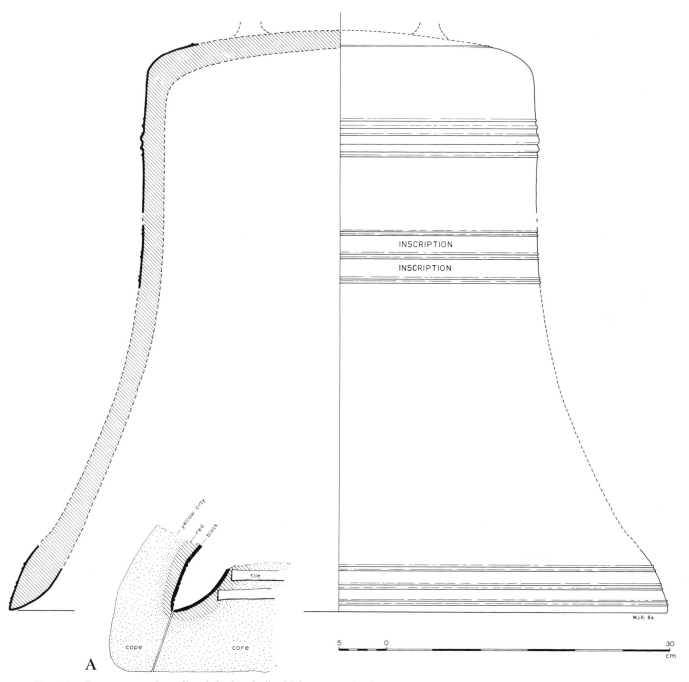

Fig. 54. Reconstructed profile of the lost bell which was cast in the excavated pit at the east end of the chapel in 1754. The reconstruction is based on mould fragments. A. Section through the lower parts of the core and cope, as found, showing the close-fitting conical joint which allowed the two components to be parted, in order to remove the wax core.

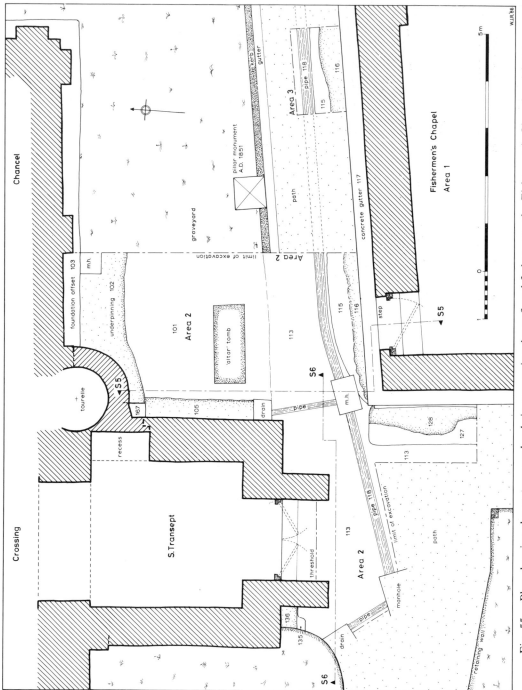

Fig. 55.   Plan showing the uppermost levels in excavation Areas 2 and 3, between the Fishermen's Chapel and Saint Brelade's Church. The positions of sections S5-S6 are also marked.

order to lay services, and for the architect's inspection of the foundations. It was readily apparent that the ground between the chapel and the church had been both considerably reduced in level by Balleine's landscaping, and further disturbed by service trenches. It was therefore uncertain whether any significant archaeological deposits had survived in this area and, if so, whether further losses of crucial evidence would be incurred during the new works.

It was against this background, supplemented by tantalising observations reported by Balleine, that a small excavation was undertaken in 1985, between the north-west corner of the chapel and the south transept of the church (Fig. 43). Two trenches were opened: an L-shaped area which took in the narrow pathway between the two buildings (Area 2), and a small trench against the north wall of the chapel, near its mid-point (Area 3: plan, Fig. 55). Only those aspects of the excavation which shed light on the chapel will be considered here; evidence bearing more directly on the history of Saint Brelade's Church is published elsewhere (Rodwell, 1987 and forthcoming).

Removal of the paths plainly revealed the wide trenches dug for the underpinning on the north and west sides of the chapel, confirming the general belief that work on the foundations had been tackled from both inside and outside the building. There is thus no doubt that all archaeological deposits abutting the chapel, at least on these two sides, have been severed. Although this is a great tragedy for the history of the chapel, it was fully anticipated.

EARLIEST FEATURES

The same geological sequence, of wind-blown sand over granite bedrock, was again encountered, although here with the addition of the predicted ancient topsoil layer (F107; p. 58). The extent to

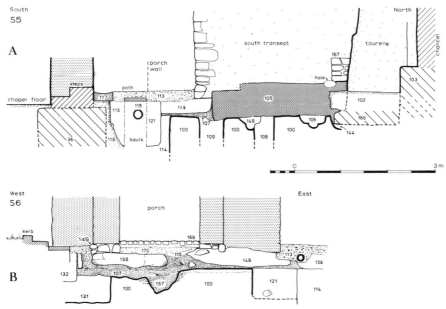

Fig. 56. Sections S5-S6 through the excavated deposits outside the chapel (Area 2). For the location of these sections, see Fig. 55.

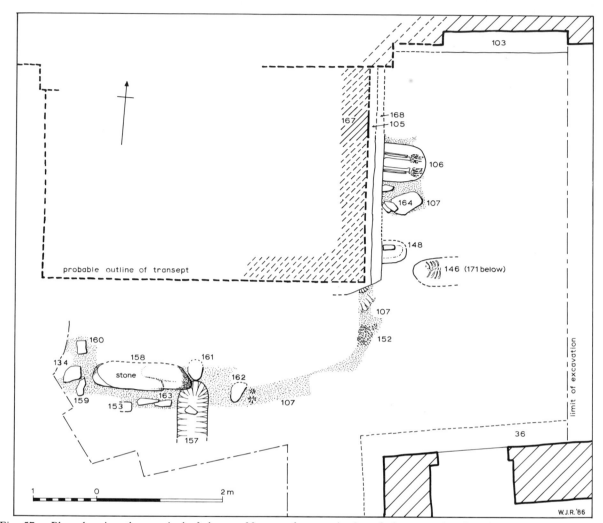

Fig. 57.   Plan showing the survival of the pre-Norman features in Area 2, between the chapel and the church. The probable outline of the Norman south transept is indicated.

which this layer survived is shown on plan in Fig. 57. On the south side of the transept the old topsoil attained a maximum depth of 55 cm, evidently its full original thickness (Fig. 56B). It was a very fine, dark grey, sandy loam, with diffuse lenses of sooty material and occasional lumps of granite, both large and small. Some of these were fire-blackened and probably derived from a hearth in the area. Towards the base of the old topsoil several concentrations of limpet shells were noted, and some animal bones were recovered, including horse. Also cut into this layer were a few small stake-holes and a round-ended gully or timber-slot (F157, Fig. 57).

Finally, a series of stones embedded in this horizon, flush with the ancient ground level, may relate to the foundation of a timber-framed building. In particular, a substantial boulder (F158), 1.6 m in length, laid perfectly flat, could well have been the threshold of a doorway (it was flanked at one end by the timber-slot F157 already mentioned, and at the other by a group of upright stones which appeared to have been the packing around the foot of a post). There is possibly just enough evidence to suggest that we have here the north-east corner of a timber building, with a north-facing door. This was certainly separate from the early building which, it has been argued, underlay and preceded the present chapel (p. 60).

A little more dating evidence is available for the early features outside the chapel, than for those inside it. Two sherds of late Gallo-Roman pottery were found in the old topsoil beside the possible threshold stone, and two more were unstratified in later deposits close by. A sample of the limpet midden from the old topsoil was submitted to Harwell Laboratory for radiocarbon testing, and returned an uncalibrated date centring on A.D. 440,[4] and animal bones from the same deposit returned a date of A.D. 720–900.[5] There can be little doubt that the occupation evidence outside the chapel relates to the so-called 'Dark Ages'.

THE CEMETERY

Evidence for thirty-seven graves was encountered during the excavations, and in most cases the remains were extremely fragmentary, either as a result of one grave cutting into another, or in consequence of the trenching connected with drainage and underpinning operations. The majority of these burials belonged to the medieval and later cemetery associated with the parish church, and are not therefore of immediate relevance here. Nevertheless, there are four, or possibly five, graves belonging to the stratigraphically oldest phase of interment, which may help to shed light on the early Christian history of the site. Two of these are actually severed by the foundations of the first transept of Saint Brelade's Church (plan, Fig. 57). They contained an adolescent, of whom only the lower legs and feet survived (F106, Fig. 58), and a new-born baby (F148).

The characteristics of these graves are threefold. First, they were very shallow when dug, being

Fig. 58. The surviving foot-end of a pre-Norman grave (F106) underlying the south transept of Saint Brelade's Church.

Photo: Warwick Rodwell

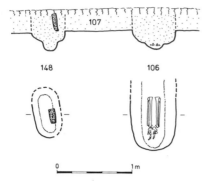

Fig. 59.   Reconstructed plans and sections through a pre-Norman grave (F106) and infant burial (F148), showing their relationship to the ancient topsoil which covered the site (F107).

only 40–50 cm deep, and they were cut through the old topsoil before there was a general accumulation of grave-earth over the site. Secondly, the grave-cuts were round-ended and ledged along the sides; reconstructed profiles are given in Fig. 59. Thirdly, these interments were uncoffined. In the case of the baby's burial (F148) there appears to have been a wooden marker set upright within the grave filling. A fragmentary grave (F146), just east of the infant burial, should belong to this group, as must another grave directly beneath it (F171, not excavated). Finally, there was a burial to the south of the transept, where only a pair of heels survived in the butt-end of a very narrow grave. There were doubtless further interments associated with this primary cemetery phase within excavation Area 2, but their shallowness did not permit survival amongst the maze of later and deeper features.

A bone sample from the adolescent's grave (F106) was submitted for radiocarbon determination, and returned a date centring on A.D. 850.[6]

THE FOUNDATIONS OF THE CHAPEL

Unlike the evidence recorded inside the chapel, there was hardly any of the external medieval masonry of the foundations available for inspection. Complementing the internal offset was an external one, *c.* 25–30 cm wide, but the top was obscured by the cast-concrete eavesdrip gutter (F117), and the outer face of the foundations was mostly concealed behind a skin of shuttered concrete, and the battered underpinning of boulders set in concrete (F116, north; F118, west). Where examined in detail, by emptying Balleine's trenches (F115 and F127), the underpinning was found to extend down to the surface of the bedrock, at *c.* 1.2 m below path level in Area 3. As with the internal work, underpinning was carried out in a series of short lengths; the sequence of operations is outlined on pp. 150–1.

5. STRUCTURAL ANALYSIS

A brief description of the chapel has already been given in chapter 2, and this may now be augmented with a detailed account and critical analysis of all the component parts of the structure. This study was carried out before the walls of the chancel were replastered, and while the ceiling vault was accessible from scaffolding.

The Ground Plan (Fig. 60A)

It was surprising to discover that the truly rectangular plan of the foundations is not reflected in the superstructure. While the north and south walls of the chapel are virtually parallel and rest squarely and centrally upon their foundations, the east and west walls, together with the chancel or pilaster-arch, are all skewed in a north-east to south-west direction, but by differing amounts. The west wall and the chancel arch are nearly parallel, and thus the nave is not far from being a parallelogram in plan. The chancel is, however, much less regular, owing to its south wall being some 30 cm shorter than its north wall. It would thus appear that when the walls of the chapel were marked out not only were false right-angles established, but a foot-measurement was also lost in the length of the south wall.

It can be seen from the excavation plan (Fig. 46D) that the error introduced at the west end was sufficient only to skew the wall on its foundation, which would scarcely have been noticeable, and of no practical significance. At the east end, however, a much greater problem arose, and the wall was skewed to such an extent that its inner face actually oversailed the foundation at the south-east corner of the building. The extent of this oversailing may have been in the order of 30 cm, but this cannot now be precisely verified on account of the underpinning.

Although the practical effects of the planning error are clearly to be seen, we cannot necessarily explain the cause in human terms. Setting-out errors of this kind are by no means uncommon in medieval buildings (Rodwell, 1989, 66). Despite these difficulties, there is no doubt that the four walls of the chapel are of a single build, and without alteration. It is less easy to be dogmatic about the relationship between the foundations and the superstructure. Attention was first drawn to the misfit between the chapel and its foundations at the east end by Oppenheim (1916, plan), who must have seen an excavation outside the south-east corner of the chapel when he drew his plan. He evidently supposed that the chapel had been at least partially rebuilt on older foundations, and archaeological evidence now lends support to such a notion. There are three features which suggest that the foundations belong to an earlier chapel. First, the excessive nature of the misfit; secondly, the lack of any mortar, even in the uppermost courses of the foundations, to match that of the walls; and thirdly, the considerable diagonal slope of the foundations towards the south-east. While this was of little consequence to a building with a timber-framed roof, a levelling out of the walls had to be achieved before springing-level in a stone-vaulted structure.

An explanation for the anomalous layout, together with a discussion of dimensional aspects of the plan and elevations is offered on pp. 94–7.

Walls, Windows and Doorways

THE WALLS

The chapel walls are of two thicknesses, the significance of which will be examined in connection with the vault. The end walls measure 75–78 cm ($2\frac{1}{2}$ ft), but the side walls are substantially thicker, at 92–95 cm (3 ft). They are constructed throughout in local pink granite set in a hard, creamy-white lime mortar which contains sand grains up to 1.5 mm in diameter, and a profusion of both crushed and whole limpet shells, as an aggregate. This is a well-known medieval mortar type

Fig. 62.   General view of the exposed masonry of the chancel, after the removal of the 1930s furnishings and concrete floor. In the foreground is the step of Mont Mado granite, both ends of which were deeply embedded in the side walls of the chapel.

Photo: Warwick Rodwell

in the Channel Islands, but research into its manufacture and ingredients would be useful. Indeed, where the mortar has been allowed to 'cure' thoroughly it still has immense strength, so much so that Balleine reported the use of small charges of gunpowder to dislodge recalcitrant stones during his restoration of Saint Brelade's Church (Balleine, 1932, 31).

He also published seemingly authoritative statements concerning the method of construction employed for the walls of Jersey churches and chapels, asserting that mortar was prepared by boiling crushed shells in sea water, and pouring the hot mixture into wooden casements that were erected as moulds for the walls. Not only is the concept of producing mortar out of boiled shells, and using it like hot glue, wholly fictitious (p. 102), but there is also no evidence for the employment of shuttering in the construction of walls. Vaults are a different matter. The walls of medieval masonry buildings in the Channel Islands were clearly constructed in horizontal 'lifts', using a stiff mix of lime mortar (see further, p. 88).

The masons' technique could best be studied in the exposed walls of the chancel (Fig. 62). Here, between the foundations and the impost level of the pilaster-arch, nine constructional 'lifts' could be traced;[1] they are indicated and numbered L1 to L9 on the elevation drawings, Figs. 60 and 61. The lifts vary in height from *c.* 20 to 50 cm, the average being 30 cm, which is normal for a rubble building of this kind. The visible continuity of lifts through the south, east and north walls, and especially into the pilasters, provides unequivocal proof that all these elements belong to a single building campaign (Figs. 63 and 64). The construction of the north pilaster and its integration with the adjacent walling was particularly clear. The south pilaster was more obscured by residual plaster, but its contemporaneity with the wall is no less certain.

In general, the lifts follow both the eastward and southward tilt of the foundations, with no attempt to establish a true horizontal until impost level was reached. There, it is noticeable,

Fig. 63.   The north wall of the chancel and its junction with the pilaster-arch, in which several of the building lifts are clearly visible.

Photo: Warwick Rodwell

Fig. 64.   The base of the chancel arch (south side), resting on the internal foundation offset. The depth of the medieval foundation can be seen here, and beneath it the two types of underpinning constructed in 1927–34: on the left is a length of vertically-shuttered concrete, while to the right is a broad apron.

Photo: Warwick Rodwell

especially on the north (Fig. 60B) that the ninth lift had to be tapered in order to bring the wall top horizontal. This was an essential preparation for the construction of the vault. Elsewhere, it is interesting to note that lifts were levelled locally, where this was necessitated by a window sill, as is particularly marked in the case of the east wall (Fig. 61B, lift L4).

Although the external appearance of the walls has been somewhat altered by modern pointing and the associated insertion of small pieces of stone between many of the joints, as already noted

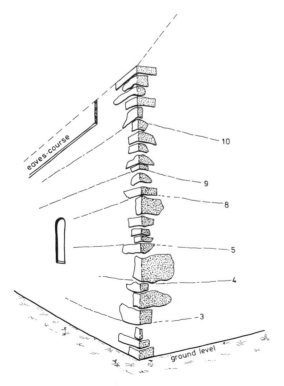

Fig. 65.   Perspective view of the south-east angle of the chapel, showing the masonry of the quoin, the projecting eaves-course at the springing of the vault, and building lifts (numbered). See also Fig. 11.

(p. 18), it is still just possible to discern some of the original building lifts in the north, east and south walls, and measurement shows that these correspond with the internally recorded evidence. The building lifts emanating from the south-east corner of the chapel are illustrated in a perspective sketch in Fig. 65. Here, a tenth lift can also be seen, corresponding to the vault springing-line. Above this, the projecting eaves-band enshrines two more lifts. It can thus be determined that the side walls of the chapel were raised from foundation to eaves in twelve lifts.

MEDIEVAL SCAFFOLDING

The scaffolding associated with the construction work was also evidenced in the internal wall faces, in the form of blocked putlog holes. There are six of these in the east wall (Figs. 10B and 61B), representing three stages of scaffolding. The first stage was erected at 1.1 m above ground level, the second at 2.0 m, and the third at 3.0 m. That gave a working platform at impost level. Two further scaffold stages were required at either end of the chapel, in order to raise the gables. These fourth and fifth stages are represented by putlog holes showing through the plaster in the west wall, at 3.4 m and 4.2 m, respectively, above ground level (Figs. 61C and 82). The putlogs in the fifth stage were set closer together (i.e. stepped in from the side walls), as is usual in gable construction. A further pair of instepped putlogs, representing a sixth and final stage, is doubtless hidden behind plaster at about 5.1 m above ground.

In each case the scaffold stage corresponds with one of the building lifts, and some putlog holes can just be discerned in the external wall faces, showing that the common practice of using through-timbers was adopted (i.e. each putlog passed right through the wall, supporting a scaffold platform on either side. As building proceeded and each new putlog was laid across the wall it was roughly encased by a pair of side stones and bridged with a capstone (all illustrated in the elevations, Figs. 60 and 61). This technique prevented the putlogs from becoming firmly mortared into the masonry, allowing their withdrawal upon completion of the work. The blocked apertures indicate that timbers of *c*. 12–15 cm square were employed.

Scaffold stages in the east gable wall were placed upon building lifts 3, 5 and 9, and in the west gable they were on lifts 10 and 12, and perhaps 14 or 15 also. In the side walls, however, the scaffolding stages relate only to lifts 4 and 6. Scars indicative of timber emplacements over lift 9 on the north side are possibly not part of the scaffolding scheme, but may be associated with the construction of the roof vault (discussed below, p. 84).

Externally, the masonry is rugged, and even the rocks used for the quoins show little hint of dressing. They are neither graded according to size, nor disposed according to any prescribed pattern: they were evidently laid – large and small – just as they came. This is well illustrated in Figs. 11 and 65. The quoins were never intended to be visible and, like the remainder of the chapel, both internally and externally, would have been plastered and limewashed. It is necessary to stress this point since Balleine, citing casual opinions given by two late nineteenth-century French antiquaries, assigned the chapel to the mid-sixth century on the allegedly diagnostic evidence of the quoin construction (p. 14). The subsequent repetition of this over-optimistic attempt at dating is regrettable. Basically, the chapel's quoins are like those on many other Jersey buildings, of the simplest possible form, and intrinsically undatable.

THE WINDOWS (Fig. 66)

The chapel retains its original full complement of five small windows which are characterised internally by widely splayed, round-headed rear-arches, and externally by low segmental-headed openings of neatly cut stone (Fig. 15). The latter have already been described and doubts cast on their antiquity (p. 18). Internal examination has demonstrated how the original windows were constructed, and the alterations that have subsequently taken place.

First, it could be seen that the rear-arches of the three windows in the chancel are integral with the construction of the walls: the north and south windows have their arch-springing level coincident with building lift L6, and the jambs of the east window rise to lift L8 (Figs. 60 and 61). The north and south windows of the chancel are an identical pair, their jambs and sills all measuring 1.08 m (3½ ft). The semi-circular rear-arches were turned on centring which rested on the jambs, and the slight ledges at springing-level consequent upon this form of construction are clearly marked. The diameter of the arch (1.12 m) was thus necessarily fractionally greater than the width of the splay below. Moreover, in the north window and south nave window channels have been preserved in the mortar at springing level, demonstrating that the centring was formed with battens having a thickness of *c.* 7 cm (Fig. 66C, E). The same two windows preserve in their arched reveals mortar impressions of the tapered battens or staves which were placed here in barrel-like formation to support the masonry above, while the mortar was setting. In the north window the form-work for the arch employed about eighteen staves (Figs. 67 and 68). Unfortunately, the restoration of 1884 removed the evidence for the form-work from the east and south chancel windows.

Fig. 67. The masonry around the north window of the chancel, exposed in 1915 and subsequently limewashed. Note the inserted stone lamp bracket on the left, and the remains of original plaster in the splay; see also Fig. 68.

Photo: Warwick Rodwell

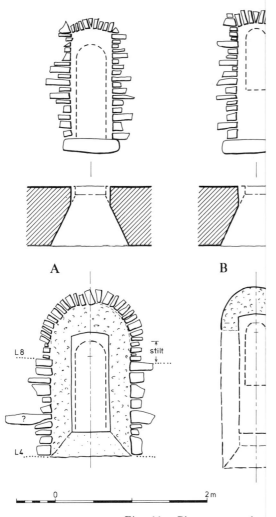

A

B

L8

stilt

L4

0   2 m

Fig. 66. Plans, external a[...]
fea[...]

Fig. 68. Detail of the arched head of the north chancel window, showing mortar impressions of the staves used to construct the centring.

Photo: Warwick Rodwell

The same form-work may have been used to construct the heads of the north and south chancel windows, but that used for the east window was slightly smaller in diameter. The latter corresponds, however, to the requirements for the south nave window and it is likely that the same form-work was employed for both. The proportions of the east window were adjusted to give it an elongated form, more suited to the gable wall than the squatter openings in the side walls. Thus a stilt of 28 cm was constructed between the tops of the jambs, as initially built, and the springing of the arch, the attenuation of the window being a modification that was introduced during construction.

The west window was set relatively high in its gable and had the narrowest rear-arch of all, being only 90 cm across. The head alone survives, heavily restored, and nothing can now be gleaned about the jambs or the overall height of the original opening. The jambs, which are built of squared stone, date entirely from 1884; and when the soffit of the arch was stripped of plaster and pointed, the joints between the stones were obscured by cementing in small water-worn pebbles. This curious and wholly inappropriate treatment was also applied to the head of the east window, and in large measure to its splays as well. The date of this work on the east window is uncertain: it may have been carried out in 1884, when the aperture was unblocked, or it could have resulted from tampering in *c.* 1915. The effect is indicated diagrammatically in Fig. 60B.

The north and south chancel windows retain evidence for the original profiles of their plastered sills, which were S-shaped in cross-section (Fig. 66C, E), and a good deal of ancient plaster remains in their splays. The east splay of the north window is the most completely preserved and exhibits a thin layer (2–4 mm thick) of fine, cream plaster applied directly to the stone. Traces of painting remain. Most of the plaster on the sills of these windows was replaced in the nineteenth century.

A feature common to all the windows is a break both in alignment and in the construction of their splays; this occurs a little more than half way through the thickness of the wall, towards the outer face. The break clearly results from the enlargement of the external apertures, and by projecting the lines of the preserved splays and heads it is possible to reconstruct the approximate original dimensions of the window openings. This exercise has been carried out in Fig. 66, where broken lines are used to indicate the reconstructed openings. There is little reason to doubt that the external openings were formerly round-headed, with the largest being the east window. Its aperture would have been *c.* 120 by 40 cm. The north and south chancel windows can be restored to *c.* 80 by 24 cm, and the south nave window to *c.* 66 by 20 cm. The width of the west window aperture seems to have been *c.* 24 cm and, if its proportions were in the order of 3:1 like all the others, its height must have been *c.* 80 cm. The reconstruction of the west window in 1884 was obviously based on the external appearance of the east window.

Altogether, the volume of light being admitted to the chapel was approximately doubled by the alterations that were carried out at a date which must next be considered. Although the external apertures were almost certainly rebuilt in 1884, following the removal of the rendering (p. 10), their general form was not altered at that time. In style, these low, segmentally-arched openings could date from the fifteenth century, or later. The remaining fragment of the west window above the intruded doorway, as depicted in illustrations prior to 1884, demonstrates that the transformation of the windows took place prior to the chapel's use by the parish militia in the second half of the sixteenth century. It is thus reasonably certain that the enlarged windows were associated with the later ecclesiastical history of the chapel, and not with its post-Reformation secular uses. Moreover, there is an indication on the earliest surviving plan of the chapel that at least two of the windows had been blocked up by the militia (Fig. 7). All the evidence points to the windows being enlarged to their present proportions in the fifteenth century, when the chapel was refurbished and repainted for its final phase of ecclesiastical use.

The original sill-stones of the north, east and south chancel windows survive, but in the south nave window a rebated stone sill was inserted, probably in the eighteenth or nineteenth century, to receive a wooden frame. Sashes and other domestic-style glazing had been introduced into the parish church (Figs. 3 and 5), and this tiny example in the chapel was doubtless part of the same general phenomenon. The stone sill remains in position, and is shown in the section drawing (Fig. 66).

The original, narrow windows would almost certainly have been unglazed, but by the time they were enlarged in the fifteenth century stained and painted glass was commonplace and would then have been fitted. This would all have been destroyed at the Reformation; a few small fragments of medieval coloured window glass were recovered during the excavations.[2] It is quite likely that all the window apertures of the chapel were filled up with masonry in the sixteenth century by the militia, partly because their glazing had been smashed, and partly for the security of the armaments that were now housed in the building. None of the windows was probably re-opened until the later 1840s or '50s, when the chapel became a carpenter's workshop (p. 4).

Finally, it may be noted that there is a pair of roughly shaped, projecting stone brackets built into the rear-arches of the north and south chancel windows (Figs. 60, 61 and 67). These are not original features, but later medieval insertions, and were intended to carry cresset oil lamps. In setting these brackets, several stones of the jambs of both windows were displaced and refixed (Fig. 66D and 66E). The soft, sandy mortar used is of orange-yellow colour, and is not found elsewhere in the chapel. This work was carried out before the plaster layer which carries the painted decoration in the northern window splay was applied. The brackets probably date from the fourteenth or fifteenth century.[3]

Alongside the northern jamb of the east window is a large, flat slab of granite, 60 cm in length and 60 cm above the sill. It is up to 10 cm thick, and projects 5 cm from the wall face (Fig. 61B). This might have been another bracket – perhaps for an image – which has later been hacked back. If so, it was an original feature of the chapel, since the stone is set in the primary mortar.

THE DOORWAYS (Fig. 69)

The original entrance at the north-west corner of the chapel has, like the windows, undergone modifications which include the formation of low, segmentally-arched heads both internally and externally (Fig. 14). In this instance a more precise indication of the date of the alterations is provided by the survival of plaster on the rear-arch and jambs. This plaster bears traces of the same fifteenth-century decorative scheme of painting as appears on the north wall of the nave. The modified doorway must, therefore, be associated with the late medieval refurbishment of the chapel. The original form of this opening may be glimpsed from a semi-circular joint in the

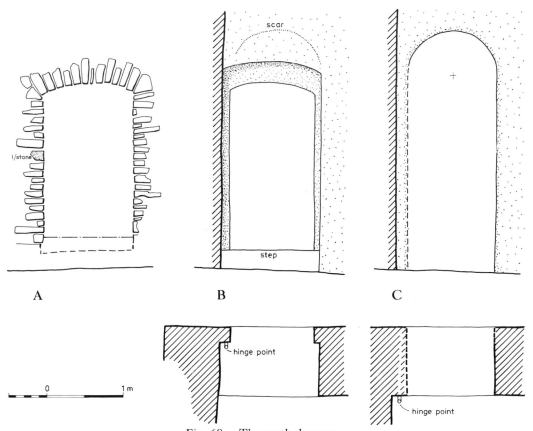

Fig. 69. The north doorway.
A. External elevation, as existing.
B. Internal elevation and plan, as existing.
C. Reconstruction of the internal elevation and plan as originally built.

wallplaster above the rear-arch (Figs. 60B and 69B), indicating the former presence of a taller, round-headed doorway. This was evidently slightly narrower than the present opening, the western jamb having been cut back to create the rebate which housed the later door and its frame. The present door and frame date from 1884.

Before the rebate for the door-frame was created the jambs were parallel and cut straight through the wall (i.e. there were no original splays or rebates), and the door would have hung on iron pintles set into the masonry in the north-west corner of the chapel. The wooden door, which would have been slightly larger than the aperture, merely closed against the flat inner face of the wall. The original arrangement is reconstructed in Fig. 69C. The primary opening measured c. 3.14 m by 1.12 m (10 by 3 ft), and the springing of its arch coincided with building lift L9.

The broad, segmentally-arched west doorway was inserted in the later sixteenth century, probably soon after 1550, and the old north doorway infilled.[4] The threshold and outline of this new doorway were internally traceable, but completely obliterated externally (Fig. 61C). The opening measured 2.1 m (7 ft) wide and c. 2.7 m (9 ft) high, although the scar formerly visible in the Victorian plaster outlined a larger area on account of the removal of the jamb-stones and arch-stones when the blocking was inserted. The threshold was c. 70 cm above post-medieval floor level in the nave (Fig. 47B), so presumably an earthen ramp was made for the entry of cannon. Externally, the churchyard sloped steeply up from the threshold, contributing even greater difficulties of access.

Vaulting and Roofing

THE CEILING VAULT

There has been a general assumption by previous commentators that the pointed barrel-vault which runs the full length of the chapel is an addition, replacing an earlier timber-framed roof. Balleine went as far as dating the changeover to the fourteenth century, believing it to be coeval with the first painted decoration. Detailed examination has failed to support this hypothesis, and several unequivocal arguments may be advanced to show that the vault and the walls upon which it rests are contemporaneous. This is an issue of such importance, not just for the architectural history of the Fishermen's Chapel, but also for the Channel Islands in general, that the evidence needs careful presentation.

First, it may be noted that there is no hint of structural discontinuity between the walls and vaulting, as might have been expected if the two elements were of different dates. Secondly, the pilasters, which are integral with the walls, would have served no function in this building if it had had a timber roof. Their imposts are too low in relation to the wall-tops to have been associated with supporting a framed roof of tie-beam construction. Plainly, the function of the pilasters has always been to carry the transverse arch of masonry, and that in turn carries the vault. Thirdly, the differences in wall thickness demonstrate that, from the outset, it was intended that the side walls would be required to contain a much greater thrust than the gable ends. A timber-framed roof on such a small building would not have required the additional thickening of the north and south walls, whereas it is a characteristic feature of barrel-vaulted churches that their side walls are either thicker, or more heavily buttressed, than their ends. The Fishermen's Chapel has never been buttressed.

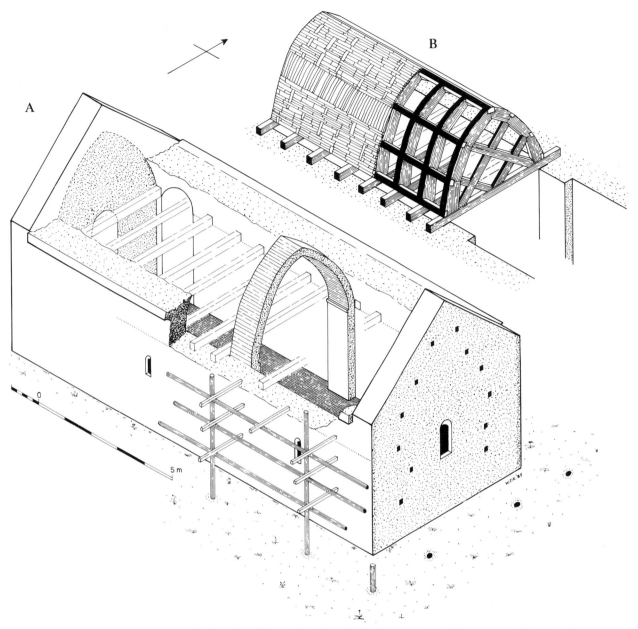

Fig. 70.   Cutaway isometric drawings illustrating the principal constructional features of the chapel.
A. The shell of the chapel with most of the stone vault removed to show the free-standing pilaster-arch and the probable positions of the beams that were built into the wall tops to support the centring for the vault. Externally, the full arrangement of putlog holes in the east wall is indicated, and a sample section of scaffolding reconstructed on the south wall.
B. A reconstruction of the seven bays of timber form-work built to support the masonry of the nave vault. Apart from the precise arrangement of cross-bracing, evidence for all the major components of this erection has been recovered from the study of the existing vault.

BUILDING THE VAULT

Detailed examination of the vault during plaster repairs in 1982–83 enabled its method of construction to be fully determined, and a cutaway reconstruction drawing has been prepared, showing all the significant features (Fig. 70). The stages of executing the work were as follows.

Stage 1

The four walls of the chapel, together with the pilasters, were raised to building lift L9, and brought to a true level. The pilasters were capped with thin, flat impost stones. In fact, perfection was not achieved, and the top of the south wall was *c.* 5 cm lower than the north, but this would have been indiscernible and immaterial.

Stage 2

Preparations were made for the construction of the vault. Exactly how the necessary scaffolding and form-work were inter-related cannot now be determined without removing plaster from the junction between the vault and the wall-tops. In the later medieval period the practice in Jersey, as elsewhere, was to place a series of large beams transversely across the building from wall to wall (Fig. 70A). These were at intervals of less than one metre, and the form-work was built directly upon them. Evidence of this arrangement is clearly displayed in the north aisle vault of Saint Brelade's Church, where the masonry is fully exposed and the sockets which housed the transverse beams remain open.[5]

On the north side of the chancel there is some evidence for timbers being placed on top of building lift L9: three scars were observed where plaster had fallen away (Fig. 60B). On the south side of the chancel old repairs to the plaster immediately above building lift L9 provide further clues to the location of infilled sockets there. Whether these features housed transverse beams or whether they were associated with the general scaffolding scheme, cannot be determined with certainty, although the former is more likely. Whatever the precise arrangement, a very rigid support structure was required at this level, with the ability to carry the principal frames for the centring for the vault. An external scaffold stage at the same level would also have been a necessity. The number of bays into which the chapel was divided for the purposes of vault construction – and hence the number of centring arches and supports – can be determined from the masonry of the vault itself (see below). The chancel vault was supported on four bays of form-work, and the nave vault on seven bays. The pilaster-arch itself comprised a narrow bay. The chapel was thus divided into twelve sections, or bays, for the purposes of vaulting, with thirteen transverse supports required for the centring, including one support at each gable end. Spacing was somewhat irregular, with the distances between centres varying from 90 cm to 120 cm.

Stage 3

Several courses of masonry were laid on the wall-tops, encasing and firmly anchoring the scaffolding and transverse beams. This took the side walls up to lift L10, and since the same lift can be traced across the east wall it demonstrates that the end gables had not previously been completed. The tenth building lift also contained the arched head of the north doorway, the highest feature in the side walls. These observations provide yet further conclusive proof that the stone vault was not an addition to an existing building.

Stage 4

The gables were probably next completed, while the carpenters were erecting the timber form-work for the vault.

Stage 5

Timber form-work was first erected for the pilaster-arch (chancel arch), before the main vault was begun. This form-work may have been supported from the scaffolding or from the transverse beams, since the diminutive imposts on the pilasters had insufficient projection for use as supports. The imposts, which project only towards the central axis of the chapel, and do not oversail the east and west sides of the pilasters, merely formed a ledge upon which the lowest shuttering boards rested. It is however clear from impressions remaining in the mortar of the arch that the form-work was fully cased at the sides (i.e. it was more than just centring). The builders intended that the pilaster-arch should be cast as a free-standing, monolithic structure, and its rectangular cross-section measured 75 by 25 cm. When the wooden form-work was complete it was lined with a thick layer of stiff lime-mortar, into which stones were then bedded. These were roughly dressed and laid radially, as voussoirs. A triangular keystone was placed at the centre (Fig. 71). The initial mortar bed – now seen as the soffit face of the arch – retains all the impressions of the horizontal shuttering boards. The average width of a board was 10 cm (Fig. 35).

When the carpenters came to erect the form-work for the arch they would have discovered that the pilasters do not stand squarely opposite one another, owing to the incorrectly laid out ground plan (p. 73). The longitudinal displacement is 30 cm. While it might have been simplest to build the arch askew, the discrepancy would have been conspicuously visible when the vault was in place. The fact that this is not the case is a result of a subtle S-curve having been introduced into the arch, so that whilst it is actually askew to the line of the vaulting, it does not appear markedly so when

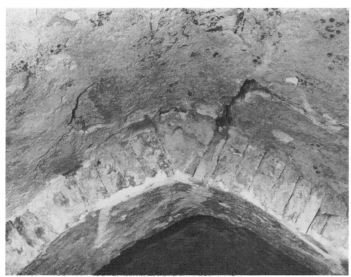

Fig. 71.   The apex of the pilaster-arch (west face), showing the radial setting
of voussoirs and the keystone.

Photo: Warwick Rodwell

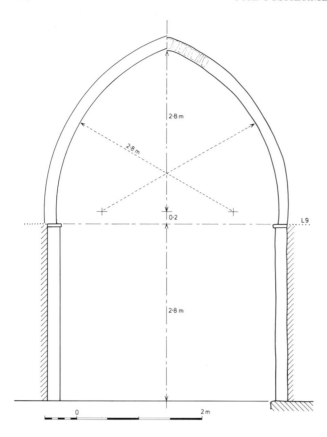

Fig. 72. The geometrical principles employed in the construction of the vault and chancel arch. The theoretical profile is shown on the left and the profile as constructed on the right.

viewed from the west end of the chapel (Figs. 60B and 61A). This was a clever device which could only have emanated from a team of carpenters and masons well versed in the art of vault building.

The profile of the transverse arch naturally reflects that of the vault itself. The vault is of simple pointed form with two centres of arcature, based on the springing line, and the radius employed can be calculated at *c.* 2.8 m (9 ft). Although it might be expected that the springing line would correspond with the top of the pilasters (i.e. impost level), this is in fact not so: the springing is at least 20 cm higher. Thus the arch has a short stilt, which is a commonly observed phenomenon in Jersey churches (Fig. 72). The explanation is almost certainly a matter of pure practicality. Thirteen sets of centring were required to support the shuttering for the vault, and these were in turn carried on the thirteen transverse beams that had been laid across the wall tops at impost level. The effective springing line of the vault was therefore raised by an amount equivalent to the thickness of the beams, or 20 cm (8 inches).

When a cross-section is drawn through the vault, its design and geometry become readily apparent, as shown in Fig. 72. It can be seen that the radius of the pilaster-arch is equivalent to the height of the pilasters, and that the height of the arch (from springing line to crown) is also the same. The two elements are separated by the silt of 20 cm. It is furthermore noticeable that the stilt in the arch, and in some places along the barrel-vault itself, does not stand quite vertical, but exhibits a slight outward lean. This imparts a suspicion of a horseshoe-shaped profile, a feature seen also in the vaulting of Saint Brelade's Church (and, on a small scale, in the east window of the chapel, Fig. 66A). The subject of horseshoe-shaped arches has generated much comment and speculation in the past, and is further considered on p. 89.

Stage 6

Timber centring was erected in the nave and chancel, dividing them into seven and four bays, respectively. The frames rested on the transverse beams, already described, and were secured in place by a series of horizontal connecting timbers, like the purlins in a roof. There were two purlins on each side, and a ridge-piece at the crown of the vault. Thus a rigid grid of timber framing was created, dividing the entire area to be vaulted into a series of compartments, or panels. There were forty-two over the nave and twenty-four over the chancel. The panels averaged one metre square, but there was considerable variation. The panels were then planked over, one by one, until the whole form-work was shuttered (Fig. 70B).

Where the medieval plaster had fallen away from the vault – and that had occurred in many places – impressions of the shuttering boards were plainly visible in the mortar. These boards varied greatly in size, the average width being *c.* 16 cm, but the greatest recorded was 23 cm. In a few cases sufficient was exposed to ascertain the full length of a board, and the longest noted was 1.05 m. It is, however, clear that shuttering boards only spanned a single panel, and that they overlapped, from one bay to the next. The shuttering seemed to stop at the end walls, and was not lodged on them. Hence the gables stood independent of the vaulting, which is often not the case elsewhere. The shuttering boards were, however, seen to oversail the edges of the chancel arch (although by no more than 2 cm in the few measurable instances). The arch, now already complete, conveniently served as the form-work for one section of the vault. It is perhaps worth

Fig. 73.   Detail of the nave vault (south side), showing the impressions of both horizontal and vertical slats used in the construction of the form-work, revealed where the plaster had fallen away. The crack on the left is a legacy of the 1926 earthquake.

Photo: Warwick Rodwell

noting here that the chancel arch was an architectural or liturgical feature, and not a structural necessity. The vaulting would stand perfectly well without it.

On the north side of the nave all the shuttering boards appear to have run longitudinally, in conformity with the axis of the vault, but the occasional vertical slat was woven between boards, presumably to give additional support in weak places. On the south side of the nave, however, there appears to have been a continuous band, 60 cm (2 ft) high, of vertical slats, halfway up the curvature of the vault (Fig. 73). Elsewhere on the south side only the occasional vertical slat was seen to be woven between the horizontal members, as on the north (Fig. 70B).

No constructional reason can be adduced for this anomaly on the south side, and it is most likely that the carpenters merely found it a convenient way of utilizing a large number of short slats which they happened to have to hand. An obvious source for these short slats would have been the shuttering that was previously erected – and now no longer needed – for the construction of the chancel arch. Some seventy slats, or almost seven metres of edge-to-edge boarding, had been required to shutter the arch, and that was exactly the quantity of vertical slatting recorded over the nave (Fig. 35).

In many parts of the vault clear impressions of wood-grain, and occasional wafer-thin slithers of timber, were preserved in the mortar. From these it was possible to deduce that the boarding was riven and averaged 2 cm in thickness, but some slats were no more than 1 cm thick. Unfortunately, the species could not be determined with certainly, but oak seems probable. The chancel vault was not studied in detail, but appeared to have been erected on boarding like that over the north side of the nave.

Stage 7
When the form-work was complete over the entire chapel the construction of the masonry vault could begin. This proceeded in horizontal bands, or lifts, running the full length of the chapel (Fig. 74). Owing to the plaster covering, it was not possible to make an accurate estimate of the

Fig. 74.   Detail of the nave vault (north side), showing horizontal joints indicating building lifts. The coarse, shelly nature and stiffness of the mortar-mix are also apparent.
Photo: Warwick Rodwell

number of lifts per side, or to be certain of the height of each lift. The general impression gained, however, is that lifts were in the order of 30–50 cm in the lower parts of the vault (i.e. closely similar to the building lifts in the main walls of the chapel). However, there was a clearly traceable lift of 90 cm just below the crown of the vault on the north side, and one of 130 cm on the south.

When building the vault, the masonry on both sides had, of course, to be raised simultaneously in order to maintain stability. The masonry was probably laid to a uniform thickness of *c.* 40–50 cm. As with the pilaster-arch, the masons' technique was to lay a thick bed of stiff mortar and then to set pieces of granite in it, voussoir-fashion. The interstices between stones were thoroughly filled, and only occasionally did a block sink sufficiently far into the mortar bed for it to come into contact with the boarding beneath. The weight of stone and wet mortar was very great; the complete vault weighed more than 80 tons, and each panel of shuttering had to support about 1.2 tons (albeit not a dead-weight load). The strain imposed on the form-work by this load is plainly discernible. Instead of maintaining a smooth curve from springing line to apex, the profile of the vault shows a tendency to rise in a series of jerks, resulting from the flattening of the unsupported boarding between purlins. Likewise, along the axis of the chapel, the vault exhibits slight sagging between the bays of form-work. Viewed at close quarters, the intrados (lower face) is markedly irregular. But it is this irregularity that encapsulates the principal evidence for the technology of vault construction in the Channel Islands.

Finally, a word must be said about the 'horseshoe' effect which is faintly discernible in the vaulting of the Fishermen's Chapel, and is somewhat more obvious in the chancel of Saint Brelade's Church; there are also slight hints of it elsewhere in the Channel Islands. Balleine was greatly excited by this subject, and referred confidently to the horseshoe effect as being deliberate and 'moresque' (Balleine, 1897, 4). Warton then proclaimed Saint Brelade's as 'Unique in possessing some mauresque arches, a suggested echo of Spanish influence, but more probably due to the Byzantine taste of some errant crusader' (Warton, 1914, 441). While the horseshoe-shaped arch is certainly a well-known feature, not just in Spain, but also in France and in other parts of Europe, it was usually of careful and clearly deliberate construction. The same cannot be said in Jersey. Indeed, the reverse is true, and there can be no serious doubt that the slight outward bulging on the pilaster-arch of the Fishermen's Chapel is purely fortuitous. The explanation is simple: when the form-work was erected, although well cross-braced, it cannot have had quite enough vertical support, directly under the apex of the arch. That is the point where the greatest dead-weight load was applied when the wet mortar and masonry were piled onto the form-work. Under this strain, the slightest depression of the apex would increase the curvature on the sides of the arch, and thus the short vertical stilt was forced outwards, creating a suspicion of a horseshoe shape.

PLASTER AND PAINT

Once the masonry of the vault was set, and the form-work dismantled, the worst of the irregularities were filled, including craters resulting from overlapping planks in the form-work. The shelly mortar used in the construction of the vault and in these patches of infilling is visually identical to that in the walls of the chapel (p. 45). The uneven, shutter-marked surface of the vaulted ceiling was then smoothed over with a thick layer of cream, sandy plaster (the *arriccio*). Over this was laid the finishing coat (the *intonaco*), and finally an application of limewash, which was finished off with a wet brush, leaving characteristic striations. The scaffolding inside the chapel was struck (dismantled) as the plasterers worked their way down the walls, and probably most of the gaping putlog holes were blocked at the same time. But it appears that the pair of putlog holes in the west gable was not properly filled (Fig. 61C), and the plasterers worked around timbers that were still *in situ* here, feathering the edge of the plaster back to the face of the stones.

When the fifteenth-century painted decoration was added scaffolding must have been erected again, and a secondary layer of white lime plaster was applied to the vault, as a preparation. This layer is of varied thickness, being in places no more than a skim. The putlog holes in the west gable were still not filled, and the painted decoration actually runs off the plaster and onto the exposed face of the stone cheeks to these holes. It was common practice in the Middle Ages to leave high-level putlog holes open, so that scaffolding timbers could be re-inserted in them when required.

A detailed, technological account of the plaster and paintwork in the chapel is given in Chapter 3, pp. 45–50.

THE ROOF

Following the completion of the barrel-vault, its extrados (outer face) had to be shaped to conform to the completed profile of the roof. As can be seen from the cross-sections of the chapel (Fig. 61B and 61C), there are two areas where a considerable extra mass of masonry was piled on: along the ridge and, more importantly, along the eaves. Whether all of this is original, or includes some later additions, cannot be determined without cutting into the structure. The additional weight of masonry on the wall-tops, above springing level helped to counter the outward thrusts exerted by the vault, and is certainly a feature of the initial build; the projecting eaves-bands are an integral part of this work (Figs. 1 and 65). They are a common feature of Channel Island churches, and of Romanesque vaulting in general. It can be seen in the Fishermen's Chapel that these bands clearly relate to the vault, and do not extend beyond it into the gable walls.

In 1983 it was possible to remove small areas of slating on the south slope of the nave for an

Fig. 75.   The south slope of the chapel roof, showing the slates of varying sizes bedded directly onto the masonry of the vault.
Photo: Deirdre Shute

examination of their method of fixing; in 1985 the entire roof was stripped and reslated, although without detailed archaeological recording. It was found that the slates were bedded directly onto the masonry of the vault, using a hard, pale cream mortar which contained fine sand, but not shell (Fig. 75). In the early eighteenth century it was recorded that many Jersey churches had blue slate roofs that were bedded on the masonry of their vaulting (Falle and Morant, 1734, 178).

Some pieces of hand-made, red clay roofing tiles were discovered, used as packing material under the slates. These tiles are unlikely to be older than the eighteenth century. The slates, which were French in origin and clearly second-hand when mortared onto the chapel, varied considerably in dimension, and many were incomplete. A full-sized slate measured 27 cm wide by 35 cm long, and averaged 2 cm in thickness. The upper corners were shouldered, and there were two nail-holes for fixing to battens. The slates were of highly micaceous, light silvery-grey fabric, which had weathered to a dark grey-blue colour.

Adolph Curry, in his report of 1905[6] states that it was not possible to strip and relay the existing slates, and recommended repair *in situ*. The Civil Assembly earmarked the sum of £40 to assist with this work, and Balleine recorded his search for suitable old slates. However, it was not until 1908 that a quantity of slates was purchased from Cherbourg (p. 10). The work specified by Curry included raking out and deep-pointing all the joints and laps between the slates, which was duly executed in strong cement, with a black colouring additive. The overall appearance of the restored roof of 1908 was very acceptable, but it still leaked. Water was drawn through the joints, and into the vault, by capillarity.

When fully stripped in 1985, the extent of these repairs could be seen: much of the slating on the north side had been relaid, but on the south only about one-tenth had been affected (Fig. 76). Balleine's characteristically hard cement-mortar had been used. At the same time it was noted that two other types of slate were represented in the roof covering. One was fine, very dense and dark grey in colour, while the other was lighter grey, more akin to a Cornish slate. Fragments of all three types of slate were found in eighteenth- and nineteenth-century levels in the excavations. In connection with the third type it may be noted that Philippe Falle, writing in the eighteenth century, observed that British slates were imported for use on Jersey churches. The roof of the Fishermen's Chapel was probably patched with the residue of salvaged slates from Saint Brelade's Church. Balleine recorded that he found a succession of roofing materials during his restoration of the church and that blue-grey slates had been the covering prior to the introduction of clay tiles (Balleine, 1907, 21).

The history of roofing on the chapel is uncertain, and the evidence has not been fully available for study. There are two alternatives for the covering of the original roof: crude tiling of local stone, mortared directly onto the extrados of the vault, or thatch tied to an arrangement of rafters and battens. The former would almost certainly not have been conducive to the preservation of painted plaster, owing to water penetration. On balance, thatch seems the more likely alternative. In due course, however, a change was made in favour of true slates, of either Norman or Breton origin, and there are indications that this may have occurred in the fifteenth century. The arrival of French slates at Saint Brelade's is firmly established in the late Middle Ages by their appearance as packing material between masonry courses in the construction of the *tourelle* (stair turret) in the parish church. This stair served the rood loft and bell chamber in the tower, and is most likely of mid-fifteenth-century date. Thus imported slates were being used on either the church or the chapel, or both, before the Reformation, and these would certainly have been hung on timber battens.

Fig. 76.   The south slope of the chapel roof during stripping in 1985, showing the mortar bedding for the slates. The
remaining areas of slating are patches that were reset in portland cement in 1908.

Photo: Deirdre Shute

Fragments of French green-glazed clay ridge tiles with decorative cresting, probably dating from
the fifteenth century, were found during the excavation inside the chapel (Fig. 113; p. 157). These
were often used on slated roofs. It is therefore very likely that both the church and the chapel were
provided with slate roofs on wooden battens and rafters from sometime in the fifteenth century.
When the timber substructure of the chapel roof decayed, in the later eighteenth or nineteenth
century, the expedient of mortaring the slates to the extrados of the stone vault was adopted. While
this was perfectly adequate for the roof of a cannon shed, it will have been highly detrimental to the
survival of the medieval paintings. It is small wonder that nineteenth-century antiquaries
persistently referred to their increasing dereliction (pp. 21–4). In the case of the church, the roof
was replaced at an uncertain date – possibly in the seventeenth century – with clay tiles, remnants
of which were observed by Balleine. These may have been similar to the fragments found in the
excavations, incorporated in the bell-mould construction. Those tiles had a greenish-brown glaze
on the outer face, and originated from south-west England (p. 65).

The ends of the ridge abut a pair of stone gable crosses. The eastern cross is made from a block
of local pink granite, 62 cm in height, and 35 cm across the arms (Figs. 13 and 77A). The cross is of
distinctive form, having three stubby arms attached to a broad, flaring base, without an intervening

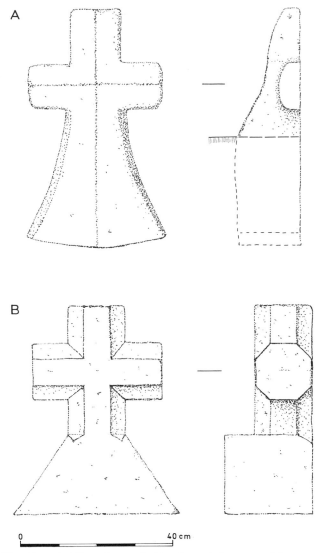

Fig. 77.   A. Elevation and side view of the east gable-cross,
showing the original setting-out lines for the axes of the arms.
B. Elevation and side view of the west gable-cross and integral
base-block.

section of shaft. On its east face, the cross is flat and retains its two axial setting-out lines, but on the west it is of irregular form and the backs of the arms are all rounded in section. While the cross is certainly medieval, on present knowledge it is not closely datable: it is unlikely to be later than the thirteenth century, and could well belong to the eleventh or twelfth. A somewhat smaller and more sophisticated example, in Normandy limestone, was found in the excavations at Saint Mary's Priory, Les Écréhous, in 1987. That example dates from the thirteenth century.

The western cross is made of Chausey granite, and was evidently placed in its present position in *c.* 1884, since all earlier illustrations of the chapel agree in showing no terminal to this gable. The cross, which rises from a triangular base-block, has four similar arms, all octagonal in section, and having a span of 34 cm (Figs. 12 and 77B). The slight asymmetry displayed by the cross-sections of the arms, and the state of weathering, strongly suggest that this is not a late Victorian product, but is more likely to be of pre-Reformation date. Antiquarian illustrations show that Saint Brelade's Church was provided with a complement of gable crosses of this type – probably dating from the fourteenth and fifteenth centuries – and although two or three still remain, others were renewed in the 1880s and '90s. It is thus not improbable that the chapel cross represents a reuse from the church (see also p. 16).

Architectural Geometry of the Chapel

At first sight, the plan appears to be wildly irregular, and might lead us to suppose that no architectural specification was followed by the builders, and no competent master mason employed to superintend the project. This is a false impression, as close analysis of the plan and elevations reveals. First, it has been shown that the foundations were laid out as a true rectangle and, secondly, it would appear that the north wall of the chapel is correct both in position and in length: the fault lies in the placing of the other three walls relative to this. The greatest error has been pinpointed at the south-east corner (p. 60), and it is worth observing that the distance by which the east wall swings out of the expected line is equal to its own thickness (Fig. 78B).

Errors of precisely this kind have been common throughout the history of building, and the circumstances giving rise to them are not difficult to reconstruct. When a new church was begun, the master mason himself would normally have supervised the measuring and pegging out of the intended wall lines, according to a drawn plan in his possession. He might then have left the labourers and masons to excavate the trenches and at least to begin laying the foundations, while he went to oversee work on another site. But if someone inadvertently displaced a marker peg at one corner, or dug a foundation trench on the wrong side of that peg (i.e. mistook an inside line for an outside line, or *vice versa*), an error equivalent to a wall's thickness could easily be introduced, throwing the overall plan out of square. In most other instances where this has plainly happened, it is the foundations that are wrongly laid out and, in consequence, often the walls follow suit. However, the curiosity about the Fishermen's Chapel is that the foundations were correctly laid out and constructed: it was the placing of the superstructure that went hopelessly awry.

This is the strongest evidence for adumbrating that the foundations and the superstructure were not contemporary components of a single building campaign, but could have been widely separated in time. Had the foundations been laid, with the superstructure following immediately afterwards, it is inconceivable that an error of the magnitude seen here could have been inadvertently introduced. In particular, the east wall would not have been built in such a way that it ran off its own foundation, as it does at the south-east corner. Such major discrepancies would have been obvious in new construction work. A wholly different situation obtains, however, on a site where demolition and rebuilding are being carried out, hand in hand. Here, it is all too easy for the true edge of an existing, unmortared foundation to become obscured amongst a confusion of trampled debris.

The evidence suggests that the first masonry phase of the chapel was constructed of drystone

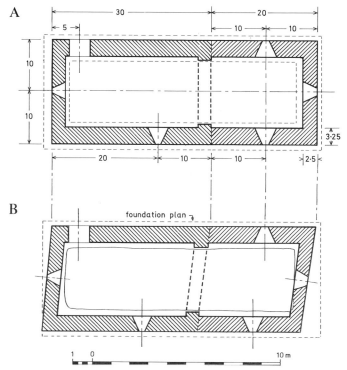

Fig. 78. The proportional system employed in setting out the plan
of the chapel.
A. The theoretical plan, showing the use of multiples of ten units
for the principal elements of the superstructure. In this case, the unit
of measurement was evidently the Jersey foot.
B. The plan of the chapel, as built, showing the discrepancy
between the foundation and the superstructure.

walling or, more likely, of masonry bonded with clay-mortar.[7] This building comprised a single, rectangular cell. When it was determined that the chapel should be rebuilt as a two-celled, vaulted structure, the old building would have been dismantled and the rubble piled in heaps around the periphery and in the central space. The tops of the old foundations would have been roughly cleared, and the lines of the new walls set out. The north wall was presumably set out first, and was correctly positioned. Then the west end probably followed, and was sited more or less on the intended line, but with a small error of angle. The drastic error came at the east end. On a clear, virgin site the misplacing of the south-east corner would have been readily detectable by eye, and the faulty setting out of right-angles at the west end would have been averted by checking diagonals. But on a construction site which is also a demolition site, the ability to spot errors and to make checks on diagonals is seriously impeded.

Once the walls started to rise, the grosser errors would have made themselves apparent, and compensations had certainly to be made when window level was reached. By this time it was too late to correct the fundamental planning error, short of pulling down the new work and setting out afresh. That is unlikely to have been contemplated: there has always been an innate resistance in the building trade to dismantle new work that has just been incorrectly constructed, and almost any amount of compromise and manipulation of the specification was seen as a preferable alternative. Time after time, archaeological surveys of buildings have shown this to be true.

If we now take the plan of the existing north wall and correct the errors at the two southern corners, it is possible to recover the intended ground plan of the new chapel (Fig. 78A). Simple as this form is, there are certain readily observable relationships between its component parts, indicative that a pre-determined specification was being followed.

Externally, the lengths of the side walls are in the ratio of 5:2. The transverse arch is sited nearer to the east end of the chapel than to its centre, and was not merely a device for separating the building into two bays for the purposes of vaulting. The division is a chancel arch, and the chapel may therefore be considered, architecturally if not liturgically, as a two-celled church, with nave and chancel. The chancel was intended to have the same external width as length. Looked at another way, the nave is a rectangle with its sides in the ratio of 2:3, and the chancel is a square, on the end of that rectangle. This is the commonest plan-form in small Anglo-Saxon and Romanesque parish churches. Frequently, the chancel and the nave are not of equal width, the former being inset by a half, or alternatively by a full, wall's thickness on either side, thus emphasising externally the two-celled nature of the building. But whether inset or not, the square chancel appended to a rectangular nave with a 2:3 plan ratio is fundamental.

Turning to other features of the plan of the Fishermen's Chapel, it can be seen that the three windows of the chancel were set centrally in their respective walls, or would have been had the south-east corner not been swung inwards. The south nave window was sited two-thirds of the way along its wall, so that its distance from the south-west corner theoretically equalled the spacing between it and the chancel window. In other words, the proportional spacing between windows on the south elevation should have been 2:2:1.

That a proportional system of design was invoked is beyond doubt, but was this also linked to a simple system of mensuration? If, for the sake of argument, we consider these observed ratios not just as proportions, but also as units of measurement, x, further simple subdivisions of this unit are not difficult to find. The distance from the centre of the north door to the corner of the nave is $0.5\,x$, and the reconstructed width of the opening is $0.4\,x$. The same figure obtains for the height and width of the jambs of the north and south chancel windows, and for the distance between their sills and the top of the foundation (i.e. height above floor level). This leads on to an examination of the geometry of the elevations, where x is also found to be the height from floor level to impost, as well as being the radius of the internal arcature of the chancel arch (Fig. 72). Wall thicknesses and other measurements fall logically in with this system too, pointing strongly towards the likely division of x into tenths. Put positively, x equals ten units of measurement.

In absolute terms, x measures $c.$ 2.80 m (9 statute feet), and thus the one-tenth division is 28 cm (11 inches). While such units are irreconcilable with recent English usage, there can scarcely be any doubt that these measurements represent the local foot which was in use in Jersey, or perhaps in Normandy, at the time the chapel was constructed. This is readily confirmed by reference to the traditional Jersey system, where the foot (*pied*) comprised eleven inches (*pouces*), and measured 27.94 cm. Thus, in Jersey terms, the overall dimensions of the chapel are 50 ft by 20 ft, of which the nave occupies 30 ft. The walls stand 10 ft high to impost level, and the centring for the chancel arch was constructed with a similar radius. The depth of the arch, like the thickness of the gable walls, measures 2½ feet. The north doorway was 4 ft wide, and centred at 5 ft from the corner; three of the rear-arches of the windows are based on a 4 ft square, with heads of 2 ft radius; and other measurements associated with the layout of the chapel equally clearly derive from the same basic system.

In conclusion, it is clear that the chapel was built with expert knowledge of an architectural specification which was current in north-west Europe in the early Middle Ages. The plan and proportional system seen here were widely used in church building, but the units of measurement employed appear to belong to the local Jersey system. The 28 cm foot employed here stands in contrast to the much longer 'northern' Roman foot of 33.5 cm that was widely used in pre-Norman buildings (Huggins, Rodwell and Rodwell, 1982).

6. ARCHITECTURAL STYLE AND DATING

All the available structural evidence bearing on the design, construction and decoration of the Fishermen's Chapel has now been presented, along with the archaeological evidence for the sequence of human activity on the site. A relative chronology for this sequence has been established with confidence, and it is the task of suggesting an absolute chronology that now confronts us. This is the most difficult facet of the whole study.

Without historical documentation, distinctive architectural detailing, or archaeologically associated artifacts of a precisely datable nature, it is impossible to tie down the chapel's date of construction within narrow limits. The problem is compounded by the fact that the present chapel is not the first building on the site, nor probably the second, but the third. The detailed evidence has already been discussed, and the suggested sequence is:

1.   Clay-floored building, probably of timber. Exact dimensions unknown, but seemingly not significantly smaller than the present structure. No direct dating evidence, but plausibly assignable to the early Christian period by virtue of its stratigraphic position. Perhaps the first church?

2.   Simple rectangular building with unmortared foundations, and presumed clay-mortared superstructure. No direct dating evidence, but securely stratified between nos. 1 and 3. There is no reason to doubt that this was a church or chapel, and is likely to have ante-dated the construction of the present parish church.

3.   The existing two-celled, barrel-vaulted church or chapel, built of mortared masonry, reusing the foundations of no. 2.

Nothing more can usefully be conjectured about the first structure. The second, a plain rectangular building, with a length-to-width ratio of 5:2 is of a size and form that readily finds analogues amongst the Celtic churches of northern and western Britain. Comparison may be made with Llandanwg Chapel, near Harlech on the west coast of Wales, which is a structurally undivided rectangle, measuring 17.1 by 6.8 m externally. Formerly a parish church, the division between nave and chancel was marked by a timber screen (RCAHM, 1921, 60–1). Of almost identical size is also Kilchieven Church, in Kintyre on the west coast of Scotland; this measures 17.5 by 6.9 m, and is also structurally undivided (MacGibbon and Ross, 1896, 100). In Ireland, the tenth-century cathedral church of Clonmacnoise measured about 22 by 9.5 m, and was therefore a little larger than the foregoing examples, but was still close to the 5:2 ratio (Radford, 1977).

Dating a simple rectangular chapel of the kind represented by these examples is impossible on architectural grounds: inevitably, vague generalisations have to suffice. We can do no more than indicate the upper and lower chronological limits that are likely to be applicable. If the building ante-dated the eighth century it would probably have been of squatter proportions, with a length-to-width ratio in the region of 3:2; and if it were a Norman construction from around the mid-eleventh century, or later, it would almost certainly have been internally divided in such a way as to leave foundation evidence. An eighth- to tenth-century date-bracket, although not proven, is the most likely.

Turning finally to the present chapel, and setting aside all preconception, the problem of dating may first be approached by establishing upper and lower limits. The upper limit, or *terminus ante quem*, is the easier to tackle, and the first phase of wallpainting demonstrates that the chapel cannot be later than the fourteenth century. There is, however, nothing in the design of the chapel to suggest that it belongs to the Gothic style at all. Had it been built in the thirteenth century it would, by analogy with other structures of that date in the Channel Islands, have been fitted with lancet windows, instead of round-headed ones, and would almost certainly have been externally buttressed at the angles, and at the junction between the nave and the chancel. Moreover, a thirteenth-century chapel might well have been given a pair of windows in the east wall, instead of a single one, as at Les Écréhous priory church and the chancel of Saint Brelade's Church. Indeed, the fashion for an axially divided and buttressed east end must have begun around the middle of the twelfth century, as evidenced at Rozel Manor chapel and Saint Martin's Church, Jersey (and at Saint Saviour's, Saint Sampson's, Saint Andrew's, Vale and Torteval Churches, in Guernsey; cf. McCormack, 1976, 55).

Fixing the lower end of the chronological scale, the *terminus post quem*, depends primarily upon a historically-based deduction. During the ninth and tenth centuries the coastal regions of France suffered appallingly from incursions by the Norse, and it is inconceivable that the chapel – with all the specialist knowledge and skills that had to be imported, particularly for the construction of its vault – could have been built during this turbulent period. The See of Coutances was not fully re-established until the 1030s, and it must have been some years before building projects in the remoter parts of the diocese could be implemented (Myres, 1978, 166). Very little church building can be shown to have taken place, either in Britain or in France, in the regions affected by Norse invasions. Equally, a pre-tenth-century date for the Fishermen's Chapel cannot be entertained on architectural grounds: the form of the building, the use of a hard mortar, and the vault all call for a later date.

Summarising the argument thus far, we may reasonably accept that the various excluding factors point to a construction date somewhere between the second quarter of the eleventh century and the mid or late twelfth century. This period must next be considered in more positive architectural terms: the chapel undoubtedly exhibits a series of features which proclaim it to be a Romanesque structure, as indeed E.A. Freeman recognised as long ago as 1845 (although he did not set out the arguments for this ascription). The simple nave, with a width-to-length ratio of 2:3, and a square, structurally separated chancel are hallmarks of the small Romanesque church; in England the junction between nave and chancel is usually emphasised externally, as well as internally. The provision of a complement of three small, round-headed windows in the chancel, to light the centrally-placed altar (i.e. one which stood forward of the east wall) is another attribute of the style.

Despite numerous assertions in the past that stone vaulting was added to existing buildings in the thirteenth or fourteenth century, there is no historical or architectural reason why it should not have been present in the Channel Islands in the twelfth century. The early history of vaulting is a keenly disputed subject, and this is not the place to embark on a substantial appraisal of it. Suffice it to say that the barrel-vaults of earlier Romanesque buildings were of semi-circular form, but at some unspecifiable time and uncertain place it was discovered that by making a vault of pointed form several considerable advantages were gained: it was more stable and exerted less lateral thrust on the walls, it gave added internal height, and it yielded a more convenient external profile for capping with a ridged roof.

In the early twelfth century the pointed barrel-vault was widely adopted by the Cistercians in France, but whence they derived it is unknown. The pointed vault had certainly reached Ireland by the 1130s, as evidenced by Cormac's Chapel, Cashel. This remarkable little chapel is two storied and, like the much simpler Saint Mochta's Oratory at Louth, is finished with a semi-circular barrel-vault on the ground floor and a pointed one at the upper level (de Breffny and Mott, 1976, 27–31). The stone-roofed church was an Irish speciality, but the date of its origin is a subject of wide disagreement. It has long been held that the corbelled roofs of buildings of the Gallarus Oratory type date back to the eighth century, and were ancestral to the truly vaulted church roof (Leask, 1955, 27–41). Both the concept and the dating have been robustly attacked, and the thesis advanced that all these 'early' Irish churches are of no earlier origin than the twelfth century (Harbison, 1970).

The uncertainties attending the dating of the first mortared vaulting in Irish churches are particularly unfortunate, since some of the simplest buildings, such as Saint Kevin's, Glendalough, may have features in common with Channel Island churches. Indeed, it is by no means impossible that the idea of vaulting as a protection against fire reached the Channel Islands from Ireland, rather than from France. Both locations have long histories of sea-borne invasion and arson attacks. The theory advanced by John McCormack that the Channel Island vaults had their derivation in Provence, and that none could be earlier than the separation of 1204 between England and France, although neat, is not sustainable (McCormack, 1976, ch. 4). First, the date is too late for some of the Jersey vaults and, secondly, architectural style and technical innovation very rarely march hand-in-hand with political history. Thus, for example, churches of Anglo-Saxon style and workmanship were still being erected in southern England for up to half a century after the Noman conquest of 1066.

Whatever the motivation and the source of inspiration for introducing the vault as an architectural fashion in the Channel Islands, it was designed and executed in the Romanesque manner. The independent construction of the transverse arch, the full-scale use of timber shuttering and form-work, the radial setting of the stones, and the projecting eaves-band are all run-of-the-mill Romanesque details. In more elaborate churches the eaves-band was carried on an ornamental corbel-table.

In conclusion, there is nothing incompatible with the suggestion that the Fishermen's Chapel was rebuilt in its present form sometime between the mid-eleventh and the mid-twelfth century, on foundations of pre-Norman date. In the light of current uncertainties about the history of the pointed vault before *c.* 1130, it is safest to posit a date for the chapel towards the middle of the twelfth century.

It is finally worth noting here that a second Jersey building of closely similar proportions and construction to the Fishermen's Chapel exists at La Hougue Bie, in Grouville parish. This important chapel needs close archaeological study, since it is clear that the structure has not been fully understood in the past. Although customarily described as comprising two separate but conjoined chapels (Notre Dame and Jerusalem), there can be little doubt that the primary structure was a two-celled arrangement, with a continuous barrel-vault of pointed form (McCormack, 1986, 289–91). The physical separation into two chapels appears only to have taken place in the early sixteenth century, when the crypted rotunda was added. Slightly smaller than the Fishermen's Chapel, that at La Hougue Bie measures 11.6 by 4.6 m externally, and has proportions very close to 5:2. It is unbuttressed and there is no external demarcation between the nave and the chancel. It is probably a later Norman building, and must be approximately contemporary with the Fishermen's Chapel.

Also of similar date was the Chapelle des Pas at Saint Helier, now known only from topographical illustrations (McCormack, 1986, 288; pl. 8). This was a two-celled building, with a stone vault and a round-headed north doorway (set close to the north-west corner, like the Fishermen's Chapel). The significant difference between the Chapelle des Pas and the other examples considered here was that it was buttressed in the manner of the twelfth century.

7. CONSERVATION AND RESTORATION

Legends from the Past
by Ursula Fuhrer

In the literature hitherto published on the Fishermen's Chapel, several intriguing stories about the construction of the building and the execution of the wall paintings keep turning up. We must begin by clarifying the scientific status of these hypotheses – focussing primarily on the wall paintings – in the light of the technological evidence described on pp. 45–50, and of the medieval sources on techniques.

THE PRODUCTION OF LIME

As with other buildings in Jersey, and wholly within the tradition of previous centuries, lime was used for mortar and plaster in the chapel. The fact that there are no natural lime deposits in Jersey – and by virtue of the geological formation of the island it is certain that there were none previously – raises the question of where the lime for mortar and plaster came from. Previous accounts refer to the probable sources of lime thus:

'The material with which the walls are compacted is most interesting. Jersey possessing no natural supply of lime, the early people, no doubt after many experiments, discovered that limpet shells, broken up and dissolved in boiling sea-water, produce a first-rate consolidating material.' (Balleine, 1932, 29)

'Having no local lime, the masons collected quantities of shells from off the beach and crushed them. Then they boiled this mixture in sea-water. This hot liquid was poured into a cased-in wall-work and the result is seen today in the wonderful solidity of these ancient walls.' (Tabb, nd, 4)

However, it is not possible by either of the two methods described above to produce lime. Simply boiling limpet shells, which do indeed consist of lime, does not produce *burnt* lime, which is required for the production of mortar. Moreover, if lime had been extracted by any means involving the use of sea water, the plaster and wall paintings in the Fishermen's Chapel would very soon have shown severe damage as a result of sea-water salts being present. Consequently, neither plaster nor paintings would have survived to the present day.

A chemical analysis of the salts contained in the plaster of the chapel has shown that only very small quantities of sea-salt (sodium chloride) are present. The proportion would have been significantly higher if sea water had been used at any stage of the mortar production.[1] An argument today against the theory that the lime was extracted from limpet shells would be the fact that there are now hardly any limpets to be found on Jersey's beaches. According to local memory, however, this was not always so, and the situation is said to have been different at the beginning of this century. Moreover, there are still plentiful supplies of limpets today on the island of Herm.

Alfred Oppenheim, who carried out the restoration of the painting on the east wall in 1915, expressed himself more precisely with reference to the production of burnt lime. In his short report of 1949, he wrote of the mortar 'being mixed with lime burned from seashells . . .'[2] Several post-medieval lime kilns are known in the island – one is on the site of the present Jersey Zoo – in which limpets and other shells were burned to produce lime for building and agricultural purposes.[3] Yet the question of from whence medieval Jersey derived its lime supply is not resolved by this observation. No documentary evidence of lime importation to Jersey in the Middle Ages has been found, either from Britain or from Normandy, although there were supplies from both countries in the eighteenth and nineteenth centuries. Nevertheless, the probability of medieval lime importation remains strong, since other building materials were brought to Jersey, such as limestone blocks, slate and Purbeck marble. Craftsmen and artists were likewise imported.

PROVISION OF LIGHTING DURING THE PAINTING PROCESS

In his report of 1949 Oppenheim wrote:

> 'How was it possible for the painter to achieve his work without having sufficient light? The answer seems to be that he must have executed his painting before the entire reconstruction of the vault and roof was terminated.'[4]

This hypothesis cannot be maintained with any justification. From early sources and records of work in churches in Europe, dating back to the time at which the chapel was built, it appears that painters submitted bills for lamp oil or tallow, from which it follows that they used oil lamps or candles as a source of light. Any suggestion that these materials were employed as a binding medium for the paintings can be rejected on the grounds there is no scientific evidence that lamp oil and tallow were ever used as binding media. Moreover, archaeological evidence shows that the walls and roof of the Fishermen's Chapel were erected all of apiece (Chapter 5).

THE PAINTING TECHNIQUE

There have been several hypotheses advanced concerning the technique used for the paintings in the chapel, again mostly propounded by Oppenheim. First, he took up a widespread theory of his time, namely that the *fresco-buono* technique had temporarily been lost in Europe, and was only rediscovered in the early fifteenth century. Pursuing this line of argument, he assumed that the fourteenth-century Annunciation on the east wall of the chapel must have been painted in *tempera*, or *secco*, technique, whereas the later decoration was executed in *fresco* technique.[5]

There are, indeed, divergent opinions about the use of fresco painting in the Romanesque and early Gothic periods; whether true fresco painting was very common at this time is a moot point. Yet current scientific opinion founded on recent research confirms that *fresco* painting was certainly very well known at the time, and it is for this reason that contemporary literary sources go so deeply into lime-painting and other *secco* techniques (Phillipot and Mora, 1984, 117–18). In the case of the Fishermen's Chapel, our technological examination shows that the painters of both periods used the technique of lime-painting (pp. 47–50).

There has also been discussion regarding the pigments which were used. Balleine, trying to explain the phenomenon of the changing visibility of the paintings, suggested that this was due not only to atmospheric conditions but also to the pigments, which he believed to contain tallow. Contemporary sources on the painting technique of the European schools during the fifteenth century describe pigments and the production of paints that were common at the time. The preparation of many paints was already then in the hands of chemists, and hence the painters did not have to concern themselves with the manufacture of every colour. In his book on painting, dated 1437, Cennino Cennini reports extensively on which pigments were suitable for use in wall paintings.

> 'You may use any of those colours which you used in fresco, in secco as well; but there are colours which cannot be used in fresco, such as orpiment, vermilion, azurite, red lead, white lead, verdigris, and lac. Those which can be used in fresco are giallorino, lime white, black, ochre, cinabrese, sinoper, terre-verte, hematite . . . .' (Thompson, 1933, 50)

Paints made from tallow, be it as a pigment component or as a binding medium, are not mentioned in any of these sources. Moreover, as Cennini's list of pigments shows, only inorganic constituents can be considered for *fresco*, as for lime-painting.

'REAPPEARANCES' OF THE WALL PAINTINGS

By the beginning of the present century, the thick incrustations and layers of dust and dirt covering the wall paintings of the Fishermen's Chapel must have obscured the visibility of the decoration to a large extent (see also p. 108). Balleine reported as follows.

> ' . . once or twice only in forty years has the 'Crucifixion' – the three figures on the crosses – been seen on the northern wall, east of the fresco 'the Scourging of Christ', and once in the same period, but on a different occasion, still more to the east and nearer the wall-base, under the grey square of plaster, three armoured soldiers holding their halberds on high – likely the guards at the foot of the crosses.' (Balleine, 1932, 34)

But why only once or twice in forty years? The Reverend William Tabb, who was rector from 1946 to 1971, gives an interesting explanation for this phenomenon.

> 'Once in about fifty years other pictures show themselves . . . this is due to atmospheric conditions. These pictures are good weather forecasters.' (Tabb, nd, 4)

But the ascription of prophetic powers to the paintings was not enough, and there was also a need for an even more dramatic moment of reappearance, and such was the case, according to Balleine and Tabb, in 1918.

> 'After a severe thunderstorm colour revealed itself under the saturated soiled plaster and led to the disclosure of "The Assumption" in a hopelessly damaged condition. But from underneath another layer of plaster, the older fresco, 'The Annunciation' was gradually recovered'. (Balleine, 1932, 33)[6]

Actually, Oppenheim had already begun to uncover the Annunciation on the east wall in 1915, a fact which Tabb does indeed mention in his account. In conclusion, one certainly does not wrong the narrators by attributing his story – like all the 'theories' discussed here – largely to the realm of erroneous, yet mysterious and charming legends of the past.

The Conservation of the Wall Paintings
by Gottfried Hauff

CONDITION BEFORE CONSERVATION

A fundamental step to save the wall paintings of the Fishermen's Chapel from total destruction was the erection of a temporary roof over the entire building in 1979 (Fig. 2). The chapel was thereby protected against further ingress of water, the main cause of the decay of the medieval plaster and paintings. By 1980 the hygrometer readings had fallen from about 80 percent relative humidity to 60 percent, and there was a great improvement in 'the feel of the chapel'.[7]

But still the appearance and condition of its interior were deplorable: there were two deep and open structural cracks in the nave walls, one over the entrance and another over the south window (Fig. 79). The original rendering was totally lost at the base of the walls (Pls. 1 and 2), and in the places where it had generally survived – that is on the upper parts of the walls and on the vault – large areas of it had fallen away. Many of these lacunae had been patched during previous restorations with cement. Although the fillings had been applied carefully, with respect for the original, the material used was entirely unsuitable for this purpose. It had not only contributed to

Fig. 79. Nave vault. Condition before conservation, showing structural crack caused by the earthquake of 1926.
Photo: Gottfried Hauff

Fig. 80.   Chancel vault: Old Testament cycle. Condition before conservation (1977), showing large, dark grey patches of cement fillings (restorations of 1915–35), and white fillings of lime mortar (emergency treatment, 1975), which spoil the legibility and unity of the painting.

Photo: Geoffrey Parker

Fig. 81. Nave vault: the Annunciation. Condition before conservation (1977), similar to Fig. 80.

Photo: Geoffrey Parker

the decay of the original lime rendering around the margins of the filled areas, but had also caused a chaos of flat, grey patches, thus spoiling the legibility and aesthetic unity of the paintings (Figs. 80 and 81). Clay pipes set in cement in the apexes of the east and west gable walls, serving as ventilation holes, added to this effect (Fig. 82).

The various layers of surviving rendering turned out, upon closer examination, to have detached themselves from one another in many places, forming flakes, hollows and blisters (Fig. 83). Along with the areas of fallen rendering much of the painted decoration had been lost, and even where the original *intonaco* was still intact, the limewashes and polychromy were to a large extent no longer preserved. In some of the surviving areas of paint the different strata showed a lack of adhesion or, in more advanced stages, had formed flakes and blisters. Most of the painted surface – and especially the west wall – was covered by a substantial incrustation of recrystallized calcium carbonate that must have been formed by the infiltrating water, which had been passing through

Fig. 82.   West wall: the Last Judgement. Condition before conservation (1977). Compare with Pl. 28.

Photo: Geoffrey Parker

Fig. 83.   Nave, south side. Detail of fragment before conservation, showing detachment of the *intonaco* and of the paint layer.
Photo: Gottfried Hauff

Fig. 84.   West wall. Detail of the Last Judgement, before conservation. The surface of the painting is covered by a thick layer of calcitic incrustations, as well as dust and dirt.
Photo: Gottfried Hauff

Fig. 85. East wall, before conservation (1977). The Annunciation, as cleaned, retouched and completed by Alfred Oppenheim in 1915. Compare with Fig. 86.

Photo: Geoffrey Parker

Plate 1.   General view of the interior of the Fishermen's Chapel in
1982, looking east, showing the refurbishment of 1935.

Photo: Warwick Rodwell

Plate 2.   The south-east corner of the sanctuary in 1982,
showing the stone altar and furnishings introduced in 1935.

Photo: Warwick Rodwell

Plate 3. General view of the interior of the chapel, looking east, after restoration (1988).

Photo: Robin Briault

Plate 4. General view of the fourteenth-century decoration around the east end of the chancel, after restoration. The central scene depicts the Annunciation to the Virgin Mary, flanked by fourteen kneeling figures, comprising the donor and his wife with with six sons (left) and six daughters (right).

Photo: Robin Briault

Plate 6. East wall. The Annunciation: the Blessed Virgin Mary against an architectural background. Behind her is a lectern, and the donor's wife and her first two daughters. Fourteenth century.

Photo: Robin Briault

Plate 5. East wall. The Annunciation: the archangel Gabriel bearing a scroll, and behind him the donor and his first two sons. Fourteenth century.

Photo: Robin Briault

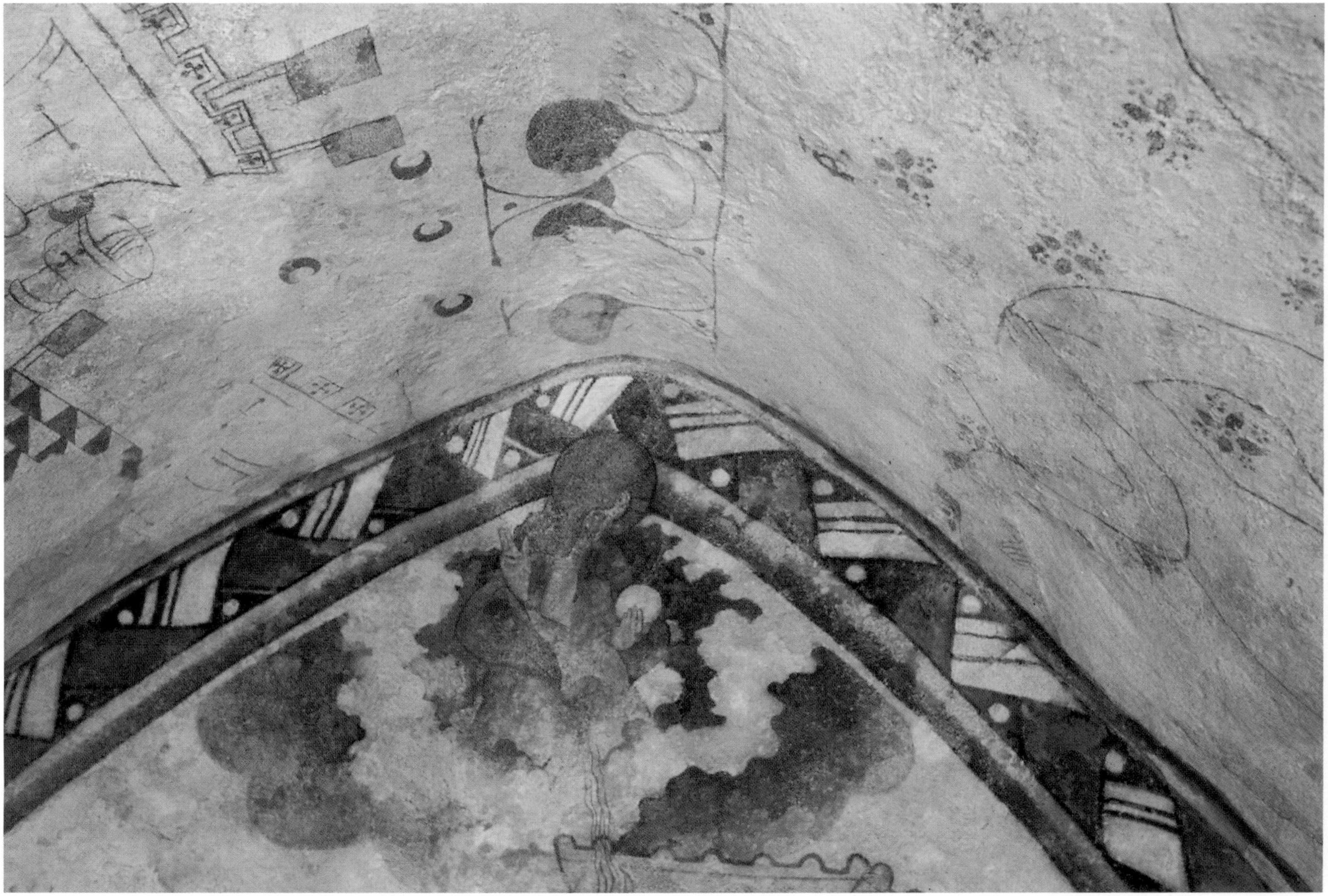

Plate 7. East wall. The Annunciation: God the Father, surrounded by clouds and looking down towards the Virgin Mary. Fourteenth century.

Photo: Warwick Rodwell

Plate 9. Chancel, south wall. The donor's third to sixth daughters, within a bent-riband framework. Fourteenth century.
Photo: Robin Briault

Plate 8. Chancel, north wall. The donor's third to sixth sons, within a bent-riband framework. Fourteenth century.
Photo: Robin Briault

Plate 10.   Chancel, south side of vault. Part of the Old Testament
cycle, showing Adam and Eve, and the Fall of Man.

Photo: Robin Briault

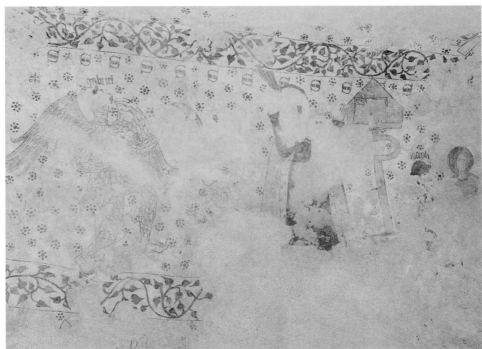

Plate 11.   Nave, south side of vault. General view of the Annunciation, with part of the
Adoration on the right (Joseph and Mary). The upper vine-scroll band and 'S' (sanctus) motif
run along the crown of the vault.

Photo: Robin Briault

Plate 12. Nave, south side of vault. The Annunciation: detail of the archangel Gabriel. The paler line running diagonally across the angel marks the line of a crack caused by the 1926 earthquake.

Photo: Robin Briault

Plate 13. Nave, south side of vault. The Adoration of the Magi: The fragmentary figures of Melchior and Caspar.

Photo: Robin Briault

Plate 14. Nave, south side of vault. The Adoration of the Magi: The remaining heads of the figures of Joseph and Mary.

Photo: Robin Briault

Plate 15. Nave, north side of vault. General view showing the Slaughter of the Innocents in the upper tier; and the Flagellation and the Carrying of the Cross in the lower tier.

Photo: Robin Briault

Plate 16. Nave, north side of vault. The Slaughter of the Innocents: the figure of King Herod.

Photo: Robin Briault

Plate 17. Nave, north side of vault. Detail of the head of King Herod.

Photo: Robin Briault

Plate 18.   Nave, north side of vault. Unidentified fragment from
the Life Cycle of Christ.

Photo: Robin Briault

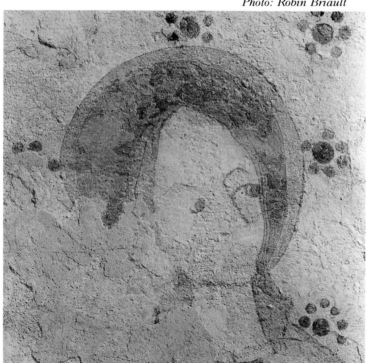

Plate 19.   Nave, north side of vault. Detail of the head of an unidentified
figure, possibly the Virgin Mary.

Photo: Robin Briault

Plate 20. Chancel, north side of vault. General view showing the Entry into Jerusalem in the upper tier, and the fragmentary remains of the Crucifixion in the lower tier.

Photot: Robin Briault

Plate 21. Chancel, north side of vault. The Entry into Jerusalem: Christ on the donkey, being welcomed.

Photo: Robin Briault

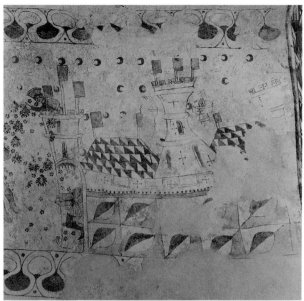

Plate 22. Chancel, north side of vault. The Entry into Jerusalem: detail of the Holy City, showing a gateway, towers with flags, battlemented walls, and the roofs of internal buildings.

Photo: Robin Briault

Plate 23. Nave, north side of vault, lower tier. The Flagellation.

Photo: Robin Briault

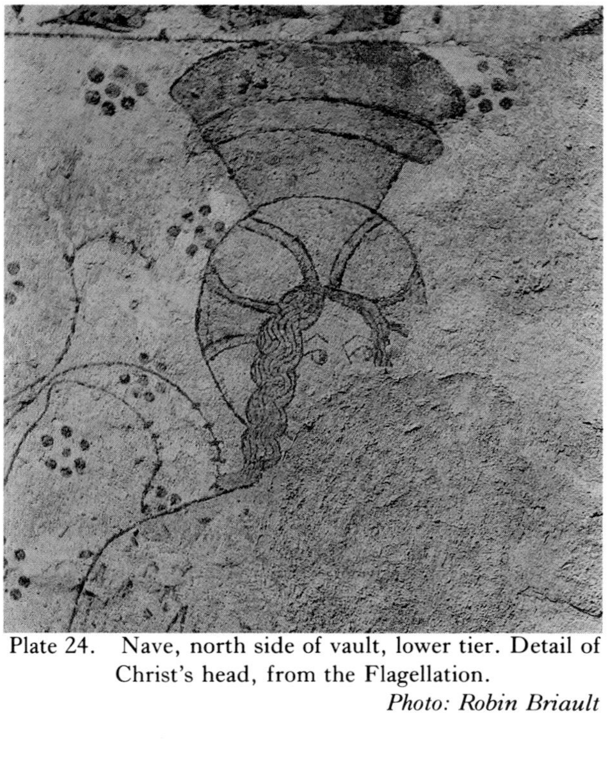

Plate 24. Nave, north side of vault, lower tier. Detail of Christ's head, from the Flagellation.

Photo: Robin Briault

Plate 27. Chancel, north side of vault, lower tier. The Crucifixion.

Photo: Robin Briault

Plate 25. Nave, north side of vault, lower tier. The Carrying of the Cross.

Photo: Robin Briault

Plate 26. Nave, north side of vault, lower tier. The Nailing of Christ to the Cross.

Photo: Robin Briault

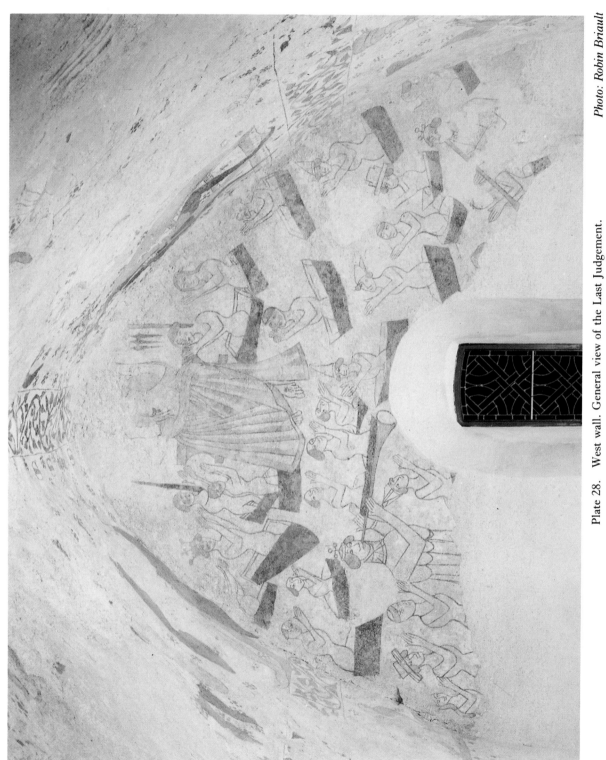

Plate 28.   West wall. General view of the Last Judgement.

Plate 30. West wall. The Last Judgement: a trumpeting archangel, flanked by a mitred bishop and a tonsured monk.

Photo: Robin Briault

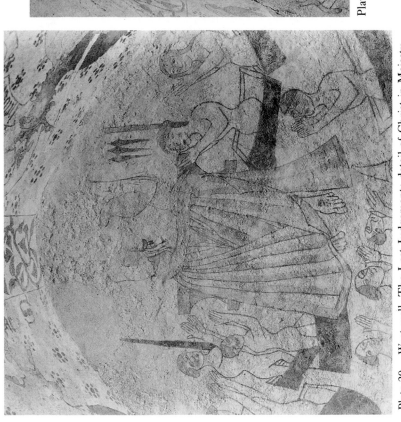

Plate 29. West wall. The Last Judgement: detail of Christ in Majesty.

Photo: Robin Briault

Plate 32. Nave, north wall, detail of the Nailing of Christ to the Cross. Cleaning test: a thick layer of calcitic incrustation, dust and dirt removed with the air-abrasive gun.

Photo: Gottfried Hauff

Plate 33. Chancel vault, detail of Adam and Eve, after reintegration. In very obvious cases – such as the shoulder of Adam (right) – losses are reconstructed in a pointillist method; other areas – such as the breast and arm of Eve (left) – where too much of the original is missing, are toned in with the surrounding plaster or limewash.

Photo: Gottfried Hauff

Plate 31. Chancel arch, south side. Detail of the foliate scroll.

Photo: Robin Briault

Plate 34.   Typical section of medieval and later trampled earth floors in the nave.

Photo: Warwick Rodwell

Plate 35.   The base of the 1754 bell-mould, as found with a fragment of the cope lying above the rim. Note the tile fragments incorporated in the clay core.

Photo: Warwick Rodwell

the lime rendering and evaporating on the surface (Figs. 82 and 84).

Strong salt efflorescence – which consisted, according to analysis, primarily of sulphates[8] – could be observed mainly near cement fillings, from which the salts had in all probability originated. In addition, algae were growing on the walls, and the whole interior surface of the chapel carried a thick deposit of dirt and dust. Only in the case of the earlier painting on the east wall, which had been uncovered and restored by Oppenheim in 1915–16, was the situation not quite so severe. The rendering there was in comparatively good condition, and the painting was adhering well to the ground. There was, however, not only the ubiquitous layer of calcitic incrustations and dirt but, additionally – and this turned out to be the major problem – there had been an appreciable amount of retouching, completion and even overpainting, of two different types (Figs. 85–87).

The first type of retouching, found especially in the upper zone of the painting, covered not only large areas of paint losses, but also fragments of the original painting, as well as flakes of limewash

Fig. 86.   East wall. The Annunciation after conservation treatment (1988).

Photo: Robin Briault

Fig. 87.   East wall: detail of the Annunciation before conservation. The painting shows many losses of paint and is covered by a layer of incrustations and dirt; some of the fillings, which are lighter in colour, carry completions.

Photo: Gottfried Hauff

which had been left *in situ* during the uncovering process. This retouching proved to be totally resistant to the regular choice of solvents used for cleaning wall paintings,[9] and could be identified as part of Oppenheim's measures.[10] The second type of retouching, present mostly on the background and on the lower parts of the painting, was easily soluble with water and can be assigned to the treatment of 1974–75.

CONSERVATION TREATMENT

In 1982, at the suggestion of Peter Burman, then Secretary of the Council for the Care of Churches, an international team of conservators was commissioned to tackle the conservation of the medieval lime-renders and mural decorations of the chapel.[11] The conservation programme was drawn up and carried out by this team over the course of four seasons, in collaboration with the church officials and other interested parties[12] (Fig. 88).

Fig. 88.   The conservation team at work on the nave vault in 1982.

Photo: Jersey Evening Post

The first step towards the actual conservation of the paintings was the securing of loose paint, especially urgent in this case since vibrations were to be expected during the drilling and breaking up of the concrete floor, prior to the internal archaeological investigation. The various layers of paint were moistened and softened with the aid of water and ethyl alcohol, and were fixed with polyvinyl acetate. In a similar way, the areas of loose rendering which had formed hollows and blisters were re-attached by injecting hydraulic lime-mortar in a fluid state, sometimes with the additional application of pressure to the outside of the blister.

For aesthetic and conservation reasons, mentioned above, it was decided to remove all previous cement fillings, most of which were extremely hard. In order to ensure minimum vibration, the cement patches were first cut into small cubes using an angle-grinder, and were then chipped out with a range of small chisels. Often the adjoining zones of medieval rendering had first to be secured with gauze and cellulose paste (Fig. 89). The algae, which must have grown on account of the excessive humidity in the chapel over a prolonged period, were treated with a 3 percent solution of formaldehyde.

The cleaning of the painted surface could generally be carried out in two stages: the superficial dust and dirt was washed off with a gentle flow of water and soft-hair brushes, while the calcitic incrustations were removed with an air-abrasive gun, using aluminium powder as the abrasive. On the west wall, however, an especially thick and more resistant incrustation could only be removed with a combination of 'AB 57' (a solution of highly alkaline salts in water, applied in a paste of

Fig. 89.   Nave vault: detail of the Slaughter of the Innocents. The edges of a lacuna are being secured with the help of Japanese paper, glued onto the surface with cellulose paste.

Photo: Gottfried Hauff

methyl cellulose or paper pulp) and the air-abrasive gun, as well as scalpels (Pl. 32 and Fig. 90).

The painting on the east wall presented a rather different situation from the rest because of its many previous retouchings and completions. Here, the concept of a reduction of the painting to the original medieval components – involving the removal of the later additions – would have created both technical and ethical problems. Not only would the original substance have been endangered in the attempt to remove the resistant overpainting, but this would also have diminished the sense of completeness of the scenic representation already established for almost seventy years. It was therefore decided to conserve the painting in its historically 'grown' version. It was only cleaned, using the methods already described, including dry dusting for areas with water-soluble retouchings (Figs. 85–86).

In order to restore the aesthetic unity of the chapel's interior, the exposed lower zones of the walls and the lacunae within the preserved areas of medieval rendering were replastered or filled to an appropriate level, according to the original make up. Losses of the *arriccio* (undercoat) were filled with a coarse lime plaster, onto which a coat of fine finishing plaster was applied; both were made to resemble the respective original layers in consistency and surface texture (Fig. 91). The structural cracks, monitored with the help of tell-tales for about two years, seemed to be stable, and were filled in the same manner.

In the case of the chancel arch and the window reveals, however, where the imprints of the

Fig. 90. West wall: detail of the Last Judgement, showing cleaning test. In the rectangular area around the head of the figure, surface incrustations, dirt and dust were removed using a poultice of 'AB 57' and the air-abrasive gun.

Photo: Gottfried Hauff

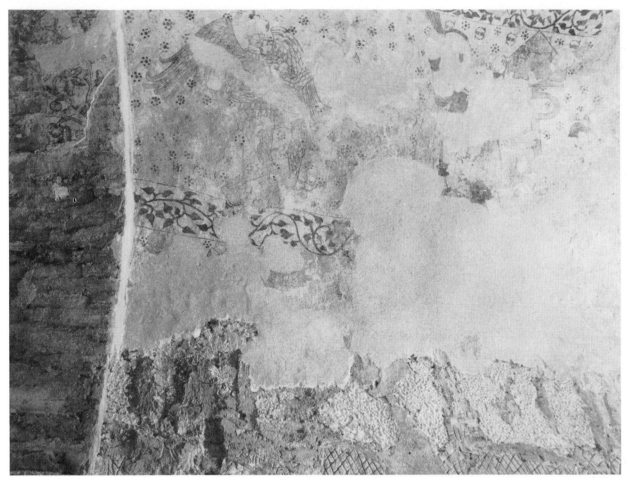

Fig. 91. Nave vault: the Annunciation. Stages of treatment, including: cement fillings (at the lower edge of the photograph) cut into cubes before being chipped away; losses of *arriccio* (above) filled with coarse lime mortar, rather white in colour, when still fresh; losses of *intonaco* and painting (above again), filled with fine lime mortar and treated to match the adjoining areas of original in surface texture.

Photo: Gottfried Hauff

shuttering boards were especially well preserved (pp. 78 and 85), the *arriccio* was covered only with a thin lime slurry in order to leave visible this interesting feature of the original construction technique.

The final aesthetic presentation of the painted decoration was based on the following considerations. Since the paintings of the later period are preserved only in fragments, a general completion or reconstruction of the scenes originally represented was out of the question. Still there remained the task to optimize the legibility and the aesthetic appearance of these fragments and their ground of limewash. In all cases, therefore, where the latter was still preserved, a new limewash was brushed onto the adjoining plaster fillings. The new limewash was integrated with, and at the same time distinguished from, the original by small dots of grey tones, in sympathy with the patina of the original work. These dots were sprayed onto the surface of the plaster (Pl. 33).

In the case of the actual paintings, two different types of losses had to be treated appropriately: first, the losses of both the painting and the rendering below and, secondly, the wear of just the uppermost pigment layer or patina, where the ground of medieval limewash was still intact. For the first type – and only within the limits of the original fragments still preserved – those losses which could be certainly interpreted as regards their content were reconstructed on the newly limewashed fillings. Again, for this a 'pointillist' method of retouching was applied, namely a system of small dots of various colours which, when seen together and from a certain distance, recreate the required form and tonal composition of the original, but which can still be readily distinguished from the latter on close inspection (Pl. 33). The losses which could not be safely reconstructed in this manner were covered only with limewash and reintegrated accordingly with sprayed-on dots of grey tones.

For the second type of losses of paint, namely the wearing away of just the uppermost layer of polychromy or patina, which resulted in distracting light-spots, the method of *aqua sporca* was applied. These spots were toned down and made to recede optically behind the pictorial plane with the help of water-colour glazes which are distinguishable from the original by having a slightly lighter, and cooler, tonality (Figs. 92–93). The painting of the earlier period on the east wall required a much less fragmentary approach: on account of its extensive and already existing completions, most of the losses could be – and for the sake of the unity of the painting had to be – reconstructed. For this again the same methods were applied.

The conservation treatment was completed in July 1985, and it is now advisable to establish

Fig. 92.   Nave vault: ivy-scroll pattern. Small superficial losses of the paint layer – with the original limewash still preserved – appear as obtrusive light spots within the black pattern.

Photo: Gottfried Hauff

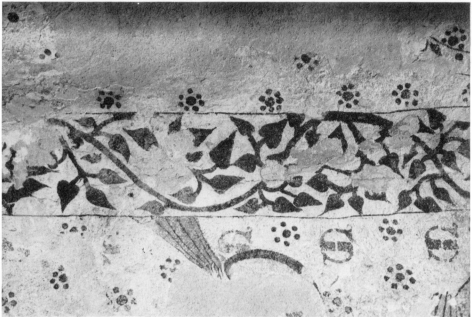

Fig. 93.   Nave vault: detail of ivy-scroll pattern, after reintegration with aqua sporca. The light spots have been toned down and made to recede behind the pictorial plane.

Photo: Gottfried Hauff

regular expert monitoring of the physical and climatic conditions of the interior of the chapel, in order to ensure the future preservation of its precious painted decoration.

Restoring the Fabric of the Chapel

While the conservation of the medieval paintings provided the principal motivation for the restoration of the chapel, there were many other factors to take into account. The roof leaked, and so did the windows. The interior was a hotchpotch of lime-plaster, cement rendering, sundry patchings, and naked rubble, all copiously marred by damp-staining and the growth of algae. A proliferation of electrical wiring contributed to the visual dereliction of the scene, and there had been no attempt to light the chapel in a manner conducive to the viewing of the paintings. The rough rubble construction of the altar (*c.* 1935) was a conspicuous display of pseudo-antiquarianism, and stood in marked contrast to the intrusive polished granite sanctuary step and altar rails. A collection of Sunday School chairs and some wooden cupboards completed the ensemble of furnishings.

The restoration of the fabric was initiated in 1979, when a temporary asbestos roof was erected over the top of the chapel; the investigations, conservation and structural works were carried out mainly between 1982 and 1985, and the refurnishing was completed by Easter, 1988. The entire scheme was carried out to the specifications, and under the supervision, of the parish's architect, Mr David Barlow.[13]

THE EXTERIOR

Apart from minor adjustments to path levels and drainage improvements, nothing has been done to interfere with the setting of the chapel. The only external alteration of substance has been the provision of an entirely new roof. The irregular, dark blue-grey slating of the chapel was aesthetically pleasing but, unfortunately, it was ineffectual as a waterproof covering. As long ago as 1905 the then-architect, Adolph Curry, recognised, on the one hand, a need to strip and relay the slating but, on the other, the impossibility of being able to save and reuse more than a small proportion of the old slates (p. 10). The chosen solution, of patching and pointing with a strong cement mix, gave temporary relief, but greatly exacerbated the difficulties of further repair today.

The possibilities of applying an epoxy resin or other proprietary waterproof coating to the existing structure were explored, but had ultimately to be rejected on several grounds. First, none of these applications can rejuvenate a decayed slate, or render it waterproof for more than a few years. Secondly, thermal movement would prevent the effective sealing of joints and laps between slates, thus allowing the ingress of water into the vault to continue. Thirdly, and perhaps most importantly, the sealing of the roof would prevent the masonry of the vault from breathing through

Fig. 94.   Reroofing the chapel in 1985. The slates have once again been hung on battens and rafters – as they probably were in the fifteenth century – instead of being mortared directly onto the stone vault.

Photo: Deirdre Shute

its upper face. If transpiration were confined to the painted plaster, this would hasten its deterioration immeasurably.

The solution adopted has, therefore, been to reinstate a slated roof which is structurally separate from the vault, aping the arrangement that was almost certainly introduced in the mid-fifteenth century, for precisely similar reasons. The old slates were removed and a full complement of rafters fixed to the vault; the new slates have been hung on battens, with a waterproof membrane beneath, as a barrier against snow and driven rain (Fig. 94). There is a ventilation gap between the membrane and the extrados of the vault, so that the latter is fully able to breathe. New hand-cut Burlington slates from Coniston, in Cumbria, were laid in 1985.

THE INTERIOR

A variety of options for floor levels and finishes inside the chapel was considered. It was decided that, since the fifteenth-century scheme of painting is the dominant feature, the internal finishes should be compatible with the work of that era, without attempting pastiche. After excavation, the floor was returned to its late medieval level, with a gentle downward slope to the east, and the foundation offsets are once again visible and form the bases of wall-benches (Pl. 3). Existing external ground level has been retained, and the chapel is entered via a short flight of steps, as it must have been in the later Middle Ages. The granite sanctuary step, raised sanctuary floor and stone altar rails – all comparatively recent introductions – have been dispensed with.

In place of red painted concrete, a floor of Jersey granite paving has been laid; this material, salvaged by the Department of Public Building and Works from local demolitions, is laid to random sizes. A small subterranean chamber has been created as an ossuary, beneath the centre of the chancel arch. The human remains gathered during excavation have been reinterred here.

Lime plaster has been applied to all internal wall surfaces that had been stripped by Balleine or rendered with portland cement.

New Furnishings (Pl. 3)

It was determined at an early stage that the chapel should be furnished with simplicity and dignity, that the furniture should be of high quality modern construction, and should not attempt to replicate any specific historical period or design. The medieval stone altar slab, brought here from Mont Orgueil Castle in 1929 (p. 13) has been retained, and is now mounted on a simple wooden frame, in preference to an immovable, pseudo-medieval masonry construction. The medieval holy water stoup has also been retained, but is not currently affixed to the fabric.

The altar slab, or *mensa*, is of considerable interest: it was made from a single block of Chausey granite[14] (now fractured) 1.50 m long, and of irregular width, but averaging 48 cm. It is also of varied thickness, but is 16 cm on average. The front edge and left-hand end are squared, and have a broad chamfer on the lower edge, which is slightly hollowed (Fig. 95). The back edge of the slab is squared, but the right-hand end is very irregular and shows no indication of having been dressed. Moreover, it is clear that when the positions of the five consecration crosses were set out on the upper face the unfinished right-hand end of the stone was deliberately disregarded. There can be no doubt that this *mensa* was made for an altar that was fitted into the south-eastern corner of an

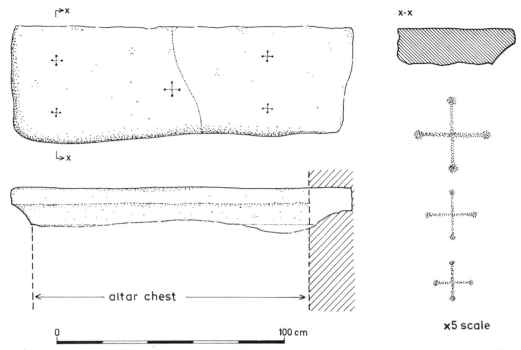

Fig. 95.   The medieval altar slab of Chausey granite. Plan, elevation and section, and details of the three different sizes of consecration crosses. The reconstructed elevation shows how the altar was designed to fit into the south-east corner of a chapel, with the rough end of the slab embedded in a wall.

aisle or side-chapel. Although there is now no means of telling for which church or chapel it was originally made, it can be seen that this slab would, by coincidence, have fitted well in the south transept chapel of Saint Brelade's Church, where the special requirement of an eastern doorway caused the altar to be displaced from its customary position against the centre-point of the wall (see plan, Fig. 43). The *mensa* probably dates from the fourteenth or fifteenth century.

There was formerly a small holy water stoup fixed to the wall in the south-west corner of the chapel, where it was undoubtedly placed as an object of antiquarian curiosity during Balleine's restoration (not being in a position of medieval liturgical relevance). There is no mention of it in published accounts of the chapel or of the church, and the origin of this object remains unknown. There is every likelihood that the stoup was discovered during work here, and that Balleine had it inserted in the corner where it remained until 1983 (Fig. 61C). The stoup is hollowed from a flat block of cream limestone of either French or English origin,[15] and is quadrant-shaped in plan; the only decoration is a pair of ring-grooves in the spandrels of the upper face (Fig. 96).

Although we have referred to this object throughout as a stoup – and it was most probably made to be one – it has also evidently served the function of piscina at some time, as shown by the presence of a drainage hole in the base. Piscinae were not usually made for corner-fixing, especially when they were of pillar-form, as the central position of the drainage hole in this example would imply. The evidence suggests that the stoup was recycled in the late Middle Ages, and was converted into a piscina. The object is likely to date from the fifteenth century.

All the new furniture for the chapel has been designed and made by Alan Peters, of Cullompton,

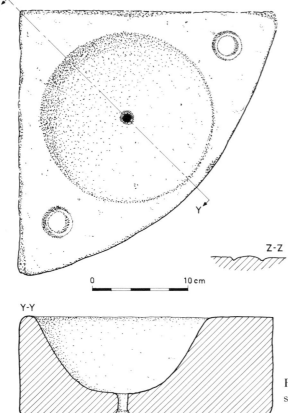

Fig. 96.   The medieval limestone stoup or piscina. Plan and section, and detail across one of the decorative ring-grooves (Z–Z).

Devon, using English oak. The full complement of furniture comprises: the altar base (supporting the medieval *mensa*), two wooden candle holders for the altar, a lectern, a prayer desk, eight chairs, and bench-tops for the stone wall-benches along the north and south sides of the chapel. There is also a small display stand and notice board. The chapel is lit by four modern electric standard lamps, manufactured by Marcatré of London; these are fixed to the floor, and direct the majority of their light upwards to the painted vault (Pl. 3). The intensity of the light can be controlled by dimmer-switches.

The decayed frames of the east and west windows were renewed with bronze casements in 1986, and a decision was taken not to reinstate the stained glass windows of *c.* 1915 and 1930.[16] Their focal positions accorded these windows considerable prominence, and their colours wrestled uneasily with the medieval paintings above them. The new glazing has been designed and made by Alfred Fisher, of Kings Langley, Hertfordshire. The leaded designs are based on a simple early medieval interlace pattern, and are filled with English hand-made reamy 'antique' glass; this is lightly tinted in order to prevent glare. The chapel's side windows have not been altered.

The total cost of the restoration works carried out between 1979 and 1988, including furnishings, archaeological investigations and reporting, falls little short of £100,000. As with the restorations of 1884 and 1927–35, the work has been entirely funded through private donations.

8. SYNTHESIS AND INTERPRETATION

An enormous quantity of data was recorded during the programmes of investigation and conservation at the Fishermen's Chapel, and much of the evidence has been analysed and presented in the previous chapters. It now remains to attempt what, in any historical research project, is the most exciting and exacting task of all, namely the final synthesis and interpretation. Here we must try to explain the whole process of the creation, development and use of the chapel, with all its vicissitudes, in relation to the historical evolution of the religious and secular life of the times. It is natural to begin with the question of origins.

Origins of the Chapel

A great volume of literature has been generated on the supposed origins of the churches and chapels of Jersey: the theories are legion, but the facts are extraordinarily few. This is not the place to attempt a searching review of the historical, topographical and place-name evidence, which might lead to fresh light being cast on the pre-Norman Church in the islands. John McCormack's *Channel Island Churches* (1986) contains the most up-to-date overview of the whole subject. Here, we can do no more than suggest possible models for the historical development at Saint Brelade, based on the evidence gleaned during the recent study, and by analogy with other sites and developments in north-west Europe.

Generally speaking, it is very likely that some of the churches and chapels in Jersey owe their foundation to the activities of Breton and western British ('Celtic') missionaries and eremitics, between the sixth and eighth centuries. But which churches were founded, when, and by whom, are specifically historical questions to which answers are unlikely to be derived from archaeological or architectural investigations. The chronological development of a particular site or building, as revealed through archaeology, is frequently difficult to marry satisfactorily with an imperfectly recorded historical outline. Such is certainly the case at Saint Brelade.

THE CELTIC DEDICATION

Saint Brelade enjoys the distinction of being the only parish church in Jersey to be dedicated in honour of a Celtic missionary, and this is certainly strong evidence for an early Christian foundation. The origin of the name has, however, caused more speculation than it merits. It has already been observed that Balleine unhesitatingly equated Brelade with the famous and much-travelled Irish missionary Brendan (p. 14). Unfortunately, there is no scholarly basis for such an equation, and the odds are substantially against it.

123

Early spellings of the name Brelade in Jersey include *Brolardi*,[1] *Breverlardi*,[2] and *Broelardi*.[3] The name also occurs at a parish adjoining Dol, in Brittany; now known as Saint Broladre, earlier spellings include *Broelardi* (1081). The Jersey and Breton names are plainly identical. Confusion arises, however, when it is appreciated that the official patron of Saint Broladre's Church is now Saint Brendan; but that has not always been the case. As long ago as 1945 Canon G.H. Doble drew attention to the assignation of 'official' dedications recalling well-known saints to churches that were previously dedicated in honour of obscure local saints. Fortunately, local tradition often preserved the true patron's name. Such is the case at Saint Broladre (Doble, 1945 and 1965). When Balleine discovered that the name of Saint Brendan was honoured at Saint Broladre, that was sufficient for him to clinch the connection between Jersey's Saint Brelade and Saint Brendan (Balleine, 1932, 7–8). He was merely following in the footsteps of medieval Bretons, by implanting the name of the famous where it had no place.

At present we can do no better than concur with Doble's analysis of the situation: neither Brelade nor Broladre is philologically connected with Brendan, but both are renderings of Branwalader who, it seems, was an associate or successor of Saint Samson, the sixth-century founder of the see of Dol in Brittany. The cult of Saint Branwalader was by no means obscure in the early Middle Ages, and it is evidenced not only in his homeland of Brittany, but also in south-west England. Traditions relating to the saint have been preserved in the Exeter Martyrology, and his name was associated with the quadripartite dedication of the monastery which King Athelstan founded at Milton, Dorset, in A.D. 933. Athelstan was renowned as a collector of relics, and amongst those which he procured from Brittany were items associated with Saints Samson and Branwalader. Both were honoured, along with Saint Mary and Saint Michael, at Milton, and there was also a cult of Branwalader at the New Minster, Winchester.

The Channel Islands lay in the diocese of Dol until its eclipse by the Norse devastations in the early tenth century. There is nothing improbable in the suggestion that a Christian community was founded at Saint Brelade in the sixth century by missionary activity from Dol, and that the saint honoured here from an early date was Branwalader. The original feast day of the saint is now uncertain: Branwalader was honoured in Brittany on 1st June, but in England on 19th January (Doble, 1945).

THE LOCAL TOPOGRAPHY

Saint Brelade is situated on a rocky ledge, overlooking a sheltered bay, in what was a very remote corner of the island (as indeed it remained until the early nineteenth century). Not only is this an archetypal situation for an early Christian monastic foundation, but it is also unparalleled amongst the other parish churches of Jersey. Most of these lie at nodal points, are centres of settlement, and have extensive fertile land close by: manifestly, none of these conditions obtains at Saint Brelade. The historic topography of the area around the church is revealed by the Duke of Richmond's map of 1795 (Fig. 97), and can be further resurrected from fieldwork. The patterns of boundaries, roads and natural drainage have all been substantially modified in modern times, destroying the sense of isolation enjoyed by Saint Brelade's Church until well into the nineteenth century.

The form and extent of the churchyard have both changed fundamentally since the Middle Ages, when it was much smaller than it is today and various topographical indicators suggest that it was near-circular in plan, with a diameter of c. 65 m. This is such a distinctive feature of early

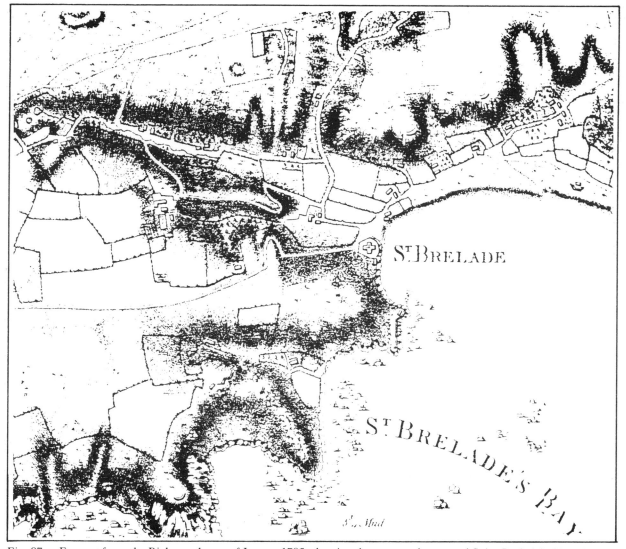

Fig. 97.   Excerpt from the Richmond map of Jersey, 1795, showing the topography around Saint Brelade's Church, and the outline of the churchyard. Compare with Figs. 99 and 108.

Christian graveyards throughout western Britain that its occurrence at Saint Brelade is worthy of further consideration. Most other Jersey churchyards were certainly rectilinear, again emphasising how Saint Brelade's differs from its neighbours. The four stages of its development are illustrated on plan, Fig. 98. The sole remaining trace of the primary circular enclosure is at the south-east corner of the churchyard, and even here some flattening has occurred through the rebuilding of boundary walls in conveniently straighter sections (Figs. 110–111). On the 1795 map, however, the entire eastern half of the circle was shown, and most of the long-since destroyed western half is perpetuated by the curvature of the 50-foot contour line, and by a pair of oak trees which are likely to be in the region of 300 and 350 years old, respectively (Figs. 103 and 108).

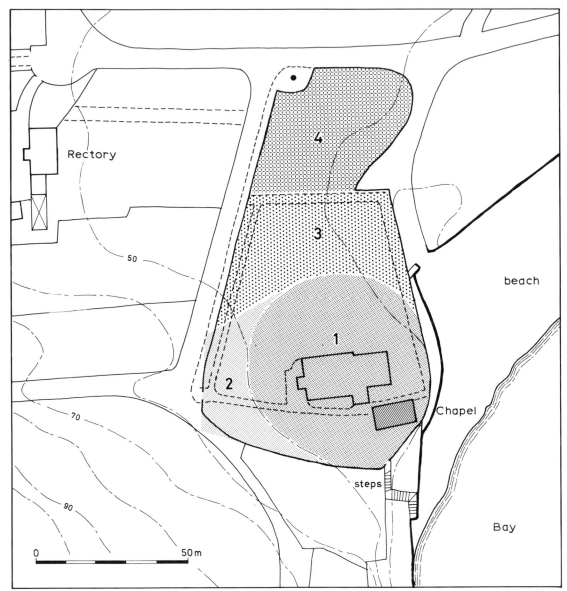

Fig. 98.   Plan of Saint Brelade's churchyard, showing the four-phase development.
1 Dark Age circular enclosure.
2 Medieval or later extension towards the west.
3 Mid-nineteenth-century extension and formal layout of roads, paths and sea wall.
4 Mid-twentieth-century addition (originating as a German war cemetery). The war memorial stands in the enclave at
the north-west corner.

The first extension to the cemetery, which was probably not before the late Middle Ages, took the form of shifting the entrance and boundary westwards, along the approach road to the church. A new west boundary was created (where the present lych-gate is), together with straight sections of north and south boundary, forming tangents to the original circle. This is the plan that appears on the 1795 map and which, at first glance, looks so unconvincing, but is in fact straightforward (Fig. 97). The third phase came in the mid-nineteenth century, when another extension of similarly trapezoidal plan was attached on the north side of the primary enclosure. With this came not only the monumental stone gateway (1852), but also the straightening of the sea wall, and the laying out of the present pattern of roads to the north and west of the churchyard. The west corners of the second-phase churchyard were clipped by these roadworks (particularly for creating access to the new houses south of the church). The final extension, again to the north, came in the present century, when a German war cemetery was created here.

In order to understand the medieval setting of Saint Brelade's Church and the Fishermen's Chapel it is necessary to recreate the historic environment, and this can be achieved to a considerable extent through the study of early maps, place-names and the existing topography. The result is shown in fig. 99. While today the church site appears to be the natural western extremity of the attenuated development that follows the road around Saint Brelade's Bay, this is a modern illusion. Down to the late eighteenth century the churchyard was sharply defined by natural features on all sides except for the west, and even access from that direction was not entirely easy. There was an extensive low-lying area of land to the north of the church, centred on the modern road junction and War Memorial; this was the mouth of a minor valley, or creek, through which ran three streams, having their confluence in the vicinity of what is now the stone gateway to the churchyard, discharging into the Bay on the site of the modern slipway.

The principal stream flowed in from the north-west, through a well-defined valley, simply called Le Val. This stream was flanked by a substantial belt of pasture and marsh, still known as Le Marais du Val (Stevens and Stevens, 1986, map 8B). The stream, now piped in its lower reaches, was diverted in or before the seventeenth century and linked with a second stream which descended the valley of La Marquanderie, the purpose of this exercise being to gain a sufficient head of water to drive a mill, Le Moulin du Grand Saut (Stevens, Arthur and Stevens, 1986, 371). The third stream entered from the west, running between the present Rectory and the church. The broad and marshy valley mouth has subsequently filled with silt to a depth of more than two metres (as may be observed from grave digging in the northern part of the cemetery). The stream, however, still flows on its old course, although now entirely subterranean: water constantly trickles through the base of the churchyard wall and flows into the bay.

Saint Brelade's Church was only readily accessible, by land, from the west, and the route around the bay cannot have been usable throughout the year, until the marsh was drained. There is no evidence for a historic village close to Saint Brelade's Church, and no particularly suitable location for one, though it is just possible that the site of the present rectory has a medieval ancestry. There can be little doubt that medieval Saint Brelade stood in topographical isolation, reflecting a situation that had obtained for many centuries. Even in the early nineteenth century, before the new road was built to the north of the churchyard and rectory in 1836, the church still appeared to stand on a promontory: 'The churchyard is washed by the sea at high tide . . . and a deep cleft that runs up from the shore' (Inglis, 1834, I, 75).

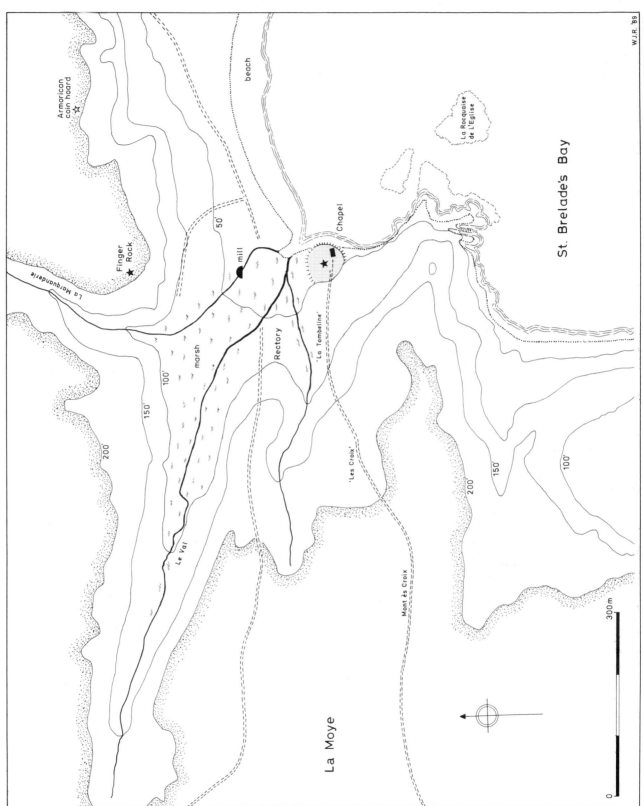

Fig. 99. Map showing the early topography in the vicinity of Saint Brelade's churchyard, together with important archaeological and toponymic evidence. The churchyard is shown here in its primary, circular form.

Earliest Settlement On The Site

Although eremitics sought to live in isolated locations, early missionaries tended to found their communities in less populous, but not deserted, places, where they could readily acquire land and where there was potential for winning local converts. We should not, therefore, expect Saint Brelade's Church to have been founded in a wholly uncleared and unoccupied terrain. Nothing was known of the archaeology of the site prior to the recent excavations, but it is now clear, from the discovery of flints and sherds of Gallo-Roman pottery, that there was prehistoric and Roman occupation on the site. Very extensive excavations would be required beneath the church and in the churchyard to establish the nature and dating of this occupation, since grave digging and other disturbances will have destroyed all but a tiny fraction of the evidence.

Fig. 100. A recumbent menhir, which appears to have formed the threshold stone of a Dark Age building to the west of the Fishermen's Chapel. The stone (F158) is now partly buried under the south transept porch of Saint Brelade's Church. Scale of 75 cm.

Photo: Warwick Rodwell

There is, perhaps, just enough evidence to hint at the former presence of a prehistoric religious or funerary monument on the site. This was first seriously considered in 1985, when the threshold stone of a Dark Age building was discovered immediately to the west of the Fishermen's Chapel (p. 70; Fig. 100). This stone, a local pink granite boulder 1.6 m (5½ ft) in length, had evidently had a previous use in a situation where it had been subjected to differential weathering. When freshly quarried, the stone had been dressed into a more-or-less rectangular block, like a gate-post; in cross-section it measured *c*. 44 by 30 cm. The pattern of weathering on the stone suggests that it once stood upright in a pillar-like position, with the lowest one-third buried in the ground. It is therefore plausible that the stone's first use was as a prehistoric menhir, as suggested in the reconstruction drawing, Fig. 101.

Without appreciating their potential significance, Balleine also reported some massive stones, only a few metres away, in the foundations of the parish church. He described them as 'pebbles, nearly six feet in length, laid transversely' (Balleine, 1907, 20). The recently-discovered stone, with its weathered profile, could have been described as a 'pebble' in Balleine's terminology. Surely, we are glimpsing here the reuse of a group of prehistoric standing stones in the foundations of religious buildings? The height of these stones is typical of the smaller menhirs of the Channel Islands. It is also interesting to note, in passing, that another presumed menhir, known as 'Finger Rock', stood on a spur of high ground overlooking Le Val marsh from the north (Fig. 99; Stevens, Arthur and Stevens, 1986, 224).

There are yet more references to possible prehistoric stone monuments: thus, when the Fishermen's Chapel was being underpinned, 'three rough stones, the longer one four feet, the others two feet in length, laid . . . at right-angles to . . . the south wall, just below the foundations' were discovered (Balleine, 1932, 36). There is no point in speculating about the feature to which these stones belonged, but it was clearly of greater antiquity than the chapel itself. Finally, in this connection, it is worth noting that massive boulders were found beneath the north-east and south-east corners of the chancel of Saint Brelade's Church; the first was described as being about 4 ft (1.2 m) square, and said to be of Chausey granite (in which case it is less likely to be from a megalithic monument), while the second block was simply noted as 'a huge corner-stone' (Balleine, 1907, 20). The reuse of large and often unwieldy boulders, deriving from pre-Christian contexts, as the corner-stones of churches is a widespread phenomenon; it is more symbolic than practical.

Although pure speculation, one might wonder whether the megalithic monument from which the Saint Brelade stones were derived was sited on the level ground immediately adjoining the church on the north, where it would not only have been at the centre of the circular churchyard, but would also account for the displacement of church and chapel to the south (Fig. 103).

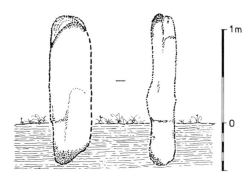

Fig. 101.   Two views showing how the large boulder (F158) found under the south transept porch probably stood, when originally set up as a menhir. The upper end is fissured and weathered, while a 'necking' towards the lower end indicates erosion at ground level.

THE EARLY CHRISTIAN ERA

In summarising the evidence for the physical association of early Christian sites with prehistoric monuments in Europe, Leslie Grinsell recently observed, 'The concentration of megalithic monuments in and around Brittany probably provides more examples of Christianisation than the whole of the Mediterranean lands, and this surely implies that some sort of megalithic religious cult was absorbed into the Christian religion' (Grinsell, 1986, 36). The force of this argument is indeed strong in the Channel Islands, with Guernsey's several Christianised menhirs, and Jersey's *pièce de résistance* at La Hougue Bie. Here, not only does a Norman chapel lie on top of the mound covering a dolmen, but the chapel is also directly above, and aligned upon, the prehistoric burial chamber. It is not implausible that the latter was adopted as a crypt.

In 1988 a new site was discovered on Les Écréhous reef, supplying further dramatic confirmation of the deliberate association between megalithic funerary monuments and early Christian foundations.[4] Although known as a small Cistercian house, Saint Mary's Priory on Maître Île was found to overlie an unrecorded church which had been so constructed that a grave containing a prehistoric-type disarticulated burial – presumably once surmounted by a stone cairn – formed the focus of its chancel (Fig. 102). This circumstance is reminiscent of the discovery of a huge boulder under the floor at the centre of the crossing of Clynnog Church, Caernarvonshire (Fig. 105C; RCAHM, 1960, 41). Moreover, at Les Écréhous a menhir, 3.35 m (11 ft) in length, had been laid to rest in a pit outside the west door of the church, and the Neolithic mother-goddess menhir at Castel, Guernsey, was discovered below the chancel step (McCormack, 1986, 6).

It is against such a milieu that the Dark Age foundation of an early Christian community at Saint Brelade must be seen, and the evidence for two buildings found in the excavations within and adjacent to the Fishermen's Chapel is almost certainly assignable to the period in question. What, then, are we to make of this scanty evidence relating to activity in Saint Brelade's churchyard prior to the erection of the chapel? That there was a previous building on the site of the chapel is beyond doubt, as shown by the traces of earth and clay floors which are both severed by the construction trench for the chapel's foundations, and are at a much lower level than its primary floor (pp. 58–60 and Fig. 49). Some 60 to 80 cm of floors and other deposits would appear to have been laid down

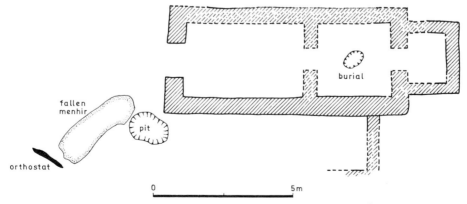

Fig. 102. Plan of the early church underlying Saint Mary's Priory, Les Écréhous, in relation to a prehistoric-type burial, recumbent menhir and other features.

over the earliest earth floor (F35), raising it to the contemporary level from which the existing chapel was built. This is likely to represent a long period of activity, and it is particularly unfortunate that the layers relating to the later part of that period were dug away when the chapel's floor level was reduced in the Middle Ages. The fact that no burials were found under the early floors (admittedly a very restricted area), no fragments of human bone were in them, and none of the graves recorded in the excavations ante-dated the late medieval period, may indicate that no early Christian cemetery had previously occupied this spot.

Whether the pre-chapel building was of religious or secular origin is indeterminable from the physical evidence. The absence of burials has no bearing on the question, since the Roman Church forbade interment within its buildings (except in special side-chambers), and the Celtic Church did not encourage the practice either. The very existence of an earlier building beneath the Fishermen's Chapel, and seemingly not of smaller dimension, must be considered strong circumstantial evidence for Christian continuity. The case is not yet proven, but we may advance, as a working hypothesis which future research may uphold or demolish, the suggestion that the present chapel is a rebuilding of a much more ancient church that was probably made of less durable materials. The fact that the earliest floor levels, under what is now the sanctuary, are hollowed slightly into the sand, and a stone footing was bedded there into the clay floor (F35), might be sheer coincidence, or evidence for the altar having remained in the same position since pre-Norman times.

The equally enigmatic evidence for a second building, immediately west of the Fishermen's Chapel, is best interpreted as domestic, on account of the deposits of animal bone and shell. Its dating to the seventh or eighth century, by radio-carbon determination (p. 71), is of fundamental interest. Again, there was no evidence for very early burials in this area.

In conclusion, none of the various stands of evidence discussed here is particularly strong in its own right but, taken together, they may be seen to support – and in no way to conflict with – the hypothesis that this sheltered rocky ledge overlooking Saint Brelade's Bay was first occupied in prehistoric times (in the Neolithic period and/or the Bronze Age), and a megalithic structure stood somewhere on the site that was later adopted as a churchyard. There was occupation in the Roman period and, subsequently – perhaps in the earlier part of the sixth century – an early Christian community was founded by Branwalader, a missionary working from the neighbourhood of Dol. A modest church was built, arguably on the site of the Fishermen's Chapel, and domestic structures were erected nearby. The contemporary cemetery, not yet located, is likely to have lain to the north, nearer to the centre of the circular enclosure defining the religious *enceinte* (Fig. 103). The whole arrangement finds parallels in the early Irish and western British monastic settlements ('lans') with their circular enclosures.

In due course, domestic settlement probably moved away from the church, leaving room for the expansion of the cemetery. The encroachment of pre-Norman burials into the area of former domestic occupation was demonstrated by excavation, and a date in the tenth century suggested by a radio-carbon determination on one of the earliest skeletons (p. 72).

The ninth and tenth centuries are a particularly difficult period in the archaeology of Jersey. Although the coastal regions of Normandy and Brittany were being devastated by the pagan Norse, there is virtually no tangible evidence for events in the Channel Islands, either indigenous or Viking. The diocese of Dol was certainly destroyed as an administrative unit, and Jersey was undoubtedly cut off from the mainstream activity of the Western Christian Church for more than a

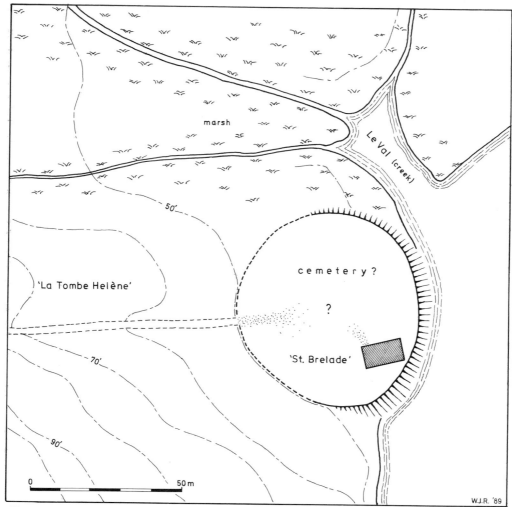

Fig. 103. Reconstructed plan of the early Christian circular enclosure in relation to contemporary topography. The church of 'Saint Brelade' shown here is the predecessor of the Fishermen's Chapel (i.e. the foundation upon which the present chapel stands).

century, not to be reabsorbed into the diocesan network until the see of Coutances was re-established in the 1020s. But this does not mean that Christianity was eclipsed in the Channel Islands, however low was its ebb. The plundering of monastic houses for their riches was an integral component of the Norse invasions, and a solitary memory of this is preserved in Jersey toponomy through one parish church dedication, *Sainte Marie d'Arsmoustier*, 'Saint Mary at the Burnt Monastery'.[5] We may suspect, but cannot yet demonstrate, that Christianity in Jersey was not totally emasculated during these difficult centuries. It is gradually becoming apparent in mainland Britain that the Viking incursions did not lead to the widespread eradication of Christianity, or to the obliteration of local churches and cemeteries. The extent of the supposed damage has been greatly exaggerated in antiquarian writing.

Saint Brelade was certainly in a vulnerable position, from the point of view of visibility to sea-borne raiders, but by virtue of its setting it was also a potentially defensible site. There was a cliff on the east, a marsh on the north, steeply rising rocks (still wooded today) on the south, and the only ready access was on foot from the west. The pre-eminent importance of that route is well authenticated in the local topography and toponomy. The principal track which crosses the La Moye plateau, running eastwards in the direction of Saint Brelade's Bay, is replete with features of early topographical interest. Most immediately obvious is the fact that the track aims directly for the centre of the circular churchyard (or, more likely in terms of origin, the megalithic monument that previously stood there: Fig. 99).

Next, the naming of the track cannot fail to arrest attention, since it is called *Mont ès Croix* ('the hill of the crosses'); and just below the 200-foot plateau a house, *Les Croix*, has stood at least since the eighteenth century. This is clearly not an instance where *les croix* could be interpreted as cross-roads, and the naming may be accepted at face value, that is an allusion to crosses of religious significance alongside the principal (only?) road leading to Saint Brelade's Church (Stevens, Arthur and Stevens, 1986, 176).

Finally, the name of the attenuated field alongside the track, immediately west of the church, is equally evocative of interest. Now known as *La Tombeline*, and previously as *Tombelaine*, this recalls an early Christian interest in *La Tombe Helène* (Saint Helen's tomb). Whether the name was applied to a prehistoric chambered tomb or to some other structure of early Christian origin is beyond speculation.

Church and Chapel: A Question of Relationship

There has been a general assumption by many historians that the Fishermen's Chapel – whatever its date – must have preceded the erection of the much larger parish church. Other writers, notably Balleine, have opted for an 'equal age' explanation, seeking to show that Saint Brelade's Church itself embodies the structure of another small, and very early chapel. A few scholars, such as Rybot, have proffered the less attractive explanation that the Fishermen's Chapel is no more than a chantry chapel in Saint Brelade's Churchyard.

The origins of Jersey parishes and churches have been discussed by the late Doctor J.N.L. Myres in a pair of papers, in which he drew attention to many of the remarkable structural similarities between the buildings (Myres, 1978 and 1981). Myres contended that the twelve parish churches originated as aisle-less, cruciform buildings, erected as a coherent group, in the middle of the eleventh century. More recent studies carried out independently by several investigators (John McCormack, Peter Bisson, and the present writer) suggest that this attractive theory needs substantial modification (cf. McCormack, 1986).

The architectural development of Saint Brelade's Church will be considered in detail in a separate paper (Rodwell, forthcoming); suffice it to say that the nave belongs to a late Romanesque church, into which the tower and crossing have been intruded, and the transepts, although probably added within the Norman period, are not a matched pair and are clearly not primary. There is nothing in the architecture or the plan of the building to sustain a date before the eleventh century. Balleine's concept of a pair of pre-Norman monastic chapels, lying side by side, is improbable: while it is true that some of the earliest Celtic religious establishments comprised a clutch of small chapels and cells, the proportions and spatial relationship of the existing buildings at Saint Brelade lend little support to such a notion.[6]

Taking all the evidence, both positive and negative, into consideration, the most plausible hypothesis that can be offered is that the Fishermen's Chapel occupies the site of the only pre-Norman church. That would have been the primary Christian focus, with its attached cemetery on the north. There may well have been other, subsidiary, foci within the encircling earthwork.

Then, when the Bishop of Coutances, through his deputy the Archdeacon of the Isles, reorganised the parochially-based church in Jersey in the middle or later years of the eleventh century, a new building would have been considered a necessity. This was, generally, a period of great church building. There would have been two options at Saint Brelade: to rebuild and extend the then-existing church or chapel, or to begin afresh on an adjacent site. Considerable difficulties would have had to be overcome if the chapel were to be enlarged into a fashionable Romanesque parish church. The chapel was small, very close to the cliff edge, and the ground rose sharply on its south and west sides. It was an impossible site in terms of contemporary liturgical requirements, particularly procession. It was logical to start building anew, on the flatter ground to the north, perhaps where the prehistoric focus had been (reverence for such pre-Christian foci was by this time passing out of liturgical fashion).

The new church could be set back further from the cliff and occupy a convenient position in the centre of the old circular graveyard. At the same time, the ancient chapel could remain in use while building work was in progress. This rational Norman practice has been revealed archaeologically at several English sites in recent years, as at Winchester, Exeter and Wells, where a new cathedral was in each case built alongside the old, so that full continuity of worship could be maintained.

In most instances of this kind, where one building was replaced by another on an immediately adjacent site, it was doubtless intended that, upon completion of the work, the old, redundant church should be demolished. But this did not always happen. It has now been appreciated, in an ever-increasing number of examples, that the venerable religious focus was not eradicated, even though it was for all practical purposes superseded. Many communities did not permit the 'clean sweep' approach of the Norman builders to destroy all physical evidence of their Christian origins, and frequently something was left as a perpetual memorial to the religious antiquity of the spot. At Winchester it was the tiny chapel of Saint Swithun, at Exeter it was the church of Saint Mary Major, and at Wells it was the chapel to the Blessed Virgin Mary; all of these relics were not only anomalously sited in relation to the new Norman buildings that for all practical purposes superseded them, but they were also maintained and rebuilt for centuries to come.

Perhaps more comparable in status and scale with Saint Brelade are the western British sites at Heysham, Lancashire, Caer Gybi and Llaneilian, on the island of Anglesey, and others in Wales. Saint Patrick's Chapel, Heysham, now only a ruin, stands on a cliff edge overlooking Morecambe Bay; it has an associated pre-Norman cemetery. Close by, but on a lower and more sheltered spot, is the parish church of Saint Peter. Although it too is a pre-Norman building, it is probably a later foundation than the chapel (Taylor and Taylor, 1965, 312–16). Saint Cybi's parish church at Caer Gybi, Holyhead, stands inside the western part of a former Roman fort, the perimeter of which delimits the graveyard (Fig. 104). Also within the Roman *enceinte*, and 20 m south of the church, is the small detached chapel, known as Eglwys-y-Bedd (RCAHM, 1937, 28–34).

Saint Eilian's parish church, Llaneilian, stands on the north coast of Anglesey, and immediately

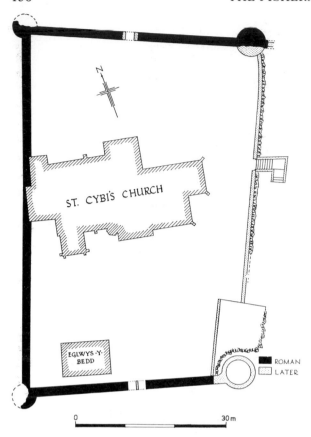

Fig. 104.   Plan of the Roman fort at Caer Gybi, North Wales, showing the centrally placed parish church and the smaller chapel in one corner.

After RCAHM, 1937

to the south-east of it is a formerly-detached (but now conjoined) chapel bearing the same dedication. The chapel is orientated north-west to south-east and stands very awkwardly in relation to the church, the earliest part of which is the Norman west tower (Fig. 105). The remainder has been rebuilt, and so has the chapel, but there can be little doubt that the latter marks an early Christian site (RCAHM, 1937, 59–61). An exactly comparable situation obtains at Clynnog, in Caernarvonshire, where there is a large, cruciform parish church dedicated to Saint Beuno, and only four metres from the south-west corner of its nave is a small rectangular chapel also dedicated to Saint Beuno (RCAHM, 1960, 36–41). This too lies on a different orientation from that of the adjacent church and, although originally detached, the two structures were later connected by a barrel-vaulted passage (Fig. 105). Furthermore, in this instance archaeological evidence has been found inside Saint Beuno's Chapel for a yet earlier and smaller chapel on the same site, as well as for other structures outside it. The comparison with Saint Brelade's is striking.

Thus, returning to Saint Brelade, there is no difficulty in positing that an early Christian chapel was superseded by a new parish church alongside, the old building remaining as a subsidiary focus. It would have held a place of importance in liturgical procession, and would have been the scene of particular veneration on the day of the patronal festival.

In terms of the relative chronology of the buildings at Saint Brelade, as they stand today, there is no doubt that the Fishermen's Chapel is older than most of the fabric of the parish church. The

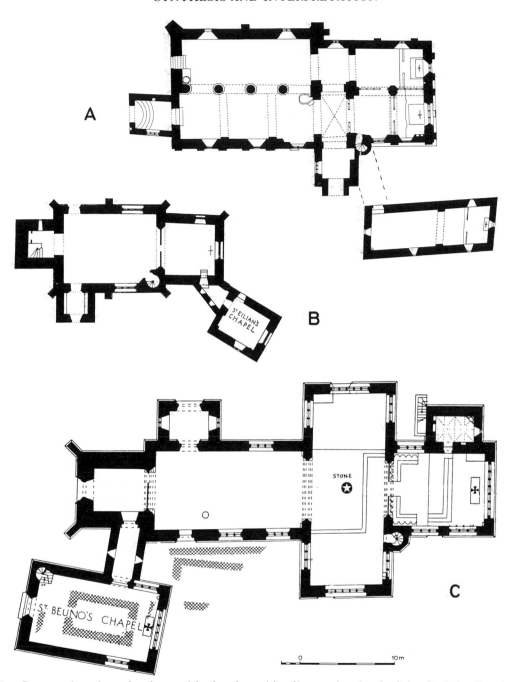

Fig. 105. Comparative plans showing parish churches with adjacent chapels: A. Saint Brelade; B. Llaneilian; C. Clynnog. In both the latter examples the structures linking church and chapel are post-medieval, but may well perpetuate earlier pentices. The cross-hatching represents foundations of yet earlier buildings, discovered during excavations.

chancel and tower are thirteenth century, as are the transepts, at least in part. The north aisle and north-east chapel are later still. That basically leaves the nave as the oldest part of the standing church, and is probably more-or-less coeval with the Fishermen's Chapel. Determining which was actually erected first is not easy on architectural grounds, but as a general principle we should not expect the chapel to have been rebuilt until the parish church which replaced it had been completed in its primary Norman form. This pattern – of building a new church, and then restoring the old structure as a secondary focus – was widespread, and applies to the examples that have already been cited. Ironically, such a sequence gives rise to an apparent chronological reversal: the older building is on the more recent site, while the *locus antiquus* is marked by a more recent structure.

Although there is now no physical connection between Saint Brelade's Church and the chapel, it is likely that there may once have been a link. The examples of Llaneilian and Clynnog well demonstrate how the doorways of the churches and their respective chapels were sited so that easy access could be gained from one to the other, and in both cases fully enclosed passages were later created. In the light of this it is interesting to note that Balleine postulated a physical link ('covered way') between Saint Brelade's Church and the Fishermen's Chapel when, during the restoration of the former, he discovered a long-disused and infilled doorway in the east side of the south transept (Balleine, 1932, 13). Certainly, this is an anomalous location for a doorway, and is only explicable in terms of access to the chapel (Fig. 105A).[7]

During the excavation and structural study of the south transept in 1985 it was established that the doorway referred to was a primary feature of the first phase of the transept, and that it was blocked in the fifteenth century, when the stair-turret was built. There could well have been a connecting pentice here between the church and the chapel, but any evidence in the ground would have been removed long ago by grave digging. After the blocking of the east doorway a new opening was created in the south wall of the rebuilt transept. This too is an unusual position, especially since there was already a door in the south side of the nave, and access to the chapel is once again to be invoked as the explanation. Any link structure that might have been erected in the later Middle Ages would have been swept away in the sixteenth century, in order to manoeuvre cannon from their store to the sea wall.

A Lost Dedication?

If the historical sequence outlined above is correct, then there is every probability that the dedication to Saint Branwalader would have been transferred (in its current linguistic form) from the old church to the new. The first recorded mention of the parish church by name is in the period 1053–66, when it was the *ecclesia Sancti Broladrii* (Stevens, Arthur and Stevens, 1986, 477). It is just possible that the new church and old chapel bore the same dedication, as at Llaneilian. This is, however, unlikely in a Norman diocese, and a fresh dedication would probably have been assigned to the now-subordinate chapel. That dedication has been lost, but it was very common in the Middle Ages for the first subordinate chapel, either physically within, or belonging to, a church to bear a dedication to Saint Mary the Virgin.

Quite independent of this line of argument is the evidence, albeit of later medieval date, provided by the mural paintings in the chapel. They proclaim in no uncertain terms that Mary held a place of special honour in the life of that building. First, the east wall was dominated by a fourteenth-century painting depicting the Annunciation to Saint Mary, and then over-painted in the following century by a representation of the Virgin and Child. Moreover, it has been shown that in the later series of paintings great emphasis was placed on the importance of not only Christ, but also his mother Mary, in salvation history (pp. 43–5). Conversely, there is nothing in the paintings to suggest an association with maritime saints, the sea, or fishermen, and this must be regarded as substantive evidence that the chapel had no serious connection with fishing guilds before the late Middle Ages, if then.

Although there is no documented evidence to support such a suggestion, it is not implausible that the chapel became associated with a fishing guild for a short period in the sixteenth century, immediately prior to the Reformation. That would conveniently account for its popular name, although, as already remarked (p. 2), the first recorded mention of *La Chapelle ès Pêcheurs* is in 1817.[8]

Finally, it should be noted that there is a possible medieval reference to the Fishermen's Chapel. It is contained in the will of Brelade Alexandre, dated 23rd January 1537:

Item do et lego thesauro capelle Sanctae Marie predicte ecclesiae superdicti Sancti Brevelardi unum grossum argentum[9]

This is probably to be translated as, 'Also I give and bequeath to the treasury of the said Chapel of Saint Mary, of the aforesaid Church of Saint Brelade, one silver groat'. While this demonstrates that there was a chapel dedicated to Saint Mary in the parish, it gives no indication as to whether it was physically within, or merely appendent to, Saint Brelade's Church. Balleine rushed to the unwarranted conclusion that the will referred to the north-east chapel in the parish church, but there is no evidence for its medieval dedication (Balleine, 1907, 16). That did not, however, deter its subsequent description, without qualification, as the 'Chapelle de la Ste. Vierge' (Warton, 1914, 443).

Further circumstantial evidence may be supplied by the Jersey Chantry Certificate of 1550: this refers to three fraternities or guilds in Saint Brelade's parish, each of which would have had its own altar, and possibly a chapel. There were fraternities of Saint Brelade, Our Lady, and the Crucifix, and the sale of their assets in 1550 yielded approximately three crowns, four crowns and eleven crowns respectively (Bisson, 1975, 36–9). The Fraternity of the Crucifix was clearly very wealthy, and that must surely be a strong contender for placement in the north-east chapel of the parish church. The Fraternity of Saint Brelade may be presumed to have had its very poorly endowed altar in the church also, perhaps in one of the transepts, or the north aisle. That leaves the slightly better-off Fraternity of Our Lady which, although it could perfectly well have been accommodated in the parish church too, might more convincingly be assigned to the Fishermen's Chapel which, at that time, was so blatantly decorated in honour of Our Lady, that it would seem perverse not to suggest the connection.

Functions of the Chapel in the Middle Ages

While the principal masses will have been held in the Norman parish church, the Fishermen's Chapel, rebuilt on old foundations, and perhaps now rededicated to Saint Mary, will still have had a variety of functions: the founder and ancient sanctity of the site will have been remembered there, it will have been an important station in liturgical processions, it may have been the focus of a local pilgrimage, and there are likely to have been holy relics displayed and venerated here too. In a sense, it was an anachronism in the Norman period, a reflection of an era when worship was not concentrated in a single, substantial building, but was dissipated amongst a group of liturgical foci which were closely inter-related, but nevertheless physically separate (in the pre-Norman era a single ecclesiastical 'site' could comprise several chapels, shrine-tombs, standing crosses, holy well, etc.). Archaic survivals such as this gradually lost their significance and disappeared with evolving liturgical fashions in the Middle Ages, and superfluous chapels where long-forgotten saints were honoured could be appropriated to new uses.

Appropriation by a prominent local family of an existing chapel or crypt was a common happening in the thirteenth and fourteenth centuries. There were two interlinked aspects of this use: first, interment and the commemoration of the dead, and, secondly, the recitation of prayers and masses for their souls. These functions constituted a chantry. Both the word and the concept have been seriously abused in Jersey historical writing, as previously observed by Bisson (1975, 6). It has frequently been stated or implied that virtually every chapel in the island originated as a chantry. The fact that the building of the Fishermen's Chapel, amongst others, demonstrably antedates the popular era of medieval chantries has not deterred some writers from making sweeping assertions. That a substantial number of the island's chapels were appropriated to chantry uses in the later Middle Ages is very likely, but that is a different matter from the history and purpose of their foundation. It is necessary to emphasise this dichotomy in order that the chantry use of the Fishermen's Chapel, as proposed here, is appreciated in context.

That use probably came in the fourteenth century, and was accompanied by the decoration of the east end and side walls of the chapel with the earlier of the two schemes of painting. There were three elements to this: first the focal composition – the Annunciation – which, it is suggested, recalls the dedication of the chapel to the Blessed Virgin Mary. This focus is supported by the two flanking rows of kneeling figures, who are not confined to the east wall but return along the north and south walls too, as far as the window openings, suggesting a deliberate attempt to enclose the altar (which at that period would have stood against the east wall). There can be little doubt that the fourteen kneeling layfolk – adults and children – represent members of a single family. They are reminiscent of the 'weepers' around the base of a late medieval tomb. This may be accepted as a strong indicator that, by about the middle of the fourteenth century, the chapel had been appropriated by a local family as their chantry and sepulchre. The third element of the decoration, now almost entirely lost, comprised saints and perhaps other figures around the walls of both chancel and nave.

At this stage it is unlikely that any alterations were made to the fabric of the chapel, except possibly the insertion of the pair of lamp brackets in the chancel walls, to provide flanking lights for the altar. With its tiny, round-headed windows, the chapel would have been decidedly gloomy, an atmosphere appropriate to its mortuary use. Whether the deceased were actually buried in the floor, under stone slabs, or whether their coffins were placed in rows on the surface, as in a crypt, cannot be determined. It would appear from English evidence that there was a revived interest in the fourteenth century in clearing out older crypts and converting them to family mortuaries, as occurred, for instance, at Lichfield Cathedral and Repton Church, Derbyshire. The insanitary atmosphere must have been overwhelming, but that was not a major deterrent in the Middle Ages.

The era of sumptuous chantries, with marginally more sanitary conditions, was the fifteenth

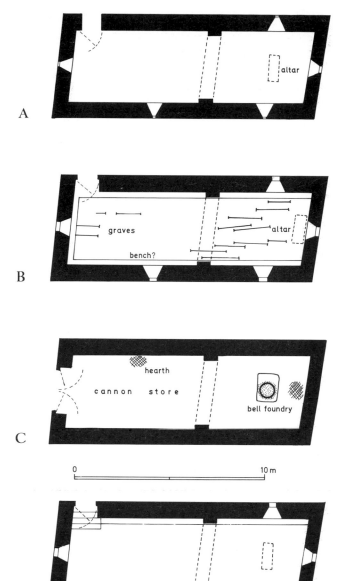

Fig. 106. The evolution of the internal arrangement and use of the Fishermen's Chapel. A. Twelfth century. The original arrangement of nave and chancel, with the altar set forward of the east wall; B. Early fifteenth to mid-sixteenth century. Graves for which evidence has been found are schematically indicated; C. Sixteenth to eighteenth-century secular uses. The windows were blocked; D. The restored plan, 1987.

century, and it was perhaps in the second quarter of that century that the chapel was refurbished. The date is suggested by the second series of paintings, which was not confined to the sanctuary and nave walls, but spread over the entire plastered surface of the chapel, including the vaulted ceiling. This must have been the time of general refurbishment, when the north doorway was reconstructed and all the window apertures enlarged, to admit more light and air, although they may have been filled with stained glass (Fig. 106B). It is very likely that the floor level was considerably lowered at the same time, doubtless to add height and elegance to the freshly decorated interior; the foundation offsets, now made visible, would have been adapted for use as wall-benches.

It is also possible that the lowering of the floor was at least partly motivated by the need to clear away a layer of shallowly buried, putrifying corpses, so that a fresh start could be made. On account of the presence of loose fragments of structural mortar in the fillings of all the graves discovered by excavation in 1982–84, it seems certain that none of these burials belonged to the fourteenth-century mortuary phase, but that they were all interments within the refurbished chapel from, say, the mid-fifteenth century onward. It is worth recalling that virtually all these burials were encoffined and were placed two or three feet below the contemporary floor surface. They conform to the general tendency in the later medieval period for graves to be a little deeper, and thus better sealed from the atmosphere of the church or chapel within which they were dug.

Whether the refurbishment of the chapel was undertaken by the same family, or whether the chantry had meanwhile passed into other hands cannot be determined with certainty. But it would be surprising to find a family obliterating the portraits of its own ancestors within three-quarters of a century of their being painted. Likewise, if we are correct in deducing that a wholesale clearance operation took place at the time of refurbishment, the balance certainly tips in favour of a change of ownership. Whether that change was from one family to another, or to a fraternity, is an interesting subject for speculation. Could this mark the inception of the Fraternity of Our Lady?

There has been a certain amount of speculation concerning the family, or families, that might have appropriated the chapel to their uses. Oppenheim sought to identify the kneeling family with the de Carterets of Saint Ouen's manor. The basis of his identification seems to have been no more than the fact their genealogy shows that seven males were living in c. 1330; and there are seven males depicted in the painting (Oppenheim, 1916, 30–5). The de Carterets had no recorded connection with Saint Brelade's parish, and this cannot have been their chapel. For the time being, at least, the family of donors must remain anonymous. In the painting the donor is represented behind the angel Gabriel, and his wife behind the Virgin, with their six sons and six daughters clearly depicted in descending order of age, as with family representations in tomb-art. From his dress, the first son can be identified as a knight.

There are no secular figures associated with the fifteenth-century paintings, but there is a curious repetition of the letter *S* along the crown of the vault over the nave. This has led to speculation that the de Sottevast family may have sponsored the chapel's refurbishment. Certainly, the de Sottevasts were connected with the parish of Saint Brelade, but the family lived in Normandy and their last recorded mention in Jersey is in the early fourteenth century (Balleine and Stevens, 1970, 108–9; Stevens, Arthur and Stevens, 1986, 503); and the name is entirely absent from the Jersey Chantry Certificate (1550). The de Sottevast family can be firmly ruled out. The other, and perhaps more obvious, interpretation of the S-monogram is *Sanctus*. The only hesitation in accepting this is the fact that Doctor Clive Rouse, in his wide experience of medieval wall-painting, has been unable to find an analogous example, although the unaccompanied use of the letter *M* (for *Maria*) is well known. Notwithstanding the singular nature of this occurrence, it is infinitely more likely that the initial stands for *Sanctus* than for any secular name, especially when it is recalled that the *S* is an embellishment confined to the first two, joyous scenes in the Life Cycle of Christ (Annunciation and Adoration; Pls. 11–13).

It is clear that the subject material of the fifteenth-century painted decoration was carefully chosen to convey a specific theological emphasis; the theme was skilfully depicted on the walls and

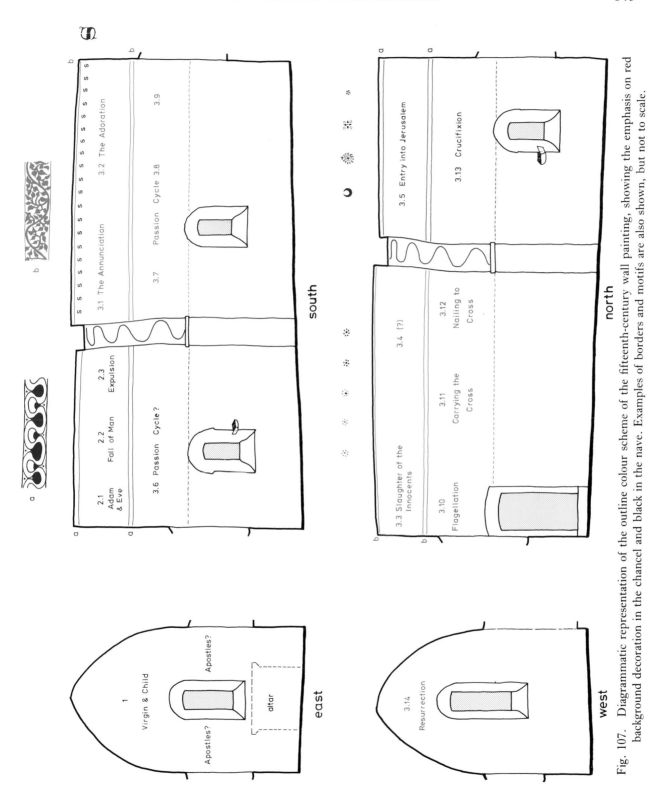

Fig. 107. Diagrammatic representation of the outline colour scheme of the fifteenth-century wall painting, showing the emphasis on red background decoration in the chancel and black in the nave. Examples of borders and motifs are also shown, but not to scale.

ceiling, with complementary scenes, archetypes and antetypes, facing one another; and the artists were at pains to achieve an aesthetically balanced composition through the fine adjustment of detail. The loss of virtually all painting from below the vault-springing line has deprived us of half the total scheme, and consequently of both its full visual impact upon entering this externally plain and simple building, and an appreciation of its many subtleties. There was, for example, an evident contrast between the border-work and background decoration in the nave and in the chancel (Fig. 107). The 30 cm wide bands of scrollwork defining the tiers of decoration are black in the nave (ivy-scroll) and red in the chancel (pelta or scallop ornament). The more elaborate forms of fleur-de-lys, floret and rosette decoration, as well as the crescentic ornaments, are all in red and confined to the chancel. Simple beaded rosettes occur ubiquitously in both chancel and nave, where they are predominantly coloured red in the former, and are a mixture of red and black in the latter. Templates were used for these repetitive background details.

It has been shown that the chapel was the scene of a considerable number of burials (p. 62) and that most, if not all of these took place after the early fifteenth-century refurbishment. Since there was barely a century to elapse before the chapel was desecrated and secularised, it follows that we cannot possibly be dealing here with the chantry of a single family. If the burials derive from multiple families the corollary must be that the chapel served a guild. Once again, identification with the Fraternity of Our Lady would be in accord with the physical evidence. If that fraternity included a substantial number of fishermen, we may glimpse the process by which the chapel acquired its colloquial name.

After the Reformation

THE MILITARY PRESENCE

Chantries and religious guilds were suppressed in 1547 and the Royal Injunctions ordering the destruction of all objects of superstition arrived in Jersey in July 1548. Latin services were dropped within months and it is recorded that Thomas Bertram, Rector of Saint Brelade, embraced the new faith enthusiastically (including marriage within the priesthood). Thus, we can be certain that by 1548–49 the Fishermen's Chapel would have passed out of ecclesiastical use. It has been shown by Bisson that Jersey parishes were generally quick to respond to the requirements of the Acts of the English Crown of the 1540s, and some even began to dispose of ecclesiastical property and spend the proceeds on defence before receiving regal authority (Bisson, 1975, 7): 'The willingness of the parishioners to provide for the defence of the living at the expense of masses for the dead suggests that faith in the efficacy of the latter was already on the wane'. Although not associated with Saint Brelade's parish, there are specific records of the purchase of arms, including cannon, by 1551 (Bisson, 1975, 10). The long struggle with France had begun, and the first attack on Jersey had been made in 1549.

A battery was established on the sea wall overlooking the bay, immediately to the east of Saint Brelade's Church; a partial straightening out of the boundary here was probably initiated by the militia, along with the restructuring of the cliff to create the two 'tiers' of walling that can be seen today (Figs. 108–110). The military wall was glimpsed by Balleine in 1927, just east of the chapel, during repair works following the earthquake (Fig. 111). He described it as being 'some four feet in

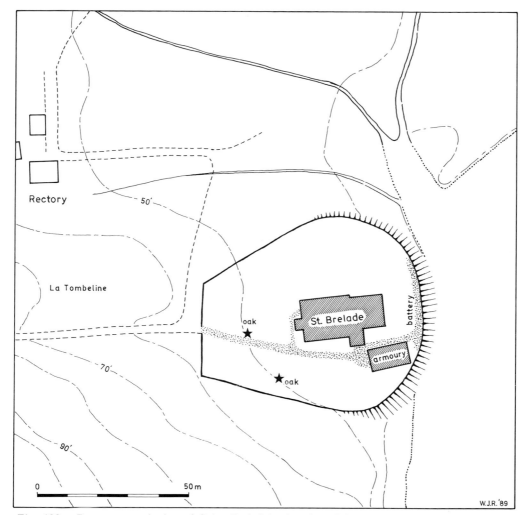

Fig. 108. Reconstructed plan of Saint Brelade's churchyard between the sixteenth and early nineteenth centuries, showing the remains of the early Christian circular enclosure and the post-medieval battery on the sea wall. The two extant oak trees – which are about 300 and 350 years old, respectively – still mark the line of the ancient enclosure (one of the trees appears in Fig. 2). The old rectory shown here was replaced in 1836, the same year as a new road system was laid out to the north of the churchyard (compare with Figs. 4 and 98).

thickness', and noted that within living memory three cannon still stood here, and that the east window of the church was known locally as 'the window above the battery' (Balleine, 1932, 35). A broad path along the edge of the churchyard still marks the approximate line of the military wall and its access track.

Each Jersey parish had to make provision for its own defence, and most stored their cannon in the safest building they had, which was the church. There is evidence remaining in the architecture of several churches for the wide doorway that had necessarily to be created for the entry of the cannon. This is particularly well seen in the west end of the north aisle of Saint Lawrence's

Fig. 109.   Saint Brelade's Church from the north-east in 1852, showing the remains of the former circular churchyard below the site of the battery (marked by the tall trees), and the newly built monumental entrance associated with the northern extension of the cemetery (for the plan, see Fig. 98).

Fig. 110.   Saint Brelade's Church and the Fishermen's Chapel (left) from the south-east (1989), showing the two tiers of curving wall. The original circular form of the churchyard is preserved by the lower wall, which can be seen to disappear beneath the nineteenth-century straightening and extension of the upper (military) wall on the right-hand side.

Photo: Warwick Rodwell

Church. At Saint Brelade there was no need to take the cannon into the church, since a ready-made gun shed was available on the sea wall, in the form of the redundant chapel. The north door and windows were blocked, for security, and a new west entrance with double-doors was provided. The precise date of this 'conversion' is not recorded, but it must surely have taken place soon after the middle of the sixteenth century, and quite possibly in the early 1550s (Fig. 106C).

BELL FOUNDING

Occasionally, the former chapel was pressed into use for other purposes, such as the casting of a bell in the eighteenth century, for which the archaeological evidence has been described (p. 64; Fig. 106C). This discovery opens the door to an intriguing historical enquiry, since the present bell in Saint Brelade's Church dates only from 1883. By coincidence, an account of casting a replacement bell for the church is recorded in Thomas Le Maistre's notebook for 1754 (Stevens, 1967, 250). He reports that on 10th–11th September two bells were cast in the garden of a house called La Fioterie, at Saint Helier. One bell, weighing 1200 lbs, was for Saint John's Church, the other, weighing 966 lbs, was for Saint Brelade's. The casting of the former failed, but the latter seems to have been a success, and the six-lugged bell was taken out of the ground on 12th September. It was said to be inscribed : *La Cloche de Saint Brelade fondue par Maitre Jacque Pitel. Lan 1754*. On 14th–15th September the Saint John's bell was cast again, and made heavier by 76 lbs. It was successfully raised from the ground on 17th September.

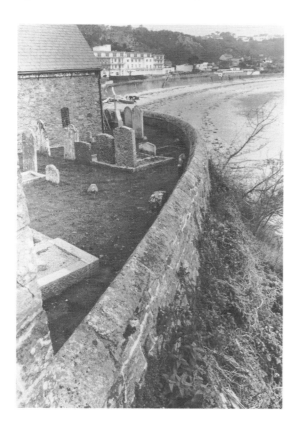

Fig. 111.   Detail of the curving churchyard wall on the cliff edge to the south and east of the Fishermen's Chapel. Rebuilt in 1927, this wall follows the line of the earlier military wall, which in turn reflected the circularity of the early Christian enclosure.

Photo: Warwick Rodwell

That might have been the end of the matter, were it not for an anonymous manuscript[10] which mentions a man called La Source from Dinan, in Brittany, who cast bells for Saint Ouen's and Saint Martin's. The manuscript also records that in November 1754 La Source cast one bell each for Saint Brelade's and Saint John's, and that the latter failed. Moreover, he is specifically recorded as having cast the Saint Brelade's bell 'in the churchyard'.

In discussing the conflicting evidence, Mrs Stevens presumed that the two accounts referred to the same events, and that the second report was largely in error. The Saint John's bell is still extant, is inscribed with Pitel's name, and is dated 1754. That certainly confirms Le Maistre's account in one respect, and the survival of La Source's bell at Saint Ouen's, also dated 1754, is confirmatory evidence for part of the anonymous account. Moreover, the unexpected discovery of an eighteenth-century bell foundry inside the Fishermen's Chapel suggests that there is yet more truth in the anonymous manuscript. How are we to reconcile the conflict here? Plainly Pitel was the successful founder of the Saint John's bell and, from the precision of the details given by Le Maistre, it must be accepted that he cast a good bell for Saint Brelade's too. The apparent duplication of the casting, two months later, must be explained in one of two ways. First, an accident may have befallen Saint Brelade's new bell (it was not unknown for a seemingly perfect bell to be raised into a tower, and then for it to crack almost immediately upon being rung, as a result of an unseen flaw in the casting). That would be a satisfactory explanation for the sequence of events at Saint Brelade's, but not at Saint John's, where there was certainly no need for La Source to recast Pitel's bell.

The alternative explanation is that both churches ordered one bell from Pitel and, two months later, a second bell from La Source. This is almost certainly what happened. In 1551, by Order in Privy Council, Jersey churches were stripped of superfluous bells, and only one was permitted to remain in each, a situation which long obtained (Bisson, 1975, 10). No medieval bells have survived in the island, the earliest extant being that of 1592 at Saint Lawrence. Single examples of seventeenth-century bells also occur at Saint Helier, Saint Saviour, Trinity and Saint Peter (recast). The first post-Reformation evidence for additional bells in Jersey churches does not appear until 1754. It would then have been considered a novelty worthy of record: hence the entry in Le Maistre's diary, and the anonymous manuscript.

There is no doubting that Saint Peter's Church received its second bell in 1754, the same year as two were cast for Saint Brelade's, two for Saint John's, and one each for Saint Ouen's and Saint Martin's. The founding of seven bells in a single year is indeed remarkable and there can be no serious doubt that the casting pit discovered in the Fishermen's Chapel was a product of this flurry of activity, and was the work of La Source. The fact that the second Saint Brelade's bell was described as being cast in the churchyard is not in conflict with the discovery of the foundry in the chapel. Whenever possible, bells were always cast inside buildings, so that the climatic conditions surrounding the crucibles of molten metal, the pre-heated mould, and the slowly cooling bell were controllable, and not subject to catastrophic variations caused by wind or rain. For La Source, the disused chapel was merely an ideal shed in the churchyard, which he could press into temporary use. Where no such conveniently situated building was available, a makeshift shed might be erected or, more commonly, the church itself had to serve as the foundry house. That is specifically recorded in the case of Saint Saviour's; here, the surviving bell was cast inside the church, at the west end, by Martin Huard in 1656.[11]

Most of the remains of the broken-up clay mould for the Saint Brelade's bell were dispersed and lost, but the fragments excavated from the casting pit show that there was a two-line inscription, incorporating scrolled decoration (Figs. 54 and 112). The few fragments that still bear lettering are insufficient for any word to be reconstructed, but even so it is clear from the juxtapositioning of the letters that there cannot be a correlation with Pitel's text, as recorded by Le Maistre. It would have been valuable to compare the calligraphy and decoration on the mould fragments with any surviving bells cast by La Source, but none of his work is extant in the Channel Islands. The bell he made for Saint Ouen's was recast in 1812, again in 1844, and for a third time in 1971. There appears to be no record of the fate of his bell for Saint Martin's, where the present one is dated 1768.

Finally, it is interesting to note that a few pieces of a clay mould (in a different fabric from the 1754 bell-mould), and some casting dross, were found in the excavations, in layers that were earlier than the bell pit. These testify to founding having been carried out on a previous occasion, perhaps in the Middle Ages.

SUNDRY USES FOR THE CHAPEL

When the States opened the new central arsenals in 1844, it was no longer necessary to store cannon and other munitions in the parish churches, and the Fishermen's Chapel will once again have become redundant. Its uses as a lumber room and carpenter's workshop have been noted (p. 4). There is also evidence, in the form of a pair of horizontal chases cut into the north and south walls of the sanctuary, that a timber loft was erected here, most likely in the nineteenth century (Figs. 60B and 61A). This was probably a hay-loft supported on a beam which ran right across the chapel, with its ends embedded in the window jambs just above the medieval lamp brackets.

Rector Balleine's Restoration

The restorations carried out between 1877 and 1935 have already been outlined (pp. 9–15). The earliest phases of the work (1877 and 1884) appear to be wholly undocumented, but Balleine's accounts of his activities in both the chapel and the church are of considerable interest. Written soon after the work was carried out, they ought to constitute accurate, first-hand reports, but some major discrepancies have been noted between what is said to have taken place and what has in fact been revealed through archaeological investigation.[12]

Nonetheless, Balleine's accounts give the impression that his restorations of the chapel and of the church were exceedingly thorough-going, and that cannot be disputed. The use of gunpowder charges to blow apart medieval masonry as an expedient in so-called 'restoration' is unparalleled in our experience. Considering that neither building was ever deemed to be in imminent danger of collapse, the extent of Balleine's underpinning is quite extraordinary. He was plainly obsessed by the supposed need (symbolic?) for churches to have rock-based foundations: 'All the work is now solid and secure, and long may it remain so' (Balleine, 1932, 37). But, tragically, the very process of creating this solidity led to the almost total eradication of the precious architectural and archaeological evidence that lay hidden behind the wallplaster, and beneath the floors and ground around these ancient buildings. Were that evidence still intact, it would have been possible to recover a more explicit chronology for the chapel and to have provided a much fuller and less equivocal account of the successive functions it served. Modern church archaeology was, however, unborn in the 1920s, so that the opportunities missed at the time can only now be fully appreciated (Rodwell, 1989, 26–37).

An unfortunate component of nineteenth- and early twentieth-century restorations was the widespread use of portland cement for pointing, crack-filling and internal rendering. While at the time the dangers were not foreseen, it has been appreciated in recent years that cement is incompatible with the lime-mortars used in ancient buildings. It is not merely a matter of aesthetics, since there are also physical and chemical inter-actions which rapidly accelerate the decay of the original work. This is particularly disastrous in a building such as the Fishermen's Chapel, where medieval paintings survive on lime plaster. Cement was used prodigiously for repairing, patching and rendering in the chapel, and one of the urgent necessities of the recent restoration was to cut out as much of this alien material as possible. All fresh and replacement repairs and rendering have been carried out using lime-based mortars and plasters.

Below ground, one of the aims of the archaeological study was to ascertain whether the entire chapel had been underpinned, since surviving records were ambiguous on this point. Apart from knowing that the work was carried out in stages, as funds permitted, over the course of about seven years, no detailed documentation has survived. However, it has now been established that the internal underpinning, at least, was fully completed, save a tiny area under the north end of the sanctuary step. It may be of interest to record here the procedure adopted for the work, as revealed by archaeology.

The individual stages of the internal underpinning are all shown in fig. 46A. The first, presumably experimental, area tackled was a three-foot length between the south chancel window and the pilaster. A small hole was dug (F25) and a vertically shuttered concrete foundation constructed (F24). This was the only part of the work carried out in that fashion. The main underpinning was then begun to the west of this trial area, and carried along the south wall, working in short stages (labelled F22a-g). The method adopted here, and subsequently, did not involve shuttering; instead, the foundations were under-built, and a sloping apron of boulders set in concrete was constructed in the base of the underpinning trench. The uppermost edge of the apron approximately corresponds with the base-level of the original chapel foundation (Fig. 45).

Underpinning on the north side began at the sanctuary step and progressed westwards, again in short stages (F23a-h). In this phase work did not stop at the north-west corner of the chapel, but continued down the west side. Finally, the sanctuary was tackled in three stages. First, a trench was dug along the south wall, eastward from the trial area, to the south-east corner, passing under the sanctuary step. Underpinning was inserted and a concrete apron formed, as elsewhere (F17). Next, the north wall was given similar treatment, but without digging under the sanctuary step (F20).

The second stage of the work involved trenching across the east end, and that is when the bell-metal furnace (Balleine's 'hearth') was discovered, causing a modification of tactics. Leaving the furnace *in situ*, trenches were dug to either side and two small areas of underpinning inserted beneath the east wall (F13 and F15). When that was accomplished, the enclosure of shuttered concrete was erected around the furnace. Finally, in a third phase, it was decided to destroy the protected furnace by digging a pit inside the concrete box, and inserting the last area of underpinning (F11).

Thus the sequence of Balleine's internal underpinning operations may be summarised as follows: trial area in the chancel; south wall of nave; north wall of chancel and nave, and west end; south side of sanctuary; north side of sanctuary; and, finally, the east end. The external underpinning, where it has been exposed around the north-west angle of the chapel, is of shuttered concrete, with an apron; this work was apparently carried out before that inside the building.

9. TECHNICAL APPENDICES

1. Human Skeletal Remains
by Juliet Rogers

Scant remains from ten articulated skeletons and two large bags of disarticulated bone from the chapel were received for examination. The latter were sorted into different types of bone in order that the minimum number of individuals represented could be estimated. These bones were also inspected for any abnormalities.

The ten skeletons, although excavated as articulated groups, had very little bone remaining, and were too few in number to be really informative. The age, sex and stature of most of the individuals was consequently indeterminable.

THE SKELETONS

Seven adults and three children were represented in this group. The children were approximately 2–3 years, 6–9 years and 8–10 years old at death. These ages were estimated from the maximum lengths of the diaphyses of the long bones present, which is a very much less certain method than age estimation by tooth eruption or fusion of epiphyses (those classes of evidence not being available from these fragmentary skeletons). In addition, the remains of two more children were found but not lifted for examination. Both were estimated by the excavator as probably being under three years of age at death. In one case (skeleton 1) the bones had dissolved, leaving only a

Table 1: Inventory of Skeletons

Skeleton	Grave	Bones Present	Age	Abnormalities
1	F72	Soil silhouette and crumbs of femora only	up to 3	–
2	F71	Possibly complete, but sealed by concrete	up to 3	–
3	F73	Legs and pelvis	8–10	–
4	F74	Lower legs	adult	–
5	F80	Tibiae and other leg fragments. Poor condition	6–9	–
6	F81	Left foot and a few hand bones	adult	–
7	F82	Fragments of child's skeleton	2–3	–
8	F76	Pair of femora, left humerus, pair of fragmentary ulnae, hand fragments. ?male	adult	osteoarthritis of thumb
9	F66	Left femur and patella	adult	–
10	F67	Fibula fragment	adult	
11	F77	Left humerus and lower legs	adult	healed fracture of ankle joint
12	F75	Right femur and fibula fragment	adult	–

152

few crumbs and a silhouette-stain in the sand, while the other (skeleton 2) appeared to be intact, but was almost entirely sealed by concrete.

There was very little bone disease present, or other evidence of abnormalities. Skeleton 8 had eburnation and osteophytes on the head of the first metacarpal (thumb); these are the bone changes seen in osteoarthritis. Skeleton 11 showed signs of a healed fracture of the medial malleolus of the left tibia (shin).

DISARTICULATED BONE

Two large sacks of bone were examined, comprising over five hundred fragments in all. This material was entirely recovered from the backfilling of Balleine's trenches of 1927–35, but was evidently derived from medieval graves within the chapel. The bones were sorted into their different types and the minimum numbers of individuals represented in each category estimated. Bones from all parts of the body were present, from both adults and children. There were no pathological abnormalities which would enable dismembered skeletons to be reconstituted.

The minimum number of individuals present was eighteen, of which eleven were adult, three were immature (aged 14–18), and four juvenile. In all this material there was only one bone with an abnormality, a humerus shaft with signs of a healed fracture.

A full inventory of the disarticulated bone has been made, and a summary of the types of bone present and the numbers of individuals represented is given in Table 2.

A note on the skeletal remains from the 1985 excavation in the churchyard (Area 2) will be included with the report on Saint Brelade's Church (Rodwell, forthcoming).

Table 2: Summary Analysis of Disarticulated Bone

Part of Skeleton	Number of Individuals Represented	
Skull	8	
Mandible	7	including 2 juvenile
Maxilla	7	including 1 juvenile
Clavicle	4	including 1 juvenile
Vertebrae	5	
Humerus	14	including 3 immature
Ulna	14	including 1 juvenile
Radius	9	including 1 juvenile
Hands	5	
Pelvis	15	including 6 adult female
		5 adult male
		4 juvenile
Femur	15	including 3 immature
		2 juvenile
Tibia	10	including 1 immature
Fibula	4	
Patella	3	
Feet	5	

2. Bell Founding Equipment

The structure of the bell-casting pit (F26) has been described on pp. 64–6. Within the primary filling, around and under the fired-clay mould, were finds which indicated previous casting activity in the chapel: charcoal, splashes of copper alloy and, most distinctively, two fragments of the core of another bell mould. This core was fabricated in two stages: the inner part consists of friable, sandy clay (evidently loess) tempered with a small amount of finely chopped vegetable material; the outer surface (i.e. that which was in contact with the metal when the bell was cast) comprises a layer of harder, finer clay *c.* 4 mm in thickness. This layer is slightly micaceous and buff in colour, with a dark reddish-brown surface. There is no possibility of these fragments being derived from the excavated bell mould.

The mould found *in situ* comprised the usual two elements, the conical core, and the outer envelope or cope; the lowest 10–15 cm of these survived almost in their entirety, although some parts of the rim of the cope were displaced when the bell was withdrawn from the ground (Fig. 52). The core was built from broken pieces of red clay roof tile, bedded in coarse, yellow sandy clay (Fig. 54A and Pl. 32B). The surfaces of both the core and the cope, where they were in contact with the bell-metal, were finished with a finer layer of slightly micaceous clay which gave a smooth, dense surface, suitable for turning out a good quality casting. This layer varied from 2 mm to 6 mm in thickness, and has a near-burnished appearance. The cope wall averaged 6 cm thick and was made of coarse yellow clay, containing a considerable amount of chopped vegetable material as a binding agent. The moulding surface of both cope and core have been consistently fired black through contact with the liquid metal, to a depth more-or-less equivalent to the thickness of the finer clay layer, beyond which the colours merged from brown to red, as the effects of the applied heat diminished. The centre of the core and outermost part of the cope remained as yellow, plastic clay.

There was a clean, conical joint between the cope and the core (Fig. 54A), indicating that the two elements were capable of being separated, and perfectly reunited again. This would have been necessary for the removal of the waxen 'ghost' of the bell which initially occupied the space between the inner and outer moulds. In this instance it is clear that the wax could not have been removed from the mould by applying heat *in situ*, as was the usual medieval practice. Here, the only way to clear the mould was to lift off the cope and cut the wax out, a process described by Diderot, who was a contemporary of the Saint Brelade's bell founder. Diderot (1753, 541–2, and 1767) illustrated a casting process which differed significantly from that generally employed in the Middle Ages, and described by the Benedictine monk, Theophilus, in *De Diversis Artibus* (for a general discussion of the subject, see Blagg, 1974, 133–49).

The octagonal wooden 'box' around the mould is an unusual feature, not normally encountered in the excavation of bell foundries. It cannot have been very tall (unless it comprised a series of drum-like sections placed one on top of another) because it would have impeded the construction of the clay mould. It is likely that the box was merely a form of reinforcement lining the pit, to prevent damage and distortion while the mould-maker worked with soft clay. The soil being loose and sandy, it would have been easy to damage the mould whilst kneeling in the pit and carrying out the delicate task of forming the core and modelling the bell's detailing in wax. Also, when the cope was lifted off in order to clear out the wax, it was vital to ensure that no loose earth or stones could trickle into the pit and foul the carefully made joint between the cope and the core.

The size of the bell can be approximately calculated, basing a reconstruction on the extant fragments of the mould (Fig. 54). The diameter at the rim was 70 cm and at the crown *c.* 42 cm. The height is less certain since it was not possible to build up a full profile, most of the surviving sherds being small and badly crushed. The sound-bow was ornamented with three pairs of raised ribs, and there was a band of ribs and hollow mouldings just below the shoulder. This position was frequently occupied by an inscription, cast in the bell, but that was plainly not the case here. The lettered fragments belong to a two-line inscription, set between three pairs of raised ribs, which must have been located lower down on the waist of the bell.

Six inscribed fragments and one piece of scroll decoration were recovered; the impressions in the mould were negative and retrograde, and would originally have been sharply defined, but are now badly degraded (Fig. 112).

No. 1. Upper line inscribed]CR[4. Inscribed]DE[(*?Brelade*)
       Lower line]AI[or]AL[5. Inscribed]EDO[
    2. Upper line]AN[(*?sanctus*)   6. Probably inscribed]WEI[(rather than]VEI[ )
    3. Word beginning N[7. Upper line with fragment of running scroll motif

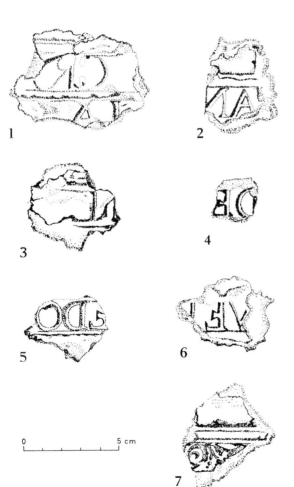

0   5 cm

Fig. 112. Fragments of inscribed and decorated bell-mould, associated with bell casting in the chapel in 1754.

Two substantial blobs of bronze, resulting from the spillage of molten bell-metal onto the earth, were recovered from the underpinning trenches in the chancel. Of irregular form, one averages 7 cm in diameter, and the other measures *c*. 15 cm by 6 cm. Metal analyses have not been undertaken.

3. Pottery and Tile
by Margaret Finlaison

The material found during the excavations came mainly from redeposited contexts. Possible interesting exceptions appear to be the sherds from graves F77 and F78, within the chapel, and from the old topsoil outside (F107). Although mainly in small sherds, the periods seen to be represented are: late Iron Age to Gallo-Roman, prior to 1100, 1100–1400, 1450–1550, and 1700 onward.

With the exception of three English post-medieval examples, all the pottery is regional French. The sample is small but, particularly within the chapel, the ceramics of the fifteenth and sixteenth centuries predominate, more specially the period 1450–1550.

A numbered catalogue of the 91 sherds has been prepared, which includes all the pottery recovered from the excavations of 1982–85; only the items capable of meaningful illustration are shown in Fig. 113.

Of the three unstratified Iron Age and Gallo-Roman sherds, one is certainly early (no. 71), one is late (no. 70), and the third is indeterminate. Iron Age traditions of form and fabric did not die out

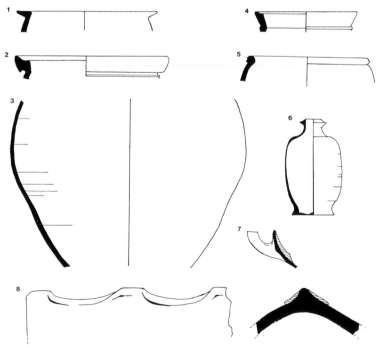

Fig. 113. Medieval and later pottery from the excavations, 1982–85. No. 8 is a crested ridge-tile. Scale 1:4.

here after the onset of Roman influence, but appear to have continued at least into the second century. This can be seen, for example, in the large Gallo-Roman assemblage from La Palaiderie, Guernsey (inf. R. Burns, under investigation). The two small sherds (nos. 90 and 91) from the old topsoil layer (F107) are late Gallo-Roman and in a fabric which anticipates the tradition of North-Western French Gritted wares, but lacks the hardness of firing which is characteristic of that pottery from the eleventh century onwards. Again, in the Normandy region, the production of thinly potted, well fired gritted wares never entirely ceased after the Roman era, and this inhibits a closer identification here.

The twelfth to fifteenth centuries are represented by various types of the well known Normandy Gritted ware (NGW). Sometimes found at sites along the south-east coast of England, it is the most common medieval pottery of the Channel Islands (Barton and Thomson, 1980; Finlaison, 1976). It is consistently a hard fired and thinly potted ware, with quartz usually being the most obvious tempering. Surface finishes range from grey-black, through orange, buff and cream, to off-white. The two visually distinct sherds from adjoining graves F122 and F131, are very likely from the same vessel, and are attributed to the twelfth-to-thirteenth century. The application of an organic wash before firing, to provide a partial or wholly grey-black finish to an otherwise oxidized pot (nos. 32 and 34), is commonly found on thirteenth-century wares in Jersey. However, there is no reason at present to assume that the practice did not continue. In the absence of any of the products of Rouen, Beauvais or the Saintonge, these sherds alone cannot give close dates.

The pottery of the fifteenth-to-sixteenth century forms a distinct and recognisable assemblage, consisting of Developed Normandy Gritted ware, North-West French Buff near-Stonewares, grey and brown Normandy Stonewares, and 'Chocolate Brown' ware. The date proposed for the greater part of this group is c. 1450–1550.

These plain wares occur on a number of sites in Jersey and Guernsey, including Mont Orgueil Castle (Barton, 1977), Vale Castle (Barton and Thomson, 1984) and Castle Cornet (inf. K.J. Barton). In Jersey, the largest stratified group, that from a domestic building in Hue Street, Saint Helier (Finlaison, under investigation), also contains Beauvais, Merida and Saintonge wares, giving a date range between c. 1480 and 1550. Another small assemblage was sealed under a paved floor when a room was refurbished in Prynnes Tower, Mont Orgueil (Finlaison, forthcoming). The walls were then decorated in a style thought by Doctor Clive Rouse to be late fifteenth or early sixteenth century. At Vale Castle in Guernsey, the group also included Saint Germain ware from Cornwall, and the date proposed for the raising of the castle is 1450–1550.

Although Normandy Stoneware (NSW) may occur in the islands in the first half of the fifteenth century, it cannot be securely dated before c. 1450. From then on it is found throughout the post-medieval period. Represented here are the plum/brown, red and grey forms. The Developed Normandy Gritted ware was still in use at least until 1480. Vessels of this fabric from Hue Street are flat-rimmed bowls or dishes with partial green glazing, and that is what sherd no. 51 may represent.

The pottery described by Ken Barton as 'Chocolate Brown' ware (nos. 15–17) occurs in all the Jersey groups. It is a light brown colour throughout and usually has a smooth finish, but the tempering can vary. It has been suggested from Brittany that the source is Lamballe – La Poterie (Côtes-du-Nord).

No parallel can be found for the crested ridge tile (nos. 45–49; Fig. 113.8). The fabric, finish and firing so closely resemble those of the other Buff wares that the tile is probably attributable to the same source. After the Normandy Stonewares, the smooth, hard fired Buff wares are the second commonest material found in these groups. Often they have a flush of reduction grey externally and a grey core, sometimes a fully reduced interior and, occasionally, partial green glazing.

What is probably a little grey Normandy Stoneware bottle (nos. 75 and 76) represents an unchanging style. Known in Guernsey in the sixteenth century, the only datable examples in Jersey come from the eighteenth or early nineteenth centuries when, amongst their many uses, they were known to hold *eau de vie*, cordial and calvados. The type is here illustrated from a mid-eighteenth-century example (Fig. 113.6).

In view of the ecclesiastical nature of the site, it is perhaps worth noting that the medieval French custom of including funeral vessels holding holy water, oil or incense with a burial has, not surprisingly, been found in Jersey. One or more pots might be placed at the head, hands or feet. This was a widespread practice did not die out in France until the eighteenth century (Cochet, 1857, 351–96). Almost any type of vessel was brought into use, including jugs. The example from Saint Lawrence's churchyard, Jersey, dates from the late eleventh century.

Catalogue

A full catalogue of the pottery found in the excavations is deposited with the excavation archive.[1] Here, only the illustrated items are described (Fig. 113).

1. Cat. no. 9. Rim of small jar. Brown Normandy Stoneware. Grave F133.
2. Cat. no. 6. Heavy rim of jar. Hard fired orange-buff Normandy Gritted ware; distinctive heavy quartz tempering, and much vein quartz. Similar to a sherd from grave F131. Twelfth to thirteenth century. Grave F122a.
3. Cat. nos. 1–2. Two large, fitting body sherds of a jug or jar. Buff Near-Stoneware. Grave F77.
4. Cat. no. 29. Rim sherd of jug or pitcher. Plum-brown Normandy Stoneware. Bell pit, F26.
5. Cat. no. 17. Two body sherds and one rim sherd of a jar. Chocolate Brown ware. Smooth red-brown, hard fired earthenware; burnt on the outer faces. Similar sherds also from the backfilling of modern trenches. Bell pit, F26.
6. Cat. nos. 75–76. Two tiny, near-eggshell-thin sherds, probably from a small bottle of the type illustrated here in full profile. Grey Normandy Stoneware. Topsoil beside transept, F101.
7. Cat. no. 37. Small solid rod handle and body sherd from a dish or cup. Buff Near-Stoneware. Partial reduction and ash glaze on outer face. Khaki green glaze on interior. Modern trench filling.
8. Cat. nos. 45–49. Five connecting sections of a crested roof ridge tile. Buff Near-Stoneware, with grey core; spatter of leaf-green glaze. *c.* A.D. 1450–1550. Modern trench filling inside chapel.

NOTES TO CHAPTERS

Chapter 1

1. *Archaeol. Journ.*, 16 (1849), 89.
2. Assemblée Ecclésiastique, 9 May 1877.
3. *ibid.*, 9 August 1883.
4. *ibid.*, 28 February 1884.
5. *ibid.*, 26 March 1884.
6. *ibid.*, 8 July 1884.
7. There was one meeting held in the chapel per annum, except in the following years: 1913, 1917, 1918, 1928–30, 1932–41 (no meetings); 1890, 1895, 1902, 1904, 1914, 1923, 1926, 1943 (two meetings); 1892, 1893, 1927 (three meetings).
8. Minute book, Assemblée Ecclésiastique, 3 January and 24 April 1905.
9. Assemblée Civile, 26 April 1905.
10. Assemblée Ecclésiastique, 7 January 1908. The completion of the work was recorded on 12 May 1908, and subsequently inspected by the president of the Island Ecclesiastical Court (minute, 20 July 1908).
11. The date given (1918) is impossible in the recorded sequence of events: see further pp. 104–5.
12. An anonymous, vituperative attack on Oppenheim was published in the *Jersey Evening Post*, 2 August 1916.
13. A.N. Oppenheim, 'The Wallpainting in the Fishermen's Chapel of St. Brelade's, Jersey, C.I.', a manuscript report dated September 1949, in the Library of the Société Jersiaise.
14. Assemblée Ecclésiastique, 22 September 1926.
15. *ibid.*, 4 February 1927.
16. *ibid.*, 11 February 1927. £70 was voted for this work.
17. *ibid.*, 24 October 1927.
18. *ibid.*, 7 January 1915. Four designs were approved on this occasion, and a fifth had been considered a year earlier, *ibid.*, 20 February 1914. The first design was that for the east window, which must have been made and installed more-or-less immediately: a photograph taken, probably in 1915, upon the completion of Oppenheim's work on the east wall painting, shows the window already in place. Balleine's dating of this window to 1906 is erroneous (Balleine, 1932, 30). The photograph is in the F. de L. Bois collection (135–106–19).
19. Assemblée Ecclésiastique, 23 September 1935; also *Jersey Evening Post* of the same date. It is curious that no fuller press coverage of Balleine's restoration seems to have been attempted. A manuscript account of the Fishermen's Chapel, written by an English architectural enthusiast, during a visit in 1933, contains no mention of the restoration: K.H. Leach, 'Notes on Church Architecture', vol. 16, 374–5 (British Library, Add. ms. 47706). The same volume contains coloured illustrations of the bent-riband decoration and quatrefoil band on the east wall.
20. *Archaeologial Journal*, 54 (1897), 410–11.
21. The first step towards this was taken in 1966, when a detailed set of plans and elevation drawings of the church and chapel was prepared by P.J.A. Winn, an architectural student. There are copies at the National Monuments Record, London: ref. BB70/6820–6826.
22. Assemblée Ecclésiastique, 4 May 1971.
23. E.C. Rouse, 'Wall Paintings in the Churches and Chapels of the Island of Jersey'. Manuscript report dated 9 May 1972, in the Library of the Société Jersiaise.

24. E.C. Rouse, 'Conservation of the Wall Paintings in the Fishermen's Chapel, St. Brelade's, Jersey'. Manuscript reports dated June 1973, and 24 June 1975.
25. W.J. and K.A. Rodwell, 'The Fishermen's Chapel, St. Brelade, Jersey: A Report on its Architectural History and Archaeology'. Manuscript report dated 26 May 1982.
26. W.J. Rodwell, *ibid.*, 'Second Report', 'Third Report' and 'Fourth Report'. Manuscript reports dated, respectively, 26 September 1982, 5 December 1983 and 20 May 1984. Also, W.J. Rodwell, 'St. Brelade's Church, Jersey: Archaeological Study of the South Transept'. Manuscript report dated December 1986.
27. M. Katkov, C. Oldenbourg, U. Fuhrer and G. Hauff, 'The Fishermen's Chapel, St. Brelade, Jersey. Conservation of Wall Paintings: nave vault, 1982'. U. Fuhrer, G. Hauff, D. Cavezzali and S. Mieth, 'The Fishermen's Chapel, St. Brelade, Jersey. Conservation of Wall Paintings: nave and chancel, 1983'. D. Cavezzali, U. Fuhrer, G. Hauff, S. Mieth and W. Schmid, 'The Fishermen's Chapel, St. Brelade, Jersey, Conservation of Wall Paintings, 1984.' U. Fuhrer, G. Hauff and S. Mieth, 'The Fishermen's Chapel, St. Brelade, Jersey. Conservation of Wall Paintings, 1985'. Manuscript reports in the Library of the Société Jersiaise.

Chapter 2

1. It is possible that the cross derives originally from the church, where it was superseded by a new one in the 1880s. The colour and texture of the Chausey granite from which it is made are consistent with other late medieval work in the church, but distinctly different from the beds quarried in the nineteenth century (inf. Doctor John Renouf).

Chapter 3

1. No traces of limewash were found over the polychromy here during the recent conservation work.
2. Again implying that the paintings on the walls were obliterated with limewash.
3. Keyser, incidentally, followed the anonymous writer in *The Builder* in giving the Fishermen's Chapel the alternative appellation of 'Notre Dame des Pas'. This is wholly erroneous, since the destroyed Chapelle des Pas was at Saint Helier.
4. Oppenheim, 1916; in nineteenth-century descriptions of the paintings no attempt was made to explain the iconographical programme: de la Croix, 1859, Anon., 1864, and Anon., 1884.
5. E.C. Rouse, 'Conservation of the Wall Paintings in the Fishermen's Chapel, St. Brelade's, Jersey'. Manuscript report, 24 June 1975.
6. Oppenheim (1916, 22) records that in his day the word *Ave* was still legible.
7. According to Oppenheim (1916, 24), the dove has not been lost: it was never there.
8. Like the olive tree, the fig tree bearing fruit was interpreted as the Tree of Life, and was associated with the Virgin Mary, or the Church; the fig tree that bears no fruit was associated with the synagogue. However, the tree can also symbolize the end of time (Kirschmann, 1970, 22).
9. Balleine, 1932, 33; E.C. Rouse, 1975 (see note 5 above). Keyser (1883) was responsible for introducing the notion that the Assumption was depicted on the east wall.
10. The Assumption of the Virgin became a main subject for churches dedicated in honour of the Virgin Mary only from the sixteenth century onwards (Kirschmann, 1970, 276).
11. For examples of this, see Kirschmann, 1970, 42.
12. See M. Thibout, 'L'Église de Marchesieux', *Congrès Archéologique de France* 214 (1966), 266 ff, 277. Paris. It is remarked that the female figure could be a washer-woman. According to popular belief in Normandy, women whose children had died without baptism were supposed to vent their grief at night and wake the sleeping villages with the noise of their washing-beaters; see, J. Cuisinier, *Récits et Contes Populaire de la Normandie*, 1 (1979), 60. Paris.
13. Looking at the more famous late Gothic paintings of the Last Judgement, we find immense conglomerations of

figures such as the Twelve Apostles, Saint Michael weighing the souls, the Blessed and the Damned, etc. (Kirschmann, 1972, 513).

14.

	Earlier Painting		Later Painting
Oppenheim, 1916, 3, 5	1300–1350		1400–1430
Borenius and Tristram, 1927, 40		–1425–	
Tristram, 1955, 187		–1400–	
Balleine, 1932, 32	1310–1315		15th century
*Rouse, 1985	1330–1340		early 15th century

*E.C. Rouse, 'The Wall Paintings in the Fishermen's Chapel, St. Brelade's, Jersey'. Manuscript report dated 20 May 1985.

15. For the changes in hairstyles, see Enlart, 1916, 186.

16. The development of the iconography of the Annunciation between 1300 and 1400 is discussed in Robb, 1936, 480ff.

17. Illustrated in Y. Bonneyfoy and P. Devinoy, *Peinture Murale de La France Gothique* (Paris, 1954), pl. 56. For dating see *ibid.* 164.

18. Consultation of the catalogue of the Congrès Archéologique de France proved fruitless.

19. A still valid picture of the development of art at that time in relation to the new piety is provided in Male, 1908, ch. 1.

20. The English translation of the text is in Ragusa, 1961.

21. It should be noted that there is still some confusion in the exact definition of the different techniques. For instance, in Phillipot and Mora (1984, 10) a distinction is made between 'lime fresco technique' and 'lime secco technique', in our opinion a rather academic distinction. We prefer the concept of the 'lime-painting technique', mentioned for instance by O. Emmenecker, 'Techniken der Wandmalerei, ihre Schäden und die Typischen Schadensursachen', in *Historische Technologie und Konservierung von Wandmalerei*, 1985, 76 (Bern).

22. *ibid.*, 131–2.

Chapter 4

1. The *Actes* of the *Assemblée Ecclésiastique* from 1828 to the present day are contained in three volumes, held at the Rectory.

2. Doctor Renouf's full report is lodged with the excavation archive; he identified the three layers as 'top clean sand' (F100a), 'gravelly lens' (F100b) and 'basal gravelly sand' (F100c). In his report he interprets the sequence as follows:

'The sand body was formed from sand blown by the wind onto a surface of decomposed granite. The sand shows little evidence of derivation from a beach, and the poor rounding and presence of original rock material still adhering to many of the quartz grains would suggest that the sand is itself derived from a decomposed granite surface nearby (hundreds of metres, rather than thousands). From time to time, little rivulets brought coarser material onto the sand surface, almost certainly from a little higher upslope from the site.

The absence of beach sand and of loess would suggest the time of accumulation to have been after the end of the last glacial, before the main growth of vegetation and rise of sea level during the post-glacial. A comparison with the sands found above the main La Cotte deposits in the North Ravine (St. Brelade) is possible though unproven.'

3. The placing of whole or fragmentary pottery vessels in graves, although commonest in pagan interments, is occasionally encountered in Christian burials down to the nineteenth century (eg. Rodwell and Rodwell, 1981, 215); see further appendix 3, p. 158.

4. Reference HAR-8617. A.D. 440±40, uncalibrated. Calibration would bring this date into the sixth century; however, radio-carbon determinations on shell are not considered as reliable as those on bone.

5. Reference HAR-8618. A.D. 730±90, uncalibrated. A.D. 720–900, calibrated (68% confidence range), or A.D. 640–1000 (95% confidence range).

6. Reference HAR-8609. A.D. 850±40, uncalibrated. This may be calibrated to A.D. 890–985 (68% confidence range), or A.D. 880–1010 (95% confidence range).

Chapter 5

1. These are the levelling joints denoting the end of each day's work; discussed in Rodwell, 1989, 137–9.
2. One piece bears red-painted decoration, and a single fragment was derived from a stratified context in floor F39 (Fig. 47B).
3. Similar mortar occurs in Saint Brelade's Church, in the *tourelle*. Here the yellow sandy mortar is confined to the masonry associated with the insertion of the high-level doorway onto the rood loft, and also some secondary patching around the lower doorway. Again, the date is fourteenth or fifteenth century. There is a late medieval stone cresset lamp, of micalamprophyre, in Saint Brelade's Church (currently in use as a miniature portable font).
4. The pair of iron-studded doors seen in the Victorian photograph (Fig. 6) probably date from the eighteenth or early nineteenth century.
5. The earlier vaulted nave in the same church, with its exposed masonry, does not now exhibit a regular series of large sockets; but that does not disprove their former existence. It may merely mean that they have been carefully blocked.
6. Minute book, Assemblée Ecclésiastique, 26 April 1905.
7. In the absence of natural lime in the Channel Islands, the local loess was commonly used (with or without an admixture of chopped straw) to form clay-mortars and clay-renders throughout the Middle Ages, and down to modern times. On present evidence, it would appear that the importing of lime began in the Norman period, and then only for use in royal and ecclesiastical works. In domestic contexts in Jersey, lime-mortars and lime-plasters are rare before the nineteenth century. A detailed study of the subject has been carried out on the buildings at Hamptonne, Saint Lawrence.

Chapter 7

1. Analyses of several plaster samples were carried out in 1982 in the Jersey States Analyst Laboratory and the Geology Department of the Open University of Jersey. Details are given in M. Katkov, C. Oldenbourg, U. Fuhrer and G. Hauff, 'The Fishermen's Chapel, St. Brelade, Jersey: Conservation of Wall Paintings, 1982'. Manuscript report in the Library of the Société Jersiaise.
2. A.N. Oppenheim, 'The Wall Painting in the Fishermen's Chapel of St. Brelade's. Jersey', p. 2. Manuscript report, dated September 1949, in the Library of the Société Jersiaise.
3. There appears to be no record of lime burning taking place before the late eighteenth century (J. Stevens, 1977, 27–8).
4. Oppenheim, *op. cit.* (note 2), p. 2.
5. *ibid.*, 1.
6. The same story was told by Rector Tabb (n.d., 4).
7. P. Burman, 'St. Brelade, Jersey: The Church and Fishermen's Chapel'. Manuscript report, dated December 1981, in the Library of the Société Jersiaise.
8. See note 1 above.
9. See, for instance, Phillipot and Mora, 1984, 294.
10. Since Oppenheim's account (1916) deals exclusively with the iconographic side of the painting, we have no record of the binding medium used. Its resistance to the solvents tried suggests that it may well have been isinglass, as Rouse assumes in his report of 1973 (see note 24, p. 160).
11. Together with the co-authors of this report (U. Fuhrer, G. Hauff and S. Mieth), two colleagues from Italy (D. Cavezzali and W. Schmid), and two from England (M. Katkov and C. Oldenbourg) took part in the conservation project.
12. For more detailed and specific information, see: 'The Fishermen's Chapel, St. Brelade, Jersey. Conservation of Wall Paintings'. Manuscript reports 1–4, 1982–85 (see note 27, p. 160).
13. Then of Nigel Biggar and Partners, now of David Barlow Associates.
14. The stone has been identified by Doctor John Renouf, whose detailed description is lodged with the site archive.

15.   Doctor Renouf reports: 'the stoup is fashioned out of a slab taken from a single bed of cream coloured, compact crystalline limestone marked with laminations. The basal few centimetres are weakly bedded, the weathering and break-down of which gives the uneven quality to this part of the vessel. Moluscan shell fragments are visible in this lower section and are probably pieces of the bivalve *Inoceramus*.

   'As to origin, the most that I would wish to say is that the limestone is Lower to Middle Jurassic in age, and would be equally at home in the cliffs and quarries of the Bessin around Bayeux and Caen or in the south of England from the Cotswolds to the coast, though with Purbeck-Portland as a particularly likely candidate.'

16.   The displaced Bosdet glass has been deposited in the Jersey Museum.

Chapter 8

1.   *Extente de l'Île de Jersey*, 1227.
2.   *Livre Noir de Coutances*, 1278.
3.   *Extente*, 1331.
4.   Rodwell, 1986; and W.J. Rodwell, 'St. Mary's Priory, La Maître Île, Les Écréhous, Jersey: An Interim Report on the Archaeological Excavations, 1988'. Manuscript report in the Library of the Société Jersiaise.
5.   Recorded in 1042: Stevens, Arthur and Stevens, 1986, 483.
6.   There has been a confusing misuse of terminology by Balleine and others: allusions to a supposed presence of 'monks', and other aspects of monastic activity, at Saint Brelade are wholly erroneous. There was certainly no monastic presence here in the Middle Ages; nor is there anything to commend the suggestion that the wall paintings in the Fishermen's Chapel were executed by monks, as assumed by Balleine (1932, 33).
7.   McCormack unfortunately mistook the feature for an altar recess, drawing erroneous comparisons with recesses in other Jersey churches (McCormack, 1986, 193).
8.   As an aside, it worth instancing the ease with which casual, or even frivolous, remarks, based on no evidence whatever, can enter the record and add to an already overburdened mythology. In 1984 a local historian mused on the possibility that an incorrectly placed accent at some earlier period, changing *pécheurs* to *pêcheurs*, could have derived 'The Fishermen's Chapel' out of 'The Sinners' Chapel'. Regrettably, this has already appeared in print as a serious proposition (McCormack, 1986, 295). Quite apart from the fact that written accents were of no relevance to the verbal transmission of local lore, and the contextual use of *pêcheurs* would have perpetuated the correct meaning, all medieval chapels were for sinners' use. Sinners were neither a suitable subject for a guild, nor a dedication!
9.   *Ann. Bull. Soc. Jersiaise*, 6, 111–14.
10.   This was formerly in the Library of the Société Jersiaise, but is now missing; it is referred to in Stevens, 1967, 250.
11.   Bois, 1976, 26; and *Ann. Bull. Soc. Jersiaise*, 23.3 (1983), 382.
12.   Cf. for example, the destruction of the hearth, p. 52, and the account of the foundation offsets, p. 60). His accounts are also replete with errors in historical fact and art-historical detail. Balleine was also responsible for misreading the king's name Caspar, as 'les Mages', and for sundry other errors in the description of the wall paintings (Balleine, 1932, 33–4). He compounded the confusion by perpetuating the incorrect identification of the fifteenth-century painting on the east wall as the Assumption (after Keyser, 1883).

Chapter 9

1.   The finds and records deriving from the 1982–85 excavations have been deposited in the Jersey Museum.

BIBLIOGRAPHY

ANON. [BAKER], 1840. *Caesarea. The Island of Jersey.* London.

ANON., 1850. 'A Few Notes on Jersey Churches', *Ecclesiologist*, 10, 176–83.

ANON., 1864. 'The Coloured Decoration of Churches', *The Builder*, 22 (No. 1131), 733–4.

ANON., 1884. 'Excursion de La Société Française D'Archéologie à L'Ile de Jersey', *Congrès Archéologique de France, en 1883*, 410ff. Paris.

BAKER, T., (publisher) 1844. *A Guide to the Island of Jersey.* London.

BALLEINE, G.R., 1946. 'Our Ancient Churches: IV St. Brelade's', *The Pilot*, 1, 115–16. Jersey.

BALLEINE, G.R., and STEVENS, J., 1970. *The Bailiwick of Jersey.* Revised edition. London.

BALLEINE, J.A., [1907]. *The Church of St. Brelade, Jersey: Its Restoration (1895–1900).* Privately printed, Jersey. Also published in *Ann. Bull. Soc. Jersiaise*, 6 (1909), 224–45.

BALLEINE, J.A., [1932]. *The Story of St. Brelade Church, Jersey.* The first of nine editions. Privately printed, Gloucester.

BARTON, K.J., 1977. 'Medieval and Post-Medieval Pottery from Gorey Castle', *Ann. Bull. Soc. Jersiaise*, 22, 69–82.

BARTON, K.J., and THOMSON, R., 1980. 'Excavations at Chateau des Marais, Guernsey', *Rep. Trans. Soc. Guernsiaise*, 20, 677–86.

BARTON, K.J., and THOMSON, R., 1984. 'Excavations at the Vale Castle, Guernsey, C.I.', *Rep. Trans. Soc. Guernsiaise*, 21, 512–19.

BISSON, S.W. (ed.), 1975. *The Jersey Chantry Certificate of 1550.* Société Jersiaise.

BLAGG, T.F.C., 1974. 'An Umbrian Abbey: San Paolo di Valdiponte, Part 2', *Papers of the British School at Rome*, 42, 99–178.

BOIS, F. DE L., 1976. *The Parish Church of St. Saviour, Jersey.* Chichester.

BONNEFOY, Y., and DEVINOY, P., 1954. *Peinture Murale de La France Gothique.* Paris.

BORENIUS, T., and TRISTRAM, E.W., 1927. *English Medieval Painting.* London.

BORENIUS, T., and TRISTRAM, E.W., 1927a. *Englische Malerei des Mittelalters.* Munich.

DE BREFFNY, B., and MOTT, G., 1976. *The Churches and Abbeys of Ireland.* London.

COCHET, E.A., 1857. *Sépultures Gauloises, Romaines, Franques et Normanes.* Paris.

DE LA CROIX, J.N.R., 1859. *Jersey: Ses Antiquités, Ses Institutions, Son Histoire*, vols. 1 and 3. Jersey.

DIDEROT, D., 1753. *L'Encyclopédie, ou Dictionnaire Raisonné des Sciences, des Arts and des Metiers*, vol. 3. Paris.

DIDEROT, D., 1767. *Recueil de Planches sur les Sciences, les Arts Libéraux et les Arts Mécaniques*, vol. 4. Paris.

DOBLE, G.H., 1945. 'Saint Branwalader', *Laudate*, 23, 22–33. Nashdorn Abbey.

DOBLE, G.H., 1965. *The Saints of Cornwall*, part 4, 116–27. Oxford.

ENLART, C., 1916. *Manuel d'Archéologie Française*, III. Paris.

FALLE, P., 1694. *An Account of the Isle of Jersey.* London.

FALLE, P., and MORANT, P., 1734. *Caesarea: or An Account of Jersey.* New edition, 1797. Jersey.

FINLAISON, M.B., 1976. 'A Medieval House at 13–13A Old Street, St. Helier', *Ann. Bull. Soc. Jersiaise*, 21, 477–93.

FINLAISON, M.B., forthcoming. 'A Buried Medieval Room in Mont Orgueil Castle', *Ann. Bull. Soc. Jersiaise*.

FOURNÉE, J., 1964. *Le Jugement Dernier. Essai d'exégèse d'une Oeuvre d'Art: le Vitrail de la Cathédrale de Coutence.* Paris.

FREEMAN, E.A., 1845. 'On the Architectural Antiquities of the Island of Jersey', *Proc. Oxford Archit. Soc., 1845*, 57–71.

GRINSELL, L., 1986. 'The Christianisation of Prehistoric and Other Pagan Sites', *Landscape History*, 8, 27–38.

DE GRUCHY, [W.L.], 1884. 'Note sur Les Édifices Religieux de Jersey', *Congrès Archéologique de France en 1883*, 339–52. Paris.

HARBISON, P., 1970. 'How Old is the Gallarus Oratory? A Reappraisal of its Role in Early Irish Architecture', *Medieval Archaeol.*, 14, 34–59.

HAYWARD, J., 1867. 'Notes on Some of the Churches of Jersey', *Trans. Exeter Diocesan Architectural Soc.* (ser. 2), 1, 199–208.

HUGGINS, P.J., RODWELL, K.A., and RODWELL, W.J., 1982. 'Anglo-Saxon and Scandinavian Building Measurements', in P.J. Drury (ed.), *Structural Reconstruction: Approaches to the Interpretation of Excavated Remains of Buildings*, 21–65. Brit. Archaeol. Reps., 10.

INGLIS, H.D., 1834. *The Channel Islands*, vol. 1. London.

KEYSER, C.E., 1883. *A List of Buildings in Great Britain and Ireland having Mural and Other Painted Decorations*. Third edition. Southampton.

KIRSCHMANN, E., et al., 1968; 1970; 1971; 1972. *Lexikon der Christlichen Ikonographie*, vols. I, II, III, IV.

LEASK, H.G., 1955. *Irish Churches and Monastic Buildings*, vol. 1. Dundalk.

MACGIBBON, D., and ROSS, T., 1896. *The Ecclesiastical Architecture of Scotland*, vol. 1. Edinburgh.

McCORMACK, J., 1986. *Channel Island Churches*. Chichester.

McLOUGHLIN, R., 1982. *Recollections of Jersey en Cartes Postales Anciennes*. Le Vey Clecy, France.

MALE, E., 1908. *L'Art Réligieux de la fin du Moyen Age en France*. Paris.

MYRES, J.N.L., 1978. 'The Origin of the Jersey Parishes: Some Suggestions', *Ann. Bull. Soc. Jersiaise*, 22, 163–76.

MYRES, J.N.L., 1981. 'The Stone Vaults of the Jersey Churches: their Historical Significance', *Ann. Bull. Soc. Jersiaise*, 23, 85–96.

NICOLLE, E.T. (ed.), 1906. 'Testament de Brelade Alexandre', *Ann. Bull. Soc. Jersiaise*, 6, 111–14.

OPPENHEIM, A.N., 1916. 'The Old Wallpaintings in the Fishermen's Chapel of St. Brelade, Jersey, C.I.' Manuscript booklet, copy no. 2, presented to the Library of the Société Jersiaise, 1918. Ref. E19/22.

PHILLIPOT, P., MORA, P., and MORA, L., 1984. *Conservation of Wall Paintings*. ICCROM, Rome.

PLEES, W., 1817. *An Account of the Island of Jersey*. Second edition, 1824. Southampton.

POINDESTRE, J., 1682 (ed. W. NICOLLE, 1889). *Caesarea, or a Discourse on the Island of Jersey*. Société Jersiaise.

RADFORD, C.A.R., 1977. 'The Earliest Irish Churches', *Ulster Journal of Archaeol.* (ser. 3), 40, 1–11.

RAGUSA, I., 1961. *Meditations on the Life of Christ*. Princeton.

ROBB, M.D., 1936. 'The Iconography of The Annunciation in the 14th and 15th Century', *Art Bulletin, 1936*.

RODWELL, W.J., and RODWELL, K.A., 1981. 'Barton-on-Humber', *Current Archaeol.*, 7 (no. 78), 209–15,

RODWELL, W.J., 1986. 'Saint Mary's Priory, Les Écréhous, Jersey: A Reappraisal', *Bull. Soc. Jersiaise*, 24, 225–31.

RODWELL, W.J., 1987. 'St. Brelade's, Jersey', *Current Archaeol.*, 9 (no. 107), 369–72.

RODWELL, W.J., 1989. *Church Archaeology*. Second edition. London.

RODWELL, W.J., forthcoming. 'Saint Brelade's Church, Jersey: An Archaeological Study', *Ann. Bull. Soc. Jersiaise*.

RCAHM, 1921. Royal Commission on Ancient and Historical Monuments, *An Inventory of the Ancient Monuments of Merioneth*. H.M.S.O., London.

RCAHM, 1937. Royal Commission on Ancient and Historical Monuments, *An Inventory of the Ancient Monuments in Anglesey*. H.M.S.O., London.

RCAHM, 1960. Royal Commission on Ancient and Historical Monuments, *An Inventory of the Ancient Monuments in Caernarvonshire*, vol. 2. H.M.S.O., London.

RYBOT, N.V.L., [1948]. 'A Description of the Church of St. Brelade, Jersey'. Manuscript booklet in the Library of the Société Jersiaise, ref. E19/21.

SCOTT, M., 1980. *The History of Dress, I: Late Gothic Europe*. London.

STEAD, J., [1798]. Caesarea. *General History and Description of the Island of Jersey*, vol. 1. London.

STEVENS, C.G., 1977. *The Vanished Chapels and Priories of Jersey*. Unpublished manuscript in the Library of the Société Jersiaise.

STEVENS, C.G., ARTHUR, J.F., and STEVENS, J.C., 1986. *Jersey Place Names: A Corpus of Jersey Toponomy*, vol. 1. Société Jersiaise.

STEVENS, C.G., and STEVENS, M.C., 1986. *Jersey Place Names: A Corpus of Jersey Toponomy*, vol. 2. Société Jersiaise.

STEVENS, J., 1967. 'An Eighteenth Century Diary: Thomas Le Maistre's Notebook', *Ann. Bull. Soc. Jersiaise*, 19, 244–53.

STEVENS, J., 1977. *Old Jersey Houses*, II. Chichester.

TABB, W.G., n.d. *St. Brelade's Church, Jersey, Channel Islands*. Jersey.

TAYLOR, H.M., and TAYLOR, J., 1965. *Anglo-Saxon Architecture*, vols. 1 and 2. Cambridge.

THIBOUT, M., and DESCHAMPS, P., 1963. *Le Peinture en France à l'Époque Gothique*. Paris.

THOMPSON, D.V., 1933 (ed. and transl.). *Cennino Cennini, The Craftsman's Handbook*. New Haven.

TRISTRAM, E.W., 1955. *English Wall Painting of the 14th Century*. London.

WARTON, R.G., 1914. 'St. Brelade's Church', *Ann. Bull. Soc. Jersiaise*, 7, 441–7.

Index of Places and Personal Names